DARK BORDERS

DARK
BORDERS

*Film Noir and
American Citizenship*

JONATHAN
AUERBACH

Duke University Press
Durham & London 2011

Library of Congress Cataloging-in-Publication Data
appear on the last printed page of this book.

Duke University Press gratefully acknowledges
the support of the University of Maryland, which
provided funds toward the production of this book.

Contents

Illustrations

Acknowledgments

I am happy to thank colleagues and friends who offered feedback and support while I was working on this project, including (in alphabetical order) Peter Beicken, Chris Cagle, Kent Cartwright, Russ Castronovo, Kandice Chuh, Stan Corkin, Caroline Eades, Astrid Franke, Oliver Gaycken, Markus Gehann, Jim Gilbert, Saverio Giovacchini, Lisa Gitelman, Lee Grieveson, Marshall Grossman, Tom Gunning, Liam Kennedy, Isabell Klaiber, Bob Kolker, Frank Krutnik, Ted Leinwand, Bob Levine, Greg Metcalf, Yoichiro Miyamoto, Alan Nadal, Howard Norman, Devin Orgeron, Marsha Orgeron, Liz Papazian, Don Pease, Dana Polan, Joshua Shannon, Jan Stievermann, Horst Tonn, Michael Tratner, Trysh Travis, Orrin Wang, Mary Helen Washington, David Wyatt, and various eagle-eyed students over the years who pointed out puzzling and peculiar features of these films that otherwise I would probably never have noticed.

My gratitude also goes to Michelle Cerullo for help compiling the bibliography. I also express my appreciation for the valuable comments made by the two anonymous readers for Duke University Press, as well as for the encouragement and guidance of my editor there, Courtney Berger. Thanks also to the

Graduate Research Board at the University of Maryland, which granted me much needed time for writing.

Earlier versions of chapters 4 and 5 of this book have been previously published, "Noir Citizenship: Anthony Mann's *Border Incident*," *Cinema Journal* 47, no. 4 (2008), 102–20, and a section on Sam Fuller's *Pickup on South Street* in "Microfilm, Containment, and the Cold War," *American Literary History* 19, no. 3 (2007), 745–68, authored with Lisa Gitelman. Thanks to Adell Aldrich for permission to reproduce the intriguing photograph of her father that I discuss near the end of my study, and to Alain Silver for helping me procure the photo.

Finally I thank my wife, Marijean, and my son, Daniel, for bearing with me as I watched one bleak black-and-white movie after another, not a passion they necessarily shared, but one especially Marijean was happy to see me indulge. This book is lovingly dedicated to them.

The Un-Americanness of Film Noir

Reporting to the FBI in late 1947 about subversive activity in Hollywood, "Confidential Informant T-10" expressed the hope that Congress "by statute" would declare American communists "a foreign-inspired conspiracy" rather than "a legal party." Collectively criminalized, communist membership could then become a definitive "indication of disloyalty," T-10 reasoned, that would in turn sanction the "cleansing of their own household."[1] As the recently elected president of the Screen Actors Guild, T-10 (aka Ronald Reagan) was in a good position to appreciate how messy such a domestic purging would be without the convenient force of law to detect and then rid the "household" (both the film community and the homeland at large) of undesirable elements.

Responding to a danger felt from within, Reagan, along with many other Americans at midcentury, sought to purify the republic by imagining a group of fellow citizens as illegitimate outsiders who warranted, awkwardly, some sort of expulsion or detention. At once an epistemological crisis (how to know the enemy?) and a moral one (what should be done?), this perceived emergency in internal security severely tested American citizenship during the 1940s and 1950s. These two decades also coincided with the development of American film noir, a cycle of moody, dark crime thrillers filled with bitterness, confusion, and doubt. Not ostensibly concerned with national politics, many of these movies in style and tone dramatized feelings of alienation—a profound sense of dispossession corresponding closely to the Cold War's redefinition of the rights and responsibilities of citizenship, as I show in this study.

An obvious link between external and internal threats, the Communist Party of America (CPUSA) was the logical focus of T-10's attention, even though the CPUSA was never directly outlawed despite the private urging of Reagan and so many others. A few months before his report, the guild president had appeared in public before the House Un-American Activities Committee (HUAC, a very different audience than the FBI) to give a far more upbeat assessment: "I do not believe the Communists have ever at any time been able to use the motion-picture screen as a sounding board for their philosophy or ideology."[2] Yet Reagan in effect got his more secret wish through a series of security measures (laws, directives, and policies) enacted initially in the late 1930s in response to impending global conflict and more rapidly imposed during and soon after the Second World War.

To consider simply the single year of the informer Reagan's confidential memo, arguably the defining moment of the Cold War, 1947 marked the Truman Doctrine proclaiming the intention of the United States to defend against Soviet incursion around the globe (March 12); the creation of the loyalty oath program for federal employees (March 21); the proposal of the Marshall Plan for rehabilitating Western Europe (June); the Taft-Hartley Act aimed to root out communist leadership in labor unions (June 18); the *Foreign Affairs* publication of George F. Kennan's influential containment thesis, "The Sources of Soviet Conduct" (July); the signing of the National Security Act, designed to administer and oversee a national system of military intelligence and surveillance, both foreign and domestic (July 26); the HUAC investigations of directors and screenwriters (October 27–30); the Waldorf Statement, in which Hollywood studios began voluntarily blacklisting their own (November 25); and the attorney general's issuing of an official list of subversive organizations (December 4).

Hundreds of books and articles have been written about the home front during the Cold War, including plenty focusing on HUAC's probing of the so-called Hollywood Ten.[3] Yet for all the attention paid to the stylized rituals of naming names, guilt by association, and the heavy consequences for the accused, it seems to me that the irrational intensity of anticommunist fervor in the late 1940s and early 1950s remains something of a mystery. After all, Reagan had reassured HUAC in 1947 that the primary medium for mass culture in the United States, the Hollywood screen, remained immune to communist ideology, so that his desire to prosecute these ideologues for their beliefs seems rather curious. What did Reagan fear if no longer just fear itself (to paraphrase Franklin D. Roosevelt's New Deal aphorism)? In what sense, exactly, did the communists jeopardize security? How to draw the line between criminal disloyalty and other kinds of legitimate dissent, or the line between subversive thought and treasonous behavior? Was mere membership in an organization a matter of ideas or action? Was communism simply a political belief or "a way of life," as the FBI director J. Edgar Hoover insisted in his own HUAC testimony?[4] Such questions revolved around social and psychological thresholds between the inner and the outer—what was inside the law as opposed to outside it, what was permissible to think but not to do. The anxiety driving this concern over uncertain boundaries attached itself centrally to issues of national belonging: who and what counted as American. The question thus became how to distinguish between foreign instigation and domestic agency, how to tell friend from foe, and, in the absence of clear markers of difference, how to uncover and deal with sedition at home. As Reagan's memo suggests, worries over delineating borders seemed more pressing than the menace of any serious "fifth column" domestic subversion itself.[5]

To address this curiosity, we might begin by pairing two concepts that seem to come from different realms (politics and aesthetics), but that in my analysis turn out to function identically: *un-American* and *uncanny*. While the first word came into play at the end of the nineteenth century, it started to pervade security debates in the mid-1930s, when war loomed in Europe and when it was given institutional status by a congressional committee (HUAC) that continued to exercise significant influence through the 1950s; the second term is one of the main ways that film noir has come to be critically identified—a certain cluster of uneasy feelings rather than a fixed cinematic genre with well-demarcated themes and features. If the affective dimension of political discourse during this period often tends to be overlooked, then conversely the substantive politics at the core of noir's mood of disquiet similarly tends to be underestimated in depth and detail.[6] Bringing these two notions together, locating the uncanny in the un-American, helps us appreciate how these crime films crucially helped shape and respond to a crisis calling into question how citizens and government construed the limits of their homeland.

While at first glance *un-American* may seem analogous to adjectives like *unpatriotic* or *uncharitable* that simply denote the absence of a particular positive attribute, in fact the term worked in far stranger ways, recently prompting one scholar to call it in passing, a bit hyperbolically, "one of the most remarkable words in the twentieth century."[7] Rather than classifying ontologically a type of person or trait, *un-American* functioned strictly by negation, a canceling out or reversing of a more nebulous set of ideals.[8] The prefix *un-* is so strange because it, unlike *anti-*, cannot signify any specific grounds for difference: to be *un-American* is not simply to be hostile toward or positioned against American values from some identifiable alternative perspective, but rather to somehow embody the very opposite of "America." Yet what exactly constitutes America's opposite? Preparing the way for the Manichaean mind-set that dominated postwar politics, the "un" in HUAC created a seamless totality with no terms to mediate between its stark polarities. These poles were at once mutually exclusive and bound together by a single quality or condition (consider the adjectival pairs happy/unhappy, friendly/unfriendly, for instance). But unlike the seemingly similar prefix *non-*, *un-* did not even work by a logic of exclusion to fix legal categories of nationality (as in the term *non-Americans*). The key is that *un-American* mostly made sense only when applied *to* Americans, so that by 1959 the former president Harry Truman was emboldened to pronounce HUAC itself "the most un-American thing in the country today."[9] In a telling circularity, Truman found it un-American for Americans to label other Americans un-American.

Coupled with the word *activities*, *un-American* became an even more curious construction. "What is meant by un-American activities?" asked the representative Dewey Johnson of Minnesota when a resolution for establishing the committee came before the House in April 1937.[10] The question was a good one. As I have suggested, *un-American* is centrally a matter of values and beliefs. To investigate thought comes perilously close to violating cherished principles of free speech; therefore ideas had to be tethered to unlawful action such as sabotage or espionage to warrant prosecution, even though there were lots of laws already on the books to prosecute such crimes, including the high crime of wartime treason as defined in the Constitution. But as a catchall concept that could be applied to a variety of perceived dangers from within, *un-Americanness* demanded probing and surveillance that superseded traditional police work. As I discuss in chapter 1, even before the founding of HUAC, FDR in 1936 issued a secret directive to the FBI's Hoover that allowed him to systematically undertake intelligence gathering aimed at tracing any links between radicalism at home and foreign agents working for international communist and fascist movements. On September 6, 1939, a week after Hitler invaded Poland, FDR issued another FBI directive in connection with a declared national emergency that permitted Hoover to substantially broaden the scope of investigation to include a wide range of "subversive activities" not previously part of the bureau's mission. A crucial category of criminality was expanded to reach beyond behavior into the realm of ideas—a potential for political thought control that film noir would register with paranoia from its inception.[11]

To put it another way, the United States during this period was a rather uncanny place. Here I invoke Freud's well-known essay "The Uncanny" (1919, in the direct aftermath of the First World War). While this essay has sometimes been applied to discussions of citizenship, it is not generally discussed specifically in relation to the Cold War and in conjunction with the closely aligned term *un-American*.[12] Freud's analysis proves especially helpful for connecting matters of affect experienced on an intimate level with large-scale political questions about national belonging. Beginning, uncharacteristically, with an extended linguistic analysis of the German adjectives *heimlich* and *unheimlich* (homely/unhomely), Freud argues that the ostensible opposition between the familiar and the unfamiliar conveyed by this pair in fact reveals a single "core of feeling": that the uncanny, far from deriving from "intellectual uncertainty" about the unknown, rather emerges from a kind of reversal, a doubling or return of the familiar that has been repressed as such. In common German usage, Freud notes, the word *heimlich* can mean both "intimate, friendly, comfortable" as well as "something concealed, secret." The adjective thus takes on the connotations of *unheimlich* without the need for the prefix *un-*: "*Heimliche* [*sic*] is a word the meaning of which develops in the direction of ambivalence, until it finally coincides with its opposite, *unheimliche* [*sic*]. *Unheimliche* is in some way or other a sub-species of *heimliche*."[13]

Although Freud does not explicitly amplify his discussion of the prefix *un-* (which he calls "the token of repression") to consider the nation-state, his emphasis on the concept of home certainly makes such an analysis available, as a number of his examples indicate: "Is it still *heimliche* to you in your country where strangers are felling your woods?" and "Freedom is the whispered watchword of *heimliche* conspirators and the loud battle-cry of professional revolutionaries."[14] While it might be argued that whether the home is comfortable or a place of concealment simply depends on whether it is viewed from within or without, the question of perspective is precisely what remains so unstable. The uncanny in this regard is primarily a matter of trespassing or boundary crossing, where inside and outside grow confused as (presumed) foreigners enter domestic space and, conversely, the home reveals dark secrets hidden within. To feel that your home is strange, or more precisely, to feel like a stranger in your own house—this is the peculiar condition of citizenship intensified by wartime security measures, as well as a primary emotion driving many films noirs of the 1940s and 1950s. Cinema scholars frequently link noir to existential alienation, abstractly or philosophically considered, but such alienation needs to be more precisely grounded in specific historical and cultural fears about enemy aliens lurking within.

Beyond the obvious anxieties created by these (in)security measures, especially the inability to decide between American and un-American, I would make two related points. First, what from the perspective of international relations looks like a dramatically shifting set of allies and foes before the war, during the war, and soon after the war, from the viewpoint of the home front seems a remarkably consistent set of developments, regardless of the specific external threat (Germany, Japan, or the Soviet Union). In other words, from roughly 1939 (FDR's directive to the FBI) to at least 1954 (passage of the Loss of Citizenship Act and the Senate's censure of Joseph McCarthy in December), the United States found itself in a single continuous state of emergency prompted by global conflict: impending, hot, and cold. In this admittedly idiosyncratic definition, the "Cold War" in the United States actually begins during the late 1930s, with the rise of an intelligence apparatus that effectively put the country on a permanent wartime basis. It is impossible to explain the intensity of anticommunism after the war without taking into account the serious anxiety many Americans felt about enemy infiltration well before their country entered the war.[15] Second, beyond secret directives, congressional committees, and national legislation aimed at catching fifth-column infiltrators, this state of exception or emergency had powerful consequences for ordinary citizens because, as I have been suggesting, the very nature of American citizenship was being transformed.

Or perhaps citizenship in the abstract was being protected *against* change. Culminating more than a decade's succession of security measures, Dwight D. Eisenhower's Loss of Citizenship law (1954), enacted when membership in the CPUSA had already dwindled to negligible numbers, simply made explicit what earlier sedition and registration acts implied—that certain persons (un-Americans) were no longer welcome in the country, despite either having undergone the legal process of naturalization or possessing a presumed "constitutional birthright" as native born.[16] But whether emphasis falls on the state (rights and contract) or on the nation (consent and community)—that is, whether we view citizenship from the perspective of the law or as a more psychological matter of belonging—for denationalization to take place, U.S. citizenship could be terminated (as opposed to being voluntarily given up by the individual) only on relatively narrow, sometimes overlapping grounds: by a breech of allegiance, as a form of punishment, or as a deemed threat to public order.

As Alexander Aleinikoff has noted in his valuable review of theories about the loss of U.S. citizenship, in 1940 Congress began adding several new grounds for denationalization, not simply divided allegiance (e.g., serving in the armed forces of another country), but now, in a more penal nature, for actions such as trying to overthrow the government. As Aleinikoff remarks, these cold war provisions (as I would call them) "were excepted from the general rule that denationalization took effect only after the citizen had taken up residence abroad [and therefore] permitted the denationalization of citizens who may not have acquired citizenship elsewhere."[17] Such preemptive legislation now meant "that citizenship could be terminated against the will of the citizen," thereby raising the specter of involuntary statelessness. This leads Aleinikoff further to notice "something quite peculiar about our constitutional doctrine": that "Congress has *no* power to remove citizenship and virtually *plenary* power to deport aliens." In this regard, efforts to criminalize native-born CPUSA members, as Reagan proposed, by treating them as disloyal agents of a foreign (Soviet) conspiracy, at once aimed to preserve but also betrayed the idealized notion of citizenship as an abstract universal. Dismissing the rights perspective as "internally incoherent," concluding "consent takes us no place" and that "contract and communitarian theory cannot rule out state power to terminate citizenship against the will of the individual," Aleinikoff is left to insist, a bit feebly and glumly, that denationalization only "be based on conduct, not belief"—precisely the sort of distinction that Freud's uncanny and FDR's emergency security measures tended to blur.[18]

Exception is what gives Aleinikoff's legal theorizing such fits. In his examination of the rule of exception that increasingly has become the norm, indeed the foundation, of state power in the twentieth century, the political philosopher Giorgio Agamben more recently has analyzed a series of paradoxes about "this no-man's land between public law and political fact," which he reads spatially as kind of "a dispute over its proper *locus*," since "what must be inscribed within the law is essentially exterior to it."[19] Following Carl Schmitt, he describes "the topological structure of the state of exception" as "*Being-outside, and yet belonging*" because "the sovereign, who decides on the exception, is, in truth, logically defined in his being by the exception."[20] One consequence of this aporia between inside and outside, Agamben asserts, quoting Schmitt, is that "the state continues to exist, while law recedes."[21] And yet if we redirect our attention from the state or the sovereign to the nation, from the exercise of power to more affective qualities centered on the governed, we might reverse Agamben's topology: for those compelled to operate under such proclaimed emergencies, the feeling is *being inside, and yet not belonging*. This is the "zone of anomie" that Agamben attributes to states of exception but does not closely consider in relation to citizens themselves.

We can better grasp what it felt like to live under such a state of exception by looking closely at how various border confusions between inside and outside emerged in a group of gloomy American movies that French intellectuals soon after the Second World War dubbed "film noir." It is the aim of the present book to show how the psychological and social effects of wartime internal national security corresponded in particular ways to central features of these movies. Because Hollywood studios at the time did not label these films as such, contrary to the ways in which they categorized and promoted their other product lines like westerns or musicals, the term *film noir* still occasions discussion among cinema scholars, with some straining to classify films as "noir" according to a predetermined array of attributes, while others argue that the very concept is suspect and of limited value as a critical construct imposed well after the fact in the United States. According to these skeptics, a kind of tedious repetition sets in when familiar tropes are invoked over and over to define noir: rainy streets, low-key chiaroscuro lighting, hard-boiled dialogue, desperate criminals, femme fatales, moral angst, betrayal, and so on. But it seems to me that the skeptics threaten to become perhaps just as predictable in their own disavowals that challenge the conceptual coherence of noir; what is most striking, in fact, is the way that both sides replay the very same sorts of anxieties about constructing and patrolling thresholds that are central to the postwar period itself. In other words, current doubts about the legitimacy of "noir" as an analytic category closely resemble, indeed largely follow from, cold war worries about how to identify and locate "Americans." One boundary dispute (over the ontological stability or purity of a kind of cinema) bears directly on another (over uncanny citizenship) and therefore needs to be examined with some care and precision.[22]

Marc Vernet, one of the most subtle of these skeptics (perhaps by virtue of his own status as a French intellectual) begins his dismantling of the concept, for example, by wryly mocking noir as a convenient "object of beauty" because "it is neatly contained in a perfect decade (1945–1955), because it is simultaneously defined by its matter (black and white) and by its content (the crime story), because it is strange (see its relation to German expressionism and to psychoanalysis) . . . because there is always an unknown film to be added to the list . . . because it is a great example of cooperation—the Americans made it and then the French invented it—," and on he continues with clichéd reason after reason, which he then proceeds to deconstruct in the rest of his essay by showing how these commonplaces about style, theme, and periodization do not stand up to close scrutiny: the fine grain of film history that he masterfully displays by invoking counterexample after counterexample. If these other films exhibit noir features but predate the cycle and/or clearly belong to other genres, then the category "noir" loses all shape and clarity, becoming little more than an "eminently lost object," Vernet eloquently concludes: "Lost for never having been given a satisfactory definition, lost for having ended in 1955, lost for representing the 1930s in a modern form."[23]

In a more systematic vein, Steve Neale similarly casts suspicion on noir's status as a cinematic genre, arguing that even if critics fairly agree on a basic canon, the criteria to delineate this corpus of films is so imprecise as to be "doomed, in the end, to incoherence."[24] Yet the approach of another contemporary theorist on film genre, Rick Altman, offers a more capacious framework that calls into question Neale's own reifying and somewhat rigid logic. Throughout his *Film/Genre*, Altman invokes the spatial metaphor of borders so frequently that it should come as no surprise when he closes his penetrating analysis with an intriguing and ambitious comparison between genres and nations. For Altman, genres and nations are not given entities with fixed qualities, but rather discursive formations or practices that depend on complex ongoing negotiations among various stakeholders or communities. In this sense his idea of a border is less a clear line of demarcation than the process by which nations and genres continually undergo recreation and reimagination.[25]

Altman's suggestive analogy between genres and nations helps us pinpoint the bee in Vernet's and Neale's bonnets. In contesting the conventional parameters of noir, both Vernet and Neale install and endorse another pair of related binaries that remain unquestioned in their own arguments—the sharp separation between countries, and the equally sharp separation between image and text, that is, between making films and talking about them. Vernet asserts this most bluntly when challenging periodization: "The dates that have been agreed upon are thus ones that concern French critical reception and not American production." Rather than seriously entertain the possibility that noir emerged from transatlantic crossings or translations (literally a "carrying over") between Europe and the United States (what he jokingly derides as "cooperation"), Vernet assumes that Hollywood is one thing, Paris another, and never the twain shall meet. This dismissal is quite curious, because elsewhere in his essay he gives a rather detailed and nuanced account of postwar French politics that helps explain why certain intellectuals were so attracted to these films. Perhaps even more astonishing is Vernet's disparagement of the date 1945 as marking the start of noir because the Second World War was "not a cinematographic event," as if cinema had its own inner workings sealed off from world affairs, when in fact Hollywood and the U.S. government were arguably more closely aligned during this war than during any other period in U.S. history.[26] Later Vernet returns to that same telling adjective, approving another scholar's hypothesis about noir and the rise of television because this explanation at least had the advantage of being "internal to the cinematographic institution." Here again a barrier between the internal and the external is erected to protect cinema and the cinematic image from contamination by supposedly outside nuisances (like global conflict).[27]

Neale's understanding of genre is similarly constrained by his conceiving of the concept primarily as a function of cinema institutions; while he does allow for "audience expectations and textual norms," his resonant notion of "inter-textual relay" tends to be limited to studio publicity, promotion, and film reviews, as if other sorts of discourse mattered little. Hence his impatience with the imprecision of various attempts to define noir by broad historical generalizations. Neale's approach is symptomatic of a much larger turn in academic film studies during the past decade away from high theory (a specialty of the French, after all, that might seem to have exhausted itself) toward looking past the screen to consider cinema's various commercial operations and practices: economics, pedagogy, exhibition, distribution, reception, censorship, star studies, and so on.[28] It is beyond the scope of this study to interrogate this trend, but despite its considerable appeal and value, it seems to me that this model risks cutting off movies from the world at large by treating cinema as self-enclosed and self-motivated. While my intention in Dark Borders is not to reiterate the same tired tropes about noir, neither is it to cancel out the concept entirely; as the punning title of this book suggests, my aim is to ask new questions about a body of films whose problematic hybridity—a lack of clear generic demarcation—I will take as a virtue in helping us appreciate the uncanniness of midcentury America.

In contrast to Vernet's effort to keep the motion picture primary and pristine, Jacques Rancière has more recently given us a better way to think about the relation between images and words. Rancière seeks to fuse aesthetics and politics not by way of psychoanalytic theory (say, Freud's uncanny), but rather by conceiving of artistic representation as arising from what he calls a "regime of visibility," a "conceptual space of articulation between these ways of making and forms of visibility and intelligibility determining the way in which they can be viewed and conceived." Instead of assuming the priority of the image at the expense of critical discourse about it, typically seen as parasitic and supplementary at best, Rancière argues that a "new regime of visibility" can "make a new pictorial practice possible."[29] In this regard, noir is not a "lost object," as Vernet would have it, but a *found* one that Parisian intellectuals brought to light after the war. And so we can take seriously the Frenchness of film noir (another sort of un-Americanness). The sudden impact on the French of previously un-available Hollywood crime thrillers, blacked out during wartime Occupation, dramatically illustrates how a regime of visibility emerges thanks to this interplay or articulation between images and critical discourse. It might be argued that critics like Nino Frank and Jean-Pierre Chartier in 1946, and Raymond Borde and Etienne Chaumeton in 1955, were no Goncourt brothers, whose nineteenth-century writing on Jean-Baptiste-Siméon Chardin's paintings Rancière cites as an example. But the fact is that these Frenchmen did make visible what Americans themselves did or could not see for themselves.

The "noir" these French found in American movies gets even more interesting once we appreciate how the term in 1946 was not a completely new coinage but taken from the Série Noire, a series of paperback thrillers published by Gallimard, mostly translations of hard-boiled American fiction. That series, in turn, borrowed its name from *romans noirs*, the generic French term for Gothic or mystery novels, mainly eighteenth-century British fiction. Beyond texts, we can add that Chartier, in his article titled "The Americans Are Making Dark Films *Too*" (emphasis added) of November 1946, alludes to "discussion of a French school of film noir," for which he gives examples from a pair of Marcel Carné movies from 1938.[30] While these promiscuous manifestations of noir might support Vernet's and Neale's suspicions that the term is too loose to be very helpful, I would argue that it speaks to the potency of the adjective as a cultural signifier crossing and crisscrossing nations and media (verbal and visual). To be more exact, surrounding or chronologically sandwiching these films of the 1940s, we have a variety of texts and images—detective fiction, primarily American in translation, from the 1920s and 1930s; earlier Gothic novels; French poetic realism; and postwar French criticism making heady claims for the significance of these wartime American movies, claims that eventually make their way back to U.S. directors and screenwriters like Robert Aldrich (in the 1950s) and Paul Schrader (in the 1970s). We can add to this circulation or reciprocity between words and images (and between cultures) a third influential medium, radio, that helped shape and was in turned shaped by the hard-boiled dialogue of the prewar crime stories of writers like James M. Cain and Raymond Chandler, who were subsequently enlisted by Hollywood to import some of that dialogue into movies.

From a theoretical perspective, this verbal, visual, and aural intermediality allowing noir to become recognizable at midcentury squares nicely with Rancière's redefining of the concept of a representational medium as a regime or articulation of practices, rather than as constituted by any intrinsic materiality or ontology. From a historical perspective, such intermediality harkens back to the late-nineteenth century emergence of the moving picture, which was initially conceived and invented as an audio-visual multimedia spectacle drawing on a range of precursors and which only later developed into having cinematographic institutions and forms seemingly its own.[31] Again, it is beyond the scope of this study to contemplate how Rancière's arguments against media-specific analysis will influence "the future of the image," as one of his recent collections of essays is titled. But if we begin, along these lines, to unsettle conventional divisions between words and images, between film commentary and film production (itself already discursive and transnational, I would insist); if we probe rather than try to protect the porous boundaries between countries and cultures (cosmopolitan Berlin, Los Angeles, Paris); if we suspend debate about whether something qualifies as a cinema genre or not, even as that "something" still continues to elicit commentary and intense interest, then we can appreciate how the dark borders of noir might warrant renewed close consideration.

For me that consideration centers on affect. To return to Vernet and Neale for a moment, it is revealing, and somewhat surprising given their distaste for imprecision, that both scholars begrudgingly come nearest to accepting a definition of noir in relation to what appears as its most nebulous attribute, that of carrying a distinctive mood or sensibility linked to the emotional vulnerability of its main characters. In the midst of his relentless excoriation of the concept, Neale pauses to grant that narrative techniques such as flashback and voice-over have "considerable merit" as a characterization of noir, insofar as these formal techniques foreground "reliability, duplicity and deception." Such enigmas of narration underscore how noir movies frequently emphasize subjectivity and interiority, a "sustained focus on the thoughts and feelings of at least one major character," as Neale puts it.[32] In related fashion, Vernet reverses himself on the question of periodization, contrasting, rather than comparing, earlier comic film versions of Dashiell Hammett's *The Maltese Falcon* in the 1930s against John Huston's wartime remake of 1941—a *locus classicus* for most film noir scholars—to admit that the latter's "domination of serious tone" accounts for the movie's classification as noir, rather than "actual plot structure or photography."[33]

Despite their overall skepticism, Neale and Vernet on this matter of affect echo the initial French response to these films, particularly the first full-length account of noir, *Panorama de film noir américain* (1941–1953) published by Borde and Chaumeton in 1955, the same year that the movie *Kiss Me Deadly* was released, a fact not entirely lost on Americans themselves, as I have already suggested: the following year the film director Aldrich was photographed on a studio set holding a copy of the book.[34] In their seminal study, Borde and Chaumeton make two basic claims about film noir—that these movies are essentially about crime and that they are strange, what they term *insolite*, along with having four other related traits: being oneiric, erotic, ambivalent, and cruel. Rather than define noir by any detailed narrative content or visual style, Borde and Chaumeton identify this cycle of movies by a predominant mood akin, if not identical, to Freud's notion of *unheimlich*. They close their definitional chapter as follows: "It is easy to come to a conclusion: the moral ambivalence, criminal violence, and contradictory complexity of the situations and motives all combine to give the public a shared feeling of anguish or insecurity, which is the identifying sign of film noir at this time. All the works in this series exhibit a consistency of an emotional sort; *namely, the state of tension created in the spectators by the disappearance of their psychological bearings.* The vocation of film noir has been to create *a specific sense of malaise.*"[35]

While Borde and Chaumeton tend to locate this alienation or insecurity in the spectator, I would argue that such a consistent emotional core or sensibility constitutes the prevailing tenor of these films themselves, whose characters, settings, compositional design, cinematography, and plots carry precise affective attributes. Taking seriously the way that a text can embody a specific tone, long dismissed by formalists as a subjective and insufficiently rigorous critical concept, Sianne Ngai has analyzed a set of "ugly feelings" such as envy and anxiety that, unlike the grander passions of anger or hate, tend to attenuate individual agency and make it difficult to take action.[36] Although as befitting the popular depiction of crime, characters in noir narratives do indeed act, the tone of many of these films works against the grain of mainstream Hollywood expectation to dwell in far less familiar territory of a more psychological, abnormal, and neurotic nature, as Borde and Chaumeton suggest.

Clearly American noir was not the only kind of film to register the uncanny. Gothic romance, horror films, and science fiction from the 1930s through the 1950s all come to mind as frequently entailing a return of the repressed.[37] But rarely do these other genres dramatize the sort of ugly feelings we find in noir—paranoia, jealousy, gall, and, most prominently, a curious type of dispossession or resentment that bears on historically specific confusions about national belonging.

To propose cold war citizenship as the overarching cultural framework for this study, I want to emphasize, is not to fall into the trap of assuming that film noir functioned unequivocally as a "dark mirror" expressing a "national mood" or monolithic zeitgeist, as many traditional advocates automatically assert. Other compelling tags for the American 1940s and 1950s have included the "age of anxiety" and the "age of doubt."[38] Cautioning against such a naïve reflection model, Richard Maltby, in perhaps the single best article on the subject, shows how these claims for a simple ideological correspondence between text and context are circular, a mutually reinforcing circuit of evidence and assertion based on metaphor and coincidence that matches films and facts at will. This partial selection process allows scholars to see what they want to see. Maltby appreciates that the United States and Hollywood were simply too complex and multifaceted to be so reduced to a single zeitgeist. But curiously his essay does end up, in somewhat conflicted fashion (akin to Vernet's essay), taking seriously what he had earlier in his argument rejected as a totalizing explanation: that postwar America found itself in a period of intense maladjustment, with Maltby's focus shifting from traumatized vets returning from the war to equally troubled American intellectuals disillusioned by the darker aspects of cold war culture, especially the rise in political intolerance.[39]

So despite the best efforts of these various academic skeptics to retire noir, the concept remains powerfully haunting, undead, like a specter that will not stay in the grave. Instead of worrying if noir is a genre, a style, or a sensibility, perhaps we should wonder if the critical concept functions more like a ghost, a vampire, or a zombie. James Naremore takes a commonsense attitude toward this stubborn persistence, recognizing film noir as a "discursive construct" (elsewhere he more harshly pronounces it a "mythology"), while going on to suggest how as such it "has heuristic value, mobilizing specific themes that are worth further consideration."[40] Here I would agree, but with a different set of themes in mind. For Naremore, film noir is culturally important because it brilliantly melds high European modernism (especially surrealism and existentialism) with hard-boiled American pulp. While I am indebted to his cosmopolitan approach, giving the French credit where credit is due, his notion of noir as transgeneric or intertextual is fairly limited to aesthetic matters (literature, art history, film, and philosophy). Instead, by concentrating on feelings, I develop and expand noir's heuristic potential in two related directions. As an emergent regime of visibility, film noir lets us see (literally) a key affective dimension of the Cold War, which I have described as a state of exception.[41] And by contextualizing noir in relation to uncanny and uncertain citizenship at midcentury, a ground for intense anxiety, insecurity, and resentment, I also hope to change the way we think about these films themselves.[42]

Because it eludes clear-cut generic definitions, film noir inevitably becomes something of a problem when it comes to selecting exemplary movies for analysis, with a tendency for scholars to pick films that simply confirm their various theses about noir. Edward Dimendberg, for instance, spends a lot of attention on the police procedural *The Naked City* (1948) because it so graphically illustrates his arguments about urban space and modernity, while hardly mentioning another well-known Mark Hellinger production made two years earlier, *The Killers* (1946).[43] Vivian Sobchack, on the other hand, bypasses *The Naked City*, presumably because it depicts family life and children (whom she claims are mostly missing from noir), to focus on *The Killers*, whose settings—diners, nightclubs, and seedy boarding houses—demonstrate her contention that noir's material premises (her pun intended) serve as surrogates for an absent home.[44] So we have two very fine cinema scholars both interested in the question of space (urban and domestic, respectively) picking different films to match their very different but not mutually exclusive conclusions about noir.

What needs to be acknowledged more openly is that such choices are less essential than pragmatic, driven primarily by what we already want to make of these crime narratives. Facing the same circularity, I have selected a body of films that center on thresholds and border crossing: from a fear that enemy (Nazi) spies, informers, strangers, and brainwashers have wormed their way into the country and refuse to leave, to a resentful salesman trying to get away with murder to spite his company, to the geopolitics of Cuba and Mexico in relation to the United States, to a series of films responding to the pressures of civic duty and patriotism more broadly. Having looked closely at hundreds of dark movies made during the 1940s and 1950s, I have selected roughly a dozen to analyze in depth, some very well known, such as *Double Indemnity* (1944), *Out of the Past* (1947), *Key Largo* (1948), and *Pickup on South Street* (1953), and others less familiar but no less illuminating for testing the foundations of citizenship, such as *Stranger on the Third Floor* (1940), *The Chase* (1946), and *Ride the Pink Horse* (1947). In my effort to get at the curious liminality or un-Americanness of these films, I trust that their range of plot, character, and setting, combined with their consistency of tone, will absolve me from the charge of capricious or arbitrary selection for the sake of a single-minded thesis. Although I pay attention to the justly celebrated look(s) of noir, my focus will be on the visceral rather than its visual aspects.[45]

To help understand this domain of feeling, I have relied on Freud's notion of the uncanny, although my readings are more political than psychoanalytically inclined.[46] Here I join a number of other cinema scholars interested in the politics of noir, most of whom tend to offer relatively transparent narrative and character analyses without much attention to the significance of affect.[47] In this view, often drawing on HUAC's investigation of the Hollywood Ten as background and starting point, the political orientation of any given film can be determined by its overt treatment of themes of law and order, so that a police procedural that ostensibly enforces the law and celebrates institutional authority is a conservative or "right-wing" noir, whereas one in which the law is represented more critically is "left-wing" or progressive. But as I have already suggested, the relation between crime and law is far too unstable in noir to sustain this sort of convenient distinction, which by so focusing on manifest content neglects the emotional undercurrents running through these films.

A brief example may be useful. In 1939 Milton Krims coscripted Warner's *Confessions of a Nazi Spy* (directed by Anatole Litvak), Hollywood's first direct attack on Hitler that was banned in Germany, Japan, Italy, Poland, Holland, Norway, and Sweden (see chapter 1). Three years later, working in a similar patriotic antifascist vein, Albert Maltz coscripted the crime thriller *This Gun for Hire* (1942), which dramatizes how a disturbed hit man prevents an aging American industrialist from selling military secrets to the Japanese (see chapter 5). Soon after the war Krims wrote the screenplay for the first major Hollywood anticommunist movie, *The Iron Curtain* (1948), while Maltz around the same time refused to name names for HUAC, was blacklisted as un-American, and jailed for contempt of Congress. How to account for such a drastic difference in the fates of Krims and Maltz? While it might seem that Krims suddenly grew more conservative after the war when Maltz held steadfast to his progressive principles, I would argue otherwise: that both writers in penning their wartime tales of international espionage unleashed the same set of strong emotions—the grave concern or hysteria that the most secure social structures in the United States were being undermined by an alien enemy dwelling in the country's midst. This excess of worry lingered well past any particular danger to which it might have been linked: psychic war surplus we might call it. While Krims could effortlessly redirect and reascribe those still powerful suspicions to a new object of anxiety (Soviet spies in North America), Maltz could and did not, and therefore was made to pay for his past. In terms of the subsequent trajectories of their lives, I do not mean to diminish the difference between Maltz, who ended up in jail, and Krims, who continued to enjoy a successful career. But without the advantage of hindsight, the movies that these writers scripted may have more in common at the level of affect than labels like *conservative* and *progressive* might allow.

In so emphasizing details of studio production and reception, retrospectively telling the story of Hollywood as a relatively autonomous set of institutional practices, historians of American cinema may overlook how these films themselves engage confusing and sometimes incongruous "structures of feeling."[48] Presuming that political positions can be clearly sourced, articulated, and summarized, this approach to cinema history, however valuable, tends to do insufficient justice to the complexity and power of film as a narrative form. It also may flatten out contradictions and ambiguity such as the flipping back and forth between American and un-American that I have been tracing. In one impressively encyclopedic account, for instance, to demonstrate the plausible thesis that after the Second World War, noir became the "only remaining [cultural] sphere open for dissenting political expression," dozens of movies from the 1940s and 1950s are identified primarily by the scriptwriter.[49] In this resolutely positivist model, once these authors can be scrupulously labeled left-wing by virtue of their championing of social causes offscreen, it logically (and somewhat reductively) follows that they must have created "left-written films" embodying progressive beliefs. But as Jerome Christiansen has shrewdly suggested, film noir might be considered the Hollywood genre of American cold war liberalism par excellence in its studious disavowal of ideology.[50] As an emblematic instance, he cites the opening diner scene in *The Killers* (1946), a key scene as well for Borde and Chaumeton, who call it "one of the most striking moments in American cinema":[51] when asked by a baffled customer "what's the idea?," one of the hired killers contemptuously, simply replies, "there isn't any idea."

Christiansen's deft reading of noir as averse to ideas is instructive, but ideas are not the only way politics, or rather political attitudes and orientations (more or less clear-cut), emerge in these films. Here I return to Freud's analysis of affect, particularly the "ugly feelings" so commonly aroused in these movies, to draw on Ngai's resonant phrase. Three examples, all from lesser-known movies, will help give a concrete sense of how I develop my arguments throughout the rest of this book. *Tomorrow Is Another Day* (1951) tells the story of the ex-con Bill Clark (played by Steve Cochran) who has spent eighteen years in prison for the murder of his father, which he committed at the age of thirteen. Having in effect slept through the Great Depression and the Second World War, Rip Van Winkle style, Clark naively walks out of prison to greet the brave new world of the cold war United States, one prosperous but deeply suspicious of outsiders. The subsequent plot is fairly typical of noir: he hooks up with a dubious dance girl, with whom he runs away after falsely believing he has killed another man. Their meeting is followed by their fugitive life on the road, which takes them (untypically) to Salinas, where they are employed as migrant workers, in a kind of Popular Front homage to *The Grapes of*

Wrath, and where people feel more solidarity and trust toward one another (as they did during the 1930s, we presume).[52]

But it is the film's opening that most interests me. As he walks the streets searching for work, even before he is betrayed by a cynical reporter looking for a sensational scoop about the now grown boy murderer, Bill experiences an intense kind of disassociation from his urban surroundings. In a series of point-of-view shots rendered through Bill's eyes, the city is seen as a strange and foreign place, filled with bewildering new commodities, persons, and noises. It is as if he were an immigrant landing on U.S. soil for the first time, compelled to undergo the harsh initiation process of assimilation or naturalization. The point is that Bill's disaffection is not primarily psychological (although he feels bitter about his incarceration) but rather stems from the passage of time, from the crucial history that he has missed (economic hardship and war) and that forces him to learn again what it means to belong to America. Stepping out of prison, he has moved in one fell swoop from the New Deal to a raw deal, a detour that eventually leads him only to "where the sidewalk ends."[53]

These scenes of dispossession are repeated in dozens of films, instances that constitute the uncanniness at the heart of noir. Take another example from an earlier movie, *When Strangers Marry* (1944). The title says it all, but unlike in a conventional gothic romance such as *Rebecca* (1940), here the uncertainty of a small-town bride suspicious about her new husband grows to a far darker and more pervasive mood of estrangement running through the entire narrative, where everybody in New York seems afraid of everybody else. The insecurity and paranoia driving the plot culminate in a very curious scene near the end that adds nothing to the plot but heightens the tension. On the lam, the two fugitives enter a Harlem bar where black patrons, ignoring the white couple, intensely listen and dance to a raucous boogie-woogie pianist. After a boxing champion enters the venue to be congratulated by all, the newlyweds quickly leave, preferring the menace of the streets to the extreme alienation they feel in the jazz club, however benign the patrons. While this confrontation with otherness is so clearly and centrally racial, I think that it extends beyond race, as if race were only a metaphor or instance of a wider kind of disenfranchisement affecting everyone in the movie, except perhaps black people—the recognition of being inside the (white) nation but feeling outside it.[54] Moments of threshold crossing—walking out of prison or into a Harlem bar—thus graphically help foreground these films' stake in delineating the homeland.

My third example is a bit different in that it is quite explicitly political. *The Red Menace* (1949) represents the most egregious sort of Hollywood anticommunism, the Cold War's answer to *Reefer Madness* (1936). Yet the increasingly lurid excess of its hysteria is so valuable precisely for casting into bold relief the question of citizenship at the center of my study. Unlike most Red Scare movies, this is not a police procedural, in that it focuses on imagining how communists might think and act, not on valiant government efforts to catch them. Too overtly propagandistic and heavy-handed to be regarded as noir by most cinema scholars, the film I think actually contains quite a few narrative and visual features familiar to noir: a disgruntled (if dimwitted) war veteran, a bevy of treacherous femmes fatales who try to seduce him into the ways of Marx and Lenin, and (male) communists at home on dark, rainy city streets who look and operate like thuggish gangsters—a common-enough association at the time. When one of these men starts to have misgivings and seeks to depart the organization, he abruptly, desperately jumps out of a window to his death. This is a fate, we presume, preferable to giving in to his criminal comrades, who have warned him that no one ever leaves the party. But the movie's most intense moment of alienation and uncanniness is triggered not by the communist thugs themselves, but during a scene of interrogation led by federal agents, otherwise absent from the narrative.

On a dark street, the top red siren Yvonne Kraus (played by Betty Lou Gerson) is accosted by two men in hats and trench coats who appear at first to be a pair of her henchmen, but who identify themselves as immigration and naturalization officers. The femme fatale's reaction is striking: in a deep, gravely voice she complains about "Gestapo methods," demands her "civil liberties," insists over and over again that "I am an American citizen," and asks to see their arrest warrant, to which one agent replies, "an immigration inspector doesn't need a warrant." Instead of ignoring the question of rights, the film curiously exaggerates the issue by locating complaints about due process in the angst of a panic-stricken woman, whose strident objections become overridden in the name of state security during the interrogation itself. Brought to INS (Immigration and Naturalization Service) headquarters to answer a few questions, Kraus is asked by the chief inquisitor about her family background, her father's naturalization, and her travel in Mexico before the war. Berated for her "loudmouthed disloyalty to the United States government," Kraus is caught by the interrogator in a more tangible crime. What gives her away as the foreign communist agent Greta Bloch (a more Jewish-sounding name), who has had the real Yvonne Kraus killed, is not her imperfect English (as in some anti-Nazi war movies) but rather her all-too-perfect German, her flawless pronunciation of *Hamburg*, as well as a signature that does not match the one on Kraus's original passport application.

At first having declared her innocence, the woman now suddenly admits her stolen identity as low-key lighting starkly illuminates her widening eyes in a composition that closely resembles the moment in *Detour* (1945) when Al Roberts (Tom Neal) stares into his cup of diner coffee and begins to narrate his sorry tale (also of assumed identity) in retrospective voice-over. But unlike the noir confession of the loser Roberts, the reaction of Bloch/Kraus is not steeped in pathos, guilt, and bitterness, but rather in a kind of mad triumph. Her voice growing louder and harsher (anticipating Gerson's future casting as Cruella Deville in the Disney cartoon *A Thousand and One Dalmatians*), the demonic, laughing femme fatale goes on to fantasize the invasion and takeover of the United States by the "red legions" of the Comintern. She shrieks, "You're too late . . . the revolution is here," as drumming, martial music fills the soundtrack—an auditory hallucination of marching soldiers that nobody else in the room can hear (although we can). Pronounced "psychopathic," she is led off by the INS officers, presumably to be locked up, deported back to Germany, or tried for murder. (Since Kraus was killed in Mexico, the film remains a bit obscure on this point.)

Both preposterous and highly unnerving, this interrogation scene is useful for revealing deep-seated anxieties in cold war America about how to detect and police subversives at home. If the threat itself is negligible, dismissed as the delusional ranting of a lunatic, it must be the difficulty of detection that causes such consternation (as it worried Reagan in his secret FBI memo). Failing to identify subversion by ideological content, the official arm of the Department of Justice that requires no warrants (the INS) relies on a foreign and criminal past, if not a strange accent, to purge the state of the unwanted outsider, whose exposed status as an alien perfectly coincides with her fit of madness, as if insanity were a foreign country. Once her raving inner life bursts forth to the accompaniment of a hallucination, U.S. citizenship as a universally available abstraction is called into question, for in order for her to be expelled from the republic, Bloch must suddenly be burdened with a particular (crazy) voice and past. That hysteric embodiment neatly captures the hysteric feelings driving the anticommunism of the movie and the cold war period as a whole.

In its allusions to the Gestapo, Germany, and deportation, *The Red Menace*'s uncanny exposure of un-Americanness paves the way for my first chapter, which examines two movies that at first glance might not seem to belong together: *Confessions of a Nazi Spy* (1939) and *Stranger on the Third Floor* (1940). By bringing these two films into conversation, I foreground the powerful political resonances echoing throughout the extraordinary *Stranger*, an early if not the earliest noir that has never been appreciated for its engagement with fifth-column fears, including the remarkable appearance of an unmistakably fascist U.S. district attorney. From this pair of panicky home-front films, I turn in my second chapter to the classic *Double Indemnity* (1944). Lacking spies and strangers, and resolutely set in prewar (1938) Los Angeles, Billy Wilder's depiction of insurance fraud would seem to have little to do with nationality or citizenship and therefore to be "the odd man out" in this study, to borrow the title of an important British noir (1947) directed by Carol Reed.[55] But in the memorable figure of the claims investigator Barton Keyes and in the company for which he labors, I argue, we have a vivid demonstration of rationalized control and surveillance that inspires his nemesis/surrogate son, Walter Neff, to try and beat the odds. Keyes may not be a corporate Gestapo, or even a corporate FBI, for that matter, but his attempt to combat white-collar crime by statistics carries enormous significance for understanding Neff's profound resentment in the movie: the malaise of nonbelonging at the core of noir.

From corporate subversion I finally move beyond U.S. borders in my following two chapters, on Americans in Cuba and Mexico, respectively. A chapter on the eerie movie *The Chase* (1946) and the better-known *Key Largo* (1948) allows me to examine the postwar relation between Cuba and the United States, with the watery Florida Keys in the case of the John Huston movie serving as a ground of mediation or twilight zone between the two nations. Focusing on an aging criminal trying to stage a comeback also enables me to trace one crucial genealogy for noir, that of the American gangster film, from immigrants (the early 1930s), to assimilated citizens (the early 1940s), to exiles (the postwar 1940s). As *Key Largo* itself registers, it is no coincidence that just as mobsters like Lucky Luciano were being deported from the United States (to end up in Havana), so were equally undesirable communists. My fourth chapter deals explicitly with border crossing, focusing on the smuggling of Mexican farmworkers in *Border Incident* (1949). I show how this illicit migration between countries parallels the generic hybridity of the film, which also helps us grasp the central role Mexico has played in many noirs as a kind of alternative, a spatial other to the United States by virtue of its geographical proximity to Hollywood. To support this claim, in addition to Anthony Mann's movie, I analyze a trio of films (including *Out of the Past*) that depict Americans meeting and courting in Mexico before returning to the United States.

My final and fifth chapter works as a kind of capstone, looking at a series of disaffected tough guys called on to play the part of civic-minded patriots during wartime (*This Gun for Hire*, 1942), soon after the war (*Ride the Pink Horse*, 1947) and at the height of the Cold War (*Pickup on South Street*, 1953). I conclude with a postscript on a trio of films from the 1950s, *Gun Crazy* (1950), *Kiss Me Deadly* (1955), and *Touch of Evil* (1958), showing how these movies in tone increasingly become prone to self-parody as the noir cycle draws to a close by the end of the decade.

Having opened this introduction by looking at Reagan's confidential FBI memo, followed by un-American subversion as conceived and probed by HUAC, I want to close by briefly discussing the more profound impact of the bureau in legitimizing and, more important, delegitimizing who and what belonged in the United States. While HUAC represented the public and political front against communism (and, to a lesser extent before the war, against fascism), the FBI worked in more secretive, darker fashion to police the nation against unwanted enemies. Built into the very center of its modus operandi for the state was an extensive network of surreptitious monitoring in fearful anticipation of imagined acts of conspiracy and treachery. I think it is safe to say, in fact, that there could be no film noir without the FBI. This is not even to mention the more literal way that G-men figure prominently in a number of the movies I discuss, from *Confessions of a Nazi Spy*, to *Ride the Pink Horse*, to *Pickup on South Street* (1953), whose director Sam Fuller claimed that he and the studio chief Darryl Zanuck were called in by Hoover himself, demanding script changes to the film.

Even before FDR's emergency directives in 1936 and 1939, the agency during the early New Deal experienced an enormous centralization and consolidation of federal authority in its battle against interstate boot-legging and bank robbing. In shifting its focus later in the 1930s from gangsters to suspected agents of foreign powers (Nazi Germany and the Soviet Union), the FBI enjoyed an explosive growth in government appro-priations, from 5 million dollars in 1936 to over 90 million in 1952, an increase in funding of more than 1,800 percent, along with a similar increase in personnel of about 1,000 percent during that same key period (from 609 agents to 6,351).[56] Once the bureau's mandate had been ex-panded beyond fighting crime to include intelligence gathering, its reach into all aspects of American culture became virtually limitless. Some of that reach is reflected in the range of transgressions depicted in the noirs I will examine, from garden-variety murder and mayhem, to espionage, to insurance fraud, war profiteering, and human trafficking across the U.S. border. By the early 1950s the bureau was also actively weighing in on juve-nile delinquency, homosexuality, mass culture, race relations, and child-rearing practices (Hoover: "The cure for crime is not the electric chair but the high chair"), among a multitude of social problems and panics per-ceived to undermine the stability of the republic.[57]

If it is difficult to imagine film noir without the FBI (or an institutional equivalent), it is harder to conceive of the bureau without Hoover, who acted as the public face of the agency as well as its behind-the-scenes executive and principal plotter—a kind of Hollywood screenwriter, publi-cist, star, studio head, and auteur all rolled into one. For nearly fifty years Hoover was arguably the most powerful man in the United States (as the bureau's director from 1924–72). Serving "under" an astonishing suc-cession of eight presidents, starting with Calvin Coolidge and ending with Richard Nixon, the consummate bureaucrat Hoover continually suc-ceeded in aggregating power to himself and the FBI, regardless if his boss was Democrat or Republican, conservative or progressive.[58] Cold war intellectuals like Arthur Schlesinger Jr., who openly decried McCar-thy's hysterical theatrics, and Harold W. Chase, who expressed skepticism about measures such as the antisedition Smith Act (1940) and government loyalty oaths (1947), were almost unanimous in their support of and trust in Hoover, whose "wise counsel," as Chase concluded, represented the proper balance between internal security and civil liberties.[59]

Domestic security for Hoover was intimately tied to the constitution of U.S. citizens. From the very start of his career in 1917, working during the First World War as a young lawyer in the immigration control section of the Justice Department, Hoover sought to rid the United States of enemy aliens. By late 1939, with a second war underway in Europe, he had begun compiling a list of suspicious "persons of German, Italian, and Communist sympathies," whether residents or citizens, on a Custodial Detention Index that within a few years grew to thousands of names, classified by presumed degree of danger to the United States.[60] At a moment's notice "in time of war or national emergency," persons on the list could be rounded up and placed in concentration camps. The point of this index, as well as others that Hoover maintained in his quest to safeguard the state by one bureaucratized technique after another, was to prepare for "emergency situations" (attack, invasion, rebellion) that might require the suspension of the writ of habeas corpus, as he explained in a letter penned in 1950 to a consultant for President Truman.[61] Detailing tensions within the U.S. government about how best to defend against subversive foreign propaganda during the crucial wartime period 1939–54, Brett Gary points to the "triumph of national security liberalism over free speech liberalism," as Hoover's FBI gradually overcame objections by civil libertarian lawyers also working in the Justice Department. The result of Hoover's dominance, Gary concludes, was "a foreboding among policy makers, opinion leaders, and intellectuals that the psychological dimension of the national security crisis had grown more ominous with the onset of the cold war."[62] We might add to the list of those who felt such foreboding Hollywood filmmakers. To mark, somewhat perversely, Hoover as the tutelary spirit for this study, epitomizing the uneasy mixture of secrecy, power, fear, and suspicion at the heart of noir, I have chosen quotations from the director as epigraphs for some of my chapters. Occasionally this makes for odd juxtapositions (Hoover and the philosopher Stanley Cavell), but then again, strange bedfellows is largely what film noir is all about.

ONE

Gestapo in America

Confessions of a Nazi Spy and
Stranger on the Third Floor

Fifth Column methods have permeated into
every walk of life.—J. Edgar Hoover, 1940

Released two and half years before the United States
officially entered the Second World War, *Confessions
of a Nazi Spy* (1939) was the first mainstream Hollywood film to directly attack Hitler.[1] It was also the
earliest movie to depict Nazi espionage on American
soil. Tracing the activities of the National Socialist
Party in the United States and around the globe
during 1937–38, *Confessions* would seem to be tan-
gential to film noir, although its director, Anatole
Litvak, would go on to make a number of important
noirs in the 1940s.[2] Yet in its feverish depiction of
the German-American Bund, "the boring of enemies
within," as a prosecuting attorney warns near the end,
the movie's combination of documentary realism and
paranoia would help articulate the foundational, affective logic of noir for twenty years to come. This is
more than simply a matter of visual style. As the
phrase "enemies within" already suggests, *Confessions*
would serve as a blueprint for representations of anticommunism soon after the Second World War, and in
fact its screenwriter, Milton Krims, subsequently co-

authored the script for *The Iron Curtain* (1948), the first Hollywood treatment of Soviet spying during the Cold War.[3]

That Nazis could so easily morph into communists is perhaps less surprising than the emergence of film noir partly from such an overt piece of wartime propaganda. To tease out the relation between the dread of enemy aliens stirred up in *Confessions* and feelings of alienation and despair so typical in noir, I will pair the Litvak film in this chapter with a movie made the following year by another Russian Jewish émigré, Boris Ingster.[4] While Litvak was a Ukrainian from Kiev, Ingster was born in Riga, Latvia, coming to the United States in the 1930s as an associate of Sergei Eisenstein. After teaming up with Nathanael West to write a few screenplays, Ingster was given the opportunity to direct *Stranger on the Third Floor* (1940). By virtue of its dark mood and look, *Stranger* is commonly regarded by cinema scholars as the first noir, an expressionist hallucination that culminates in a remarkable extended nightmare sequence.[5] Putting these two seemingly different films side by side, we can appreciate how public politics (so explicit in *Confessions*) and private fantasy (so openly on display in *Stranger*) comingle and gird one another in both these motion pictures, in 1940s noir, and in many Hollywood narratives more generally.[6]

The first five minutes of *Confessions* are astonishing. The movie opens (sans credits) with the silhouette of a radio announcer intoning in a deep newsreel voice that the story about to be told, "stranger than fiction," is based on a recent criminal case of espionage against the United States. Subsequently this portentous voice will provide commentary more than a dozen times to create a documentary feel, often in conjunction with actual newsreel footage of marching Nazi soldiers, rallies, newspaper headlines, and battle scenes spliced into the fictional narrative. As the voice-over fades, we are suddenly transported to a seemingly mundane mail delivery in a small Scottish town, one of many such moments of transport foregrounding communications technology. These sharp geographical leaps emphasize the global reach of Hitler's fascist networks. A close-up of an address on a letter enables Litvak, radically shifting scope and texture once again, to cut to New York, where we see and hear the heavily accented Dr. Karl Kassel (played by Paul Lukas) in a beer hall forcefully addressing his fellow German-American Bund (GAB) members as "patriots."[7]

His speech is fierce, passionate, mesmerizing—in clear contrast to the measured tones of the shadowy radio narrator. Energetically declaring "I love America," Kassel is in fact an American Hitler, as Litvak makes clear when the camera gradually pulls back to reveal a large Nazi swastika sandwiched between two American flags. Perhaps unprecedented for a major Hollywood studio production, this visual shock is matched by equally shocking rhetoric. Identifying himself as a U.S. reserve officer and citizen, Kassel argues that the United States is based on German blood and culture, that Germans have a "destiny" in the United States to save it from the "chaos" bred by "democracy" and "racial equality." Nazism is presented here as a pan-German movement extending beyond national borders. Kassel's references to "our America," repeated both in English and in German ("unser Amerika") bring cheers and Sieg Heil salutes from the crowd, as the camera begins to pan and focus on individuals in the audience. One of these men, unemployed, feckless, with delusions of grandeur and a nagging (non-German) wife, as we soon learn, becomes inspired to volunteer as a spy for the Nazi cause, convinced that he owes allegiance to the Führer and the fatherland. Rather than represent spying as a professional intelligence or military operation, the movie thus imagines espionage in U.S. territory as resulting directly from GAB rabble-rousing that especially affects unstable, insecure, cowardly, and inept amateurs. The result, of course, is to make the actual activity of espionage seems less of a threat, less harmful than the propaganda that triggers it.

Indeed, the movie as a whole seems far more interested in speeches than in spying, and in fact it is the blurring or collapse of this distinction between words and deeds that leads me to categorize *Confessions* as a proto-noir film. Despite the provocative title, talking is less a source of (criminal) revelation than a medium for persuasion; although government agents, led by the G-man Edward Renard (played by Edward G. Robinson) do eventually break up the spy ring, the plot's popular, generic, and action-oriented detection elements remain relatively feeble. The FBI is not even introduced until midway through the picture, and Renard's main function seems less to enforce police procedure than to indulge in a form of speechifying himself, explaining (to us and those around him) the dangers of orators such as Kassel. The movie closely follows the facts of the spy case by depicting thinly veiled versions of the real incompetent spies Dr. Ignaz Griebl (Kassel) and Günther Rumich (called Kurt Schneider in the movie, played by Francis Lederer), who actually tried to directly acquire blank passports from the U.S. government just as his bungling counterpart does in the film—passports being the clearest way to document a foreign enemy's designs on U.S. citizenship.[8] Yet beyond these similarities, Hollywood's fictional reenactment in its hysterical focus on the relationship between propaganda and citizenship would introduce a different set of concerns.

As Kassel's unsettling opening address to the Bund suggests, Litvak seems remarkably willing to show the power of unrestrained rhetoric, both oral and in print. While at various points in the movie some German Americans express skepticism, disdain, or outrage during these meetings, their opposition is swiftly shouted down and met with force from Bund supporters, indicating mob mentality rather than reasoned debate. This is a form of gangsterism that the movie charts with a mixture of fascination and dread. And as we shall see, the fate of American Nazi spies in the United States who come to express misgivings about their work is far worse than a mere silencing.

In his excellent analysis of *Confessions* as the apex of progressive Hollywood antifascism, Saverio Giovacchini focuses on the movie's production history, particularly on how Warner Bros. chose to adapt a spy case of 1938 that was publicized in New York newspaper stories written by an agent who helped solve the crime.[9] But I think another current event might have exercised a more profound sway over the movie: a Washington birthday's "Free America" rally (February 19–20, 1939) held at Madison Square Garden in which over twenty thousand people came out to hear the national leader (*Bundesleiter*) Fritz Kuhn and other GAB officials. A culmination of a series of speeches held by the GAB over the previous few years, the two-day rally in New York triggered violent clashes between protestors and Bund members in attendance that night. Representing the height of the organization's influence in the United States, this mass demonstration generated much attention and anxiety in the press.[10] The movie's Kassel was clearly modeled both on Kuhn and on Griebl, so much so that Kuhn (unsuccessfully) filed a defamation suit against Warner Bros. for 5 million dollars on behalf of the GAB soon after the movie was released.[11]

It is worth contrasting what Kuhn and other speakers actually said at the rally with Kassel's speeches in *Confessions*. Although Kuhn and other leaders were openly anti-Semitic, deriding Jewish control of the media, denouncing Jews as communists, and mocking the New Deal as the "Jew Deal," they took pains at the rally to distance themselves from Hitler, saying that the German National Socialist Party had no place in the United States and warning against attacks on the U.S. Constitution. In celebrating what he took to be American ideals, Kuhn specifically called attention to his "citizenship right" to "criticize freely and act and protest as long as I do not engage in treasonable activities." He concluded by embracing "the freedom of the pulpit, press, radio and stage," but also by demanding, interestingly enough, the "thorough cleansing of the Hollywood film industries of all alien, subversive activities."[12]

Progressives in Hollywood might have been especially peeved by this parting shot at communists; but in any case the movie's script took some serious liberties in translating Kuhn into the fictionalized Kassel, who early on explicitly attacks the Constitution and the Bill of Rights, which he says must be destroyed, not upheld. Why such a drastic change? Turning the rhetoric of his accusers against them, Kuhn sought protection in the freedom of speech, declaring his status as a true American against subversive outsiders (communists/Jews), as well as standing up for his right as a citizen to speak out. But to deny the GAB that freedom, the film had to imagine Kassel as a sheer demagogue advocating the destruction of the Bill of Rights, thereby abdicating any sort of self-protection for his own speaking. In rejecting bedrock American rights inscribed in the nation's sacred documents, Kassel, according to this logic, betrays his professed patriotism and effectively renounces his claim on U.S. citizenship.

Against Kuhn's own repeated public insistence that Nazism is reserved for Germany and not for export, Kassel expresses his obedience to a foreign sovereign (Hitler) and to an alien set of principles, even while continuing to live in the United States. Anticipating cold warriors who sought to outlaw the Communist Party of the United States (CPUSA) because its members (even those native born) were presumed by virtue of their beliefs alone to be Soviet agents, Confessions directly links the speech of the Bund leader Kassel—later shown traveling to Germany and talking with Joseph Goebbels—to the deeds of espionage: precisely the kind of "treasonable activity" that Kuhn disavowed.

The film's propaganda thus sought to render propaganda itself criminal. Of course later in the movie we see Kassel actually engaged in espionage, peering at a small model of a stolen secret American antiaircraft weapon

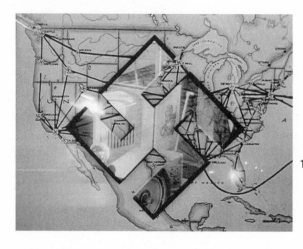

1 Nazi propaganda spreads across the United States, from *Confessions of a Nazi Spy*

that looks like a toy—not exactly the most dramatic of smoking guns to prove his criminal behavior.[13] This scene feels like a minor afterthought because the emphasis and energy throughout the film have been on the power of rhetoric. The real menace is not spying but words, which threaten to turn hundreds of thousands of law-abiding German American citizens living in the United States into potential Nazis. In the film this threat is located not only in Kassel's incendiary speech but in printed materials as well, visualized by Litvak during one powerful sequence as swastikas coming directly from Germany to spread across and overwhelm a map of the United States (see figure 1).[14] But would not this material (at least those pamphlets not directly advocating the overthrow of the U.S. government) be protected under the Bill of Rights? By drumming up a fearful state of urgency or emergency endangering national security, *Confessions* at its most hysterical would seem to answer "no." The question then becomes, who decides, who polices? It was easy enough for Hollywood filmmakers to twist Kuhn's words to match their own worst fears and suspicions, but how could the United States address a threat coming from treacherous foes, at once citizens and yet strangers, who were already firmly entrenched inside the country?

Near the beginning of his speech of February 1939, Kuhn (not Kassel) decried "the standardized order" of public opinion prescribed by the "Untermyers or Dicksteins." Since the early 1930s, alarmed by Hitler's rise to power and growing anti-Semitism at home, a Jewish representative from New York named Sam Dickstein had been lobbying for a congressional committee to investigate German Americans who might be working for the Nazi cause, creating a fifth column of support undermining the nation from within. Paralleling Dickstein was his equally persistent fellow congressman Martin Dies, whose work on House immigration and naturalization committees spurred him to introduce a number of bills advocating the expulsion of foreign communists deemed subversive.[15]

Their joint efforts helped establish in 1934 the Special Committee on Un-American Activities (the McCormack Committee), whose published report the following year indicated that Nazi propaganda circulating in the United States was aimed at "20-odd-million Americans of German birth or descent."[16] This mounting anxiety over fifth-column sympathizers would lead three years later, in June 1938 (a few months before production on *Confessions* began), to the creation of a more permanent and better-funded congressional committee headed by Dies. A staunch anti–New Dealer, Dies would turn the attention of the House Un-American Activities Committee (HUAC) almost entirely to combating communists, especially after the Soviets and Nazis signed a nonaggression treaty in August 1939. For many Americans, the Ribbentrop-Molotov Pact collapsed any nuanced distinction between communist Russia and fascist Germany. A few months after the pact, the term *Commu-Nazi* was coined to conflate the two.[17] Both Stalin and Hitler were gangster-tyrants who ruled totalitarian regimes best defined by the umbrella term *un-American*—a comprehensive category referring to anything and anyone perceived to endanger American traditions and principles. As Dickstein replied when skeptically queried about whom the proposed committee would investigate: "Everybody."[18]

Complicating the matter of who would be investigated—without the right of the accused to cross-examine a witness—was the question of what. Insisting from the start on the need to differentiate "between what is obviously un-American and what is no more or less than an honest difference of opinion," Dies defined his committee's purpose as gathering information about subversive propaganda activities, either of foreign or domestic origin, as long as this dissemination of rhetoric compromised "the principle of the form of government as guaranteed by the Constitution."[19] But short of openly attacking the Constitution, as *Confessions* has Kassel do, "propaganda activities" remained a very nebulous phrase conflating word and action. When Kuhn himself was brought before the committee in August 1939, and then again in October of that year, his often contentious testimony and cross-examination led to no new disclosures about the Bund and to no actionable evidence of crime. Like so many common gangsters before and after him, Kuhn would be indicted for and convicted of a far more mundane offense, the embezzlement of Bund funds (technically larceny and forgery), followed by his arrest and denaturalization during the war and deportation back to Germany at the war's end.[20]

The newly founded Dies Committee of course does not figure in *Confessions*, although the movie clearly partakes of its concerns; HUAC would gain far more prominence after the war investigating communist subversion in Hollywood, ironically the very kind Kuhn warned against in his Madison Square Garden speech. Because the film ostensibly centers on espionage, the forces of law and order are represented not by a congressional investigative committee but by the FBI and the justice system, institutions embodied by agent Renard and his U.S. attorney friend Kellogg (played by Henry O'Neill), who prosecutes the spies. Dedicated since its founding in 1908 to fighting crime at a national level, the FBI and its G-men civil servant bureaucrats were seemingly less given to partisan grandstanding than elected politicians such as Dies. And Edgar G. Robinson as Renard gives a fair approximation of most Americans' view of J. Edgar Hoover during the 1930s and 1940s—calm, professional, vigilant, trustworthy.[21]

And yet even for the FBI the question of what constituted a crime against the state would remain open-ended, leading to an ever-widening set of categories. Well before the founding of the Dies Committee, President Roosevelt in 1936 issued a private directive to the FBI to gather intelligence intended to track connections between domestic radicalism and foreign agents working for international fascist and communist movements.[22] On September 9, 1939, shortly after Hitler invaded Poland, FDR officially declared a provisional state of emergency. This was three days after issuing another FBI directive in conjunction with the global crisis that enabled Hoover to significantly widen the scope of investigation to examine an array of "subversive activities" not previously included in the bureau's traditional crime-fighting mandate. As if to urge FDR's secret order, the agent Renard in *Confessions* at one point in the film complains that the United States has no effective peacetime counterintelligence oper-

ations to fight this "new kind of war." Even though a subsequent directive
that the president issued in early 1943 pointedly dropped the term *subversive* to focus strictly on spying and sabotage, a crucial class of criminality
had already been expanded to extend into the domain of ideas.[23]

In fact it would not be too far-fetched to assert that FDR's declaration of
emergency in September 1939 marks the start of the Cold War (or the
Long War), understood as a state of exception and exceptionalism preoccupied with national security that, some would argue, is still in effect
today.[24] While prior to the 1936 and 1939 presidential directives FBI surveillance was authorized only when the government was preparing to
prosecute against the violation of specific federal laws, FDR's executive
enactment of emergency encouraged the bureau to pursue ongoing surveillance against suspicious un-Americans without any such intent to file
charges. This was a dramatic departure from former FBI practice, as
Hoover himself emphasized in a memorandum distinguishing between
investigative and intelligence activities: while investigations were "conducted when there is a specific violation of a Criminal Statute involved . . .
[leading to] prosecution under legislation," intelligence operations by
contrast required "an entirely different premise," since subversive activity
"does not, in the original stage, involve an overt act or violation of a
specific statute. These subversive groups direct their attention to the dissemination of propaganda and to the boring from within process, much of
which is not a violation of a Federal Statute at the time it is indulged in."[25]
What looks like a very different set of enemies, German and Soviet,
and very different kinds of war—propaganda (the 1930s), hot (1941–45),
and cold (1947–89)—from the perspective of domestic security concerns
remains remarkably continuous, seamless, and consistent. No wonder
Hollywood screenwriters like Krims could move so effortlessly from fascist
Bund members to native communist threats against the homeland.[26]

Blurring the line between thought and action, what followed the president's directive to Hoover was a series of internal security measures as
war loomed, including an antisedition statute adopted by both houses on
June 22, 1940, known as the Alien Registration Act or Smith Act. In
addition to setting up protocols for the registration and deportation of
noncitizens with radical affiliations, one key provision aimed to give the
concept of subversive activity more specificity by making it a criminal
offense to "knowingly or willfully advocate, abet, advise or teach the duty,

necessity, desirability or propriety of overthrowing the Government of the United States or any State by force or violence, or for anyone to organize any association which teaches, advises or encourages such an overthrow, or for anyone to become a member of or to affiliate with any such association."[27] Qualifying the action of overthrowing the government with strings of verbs (abet, advise, teach, encourage), strings of abstract nouns (duty, desirability, propriety), and wobbling between individuals and organizations (associations), the Smith Act was so patently vague that even when it was invoked during wartime to prosecute alleged Nazi conspirators—the "Great Sedition Trial" of 1944—a mistrial was eventually declared.[28]

But against communists both before and after the war, the Smith Act proved more successful, leading to the conviction of a dozen Minneapolis Trotskyists in a mass trial in 1941, and more important, in 1948 to the imprisonment of the leaders of the CPUSA, despite no evidence of any tangible plans to overthrow the government other than the defendant's embrace of Marxist-Leninist ideology. In 1951 this decision was upheld by the Supreme Court, whose majority opinion replaced the famous "clear and present danger" test to delimit free speech—developed by Oliver Wendell Holmes earlier in the century (1919)—with a far looser standard, concluding that conviction was justified given "the inflammable nature of world conditions" coupled with the "highly organized conspiracy" represented by the CPUSA leadership. As the dissenting justice William O. Douglas noted, under this reasoning, which abandoned Holmes's emphasis on proximity and degree, "the crime then depends not on what is taught, but on who the teacher is. This is to make freedom of speech turn not on *what is said*, but on the *intent* with which it is said."[29] Literary New Critics in the 1950s would label this kind of interpreting "the intentional fallacy." Because the defendants were U.S. citizens and not foreign spies who could be detained and deported as such, the legal protection normally afforded them had to be revised to classify their communist ideas as criminal. This logic was in perfect keeping with FDR's own tendency as war loomed to collapse the difference between the activity of enemy espionage and the isolationist rhetoric of his political opponents, whom he frequently labeled "appeaser fifth columnists," witless dupes at best, in an effort to discredit their opinions.[30]

And so in quick succession close to the making and release of *Con-*

fessions we have the congressional institutionalizing of the peculiar concept of un-Americanness (in 1938 by HUAC), a presidential declaration of
emergency (the FBI directive of 1939), and a legislative attempt to prosecute sedition (the Smith Act of 1940). As I have hinted, during this crucial
period there was a fourth governmental mechanism for containing subversion: the physical expulsion from the body politic of the enemy within,
that is, deportation.[31] Well before the Smith Act, the Immigration Act
of 1917 permitted the removal of radical aliens (noncitizens) deemed
to jeopardize national security, and it should come as no surprise that
Hoover during the First World War cut his teeth in the Justice Department, directly before his long tenure at the FBI, by reviewing the detention or deportation cases of undesirable foreigners.[32] Thanks to Hoover
and his boss, A. Mitchell Palmer, the architect of the Red Scare raids of
1919, a long-standing nativist tradition associating foreignness with criminality became institutionalized and entrenched in the FBI.

The threat of deportation is heavily pronounced in both *Confessions*
and *Stranger*, presumably stemming from the émigré sensibilities of their
respective directors. The matter of who stays in and who leaves the United
States is so curiously treated in these movies, in fact, that we might say
they exhibit a kind of deportation panic. In the case of *Confessions*, this
intense anxiety—a fate worse than death—first surfaces midway through
the film, when a German American who challenges Kassel by openly
expressing anti-Nazi sentiments is confronted in a private back room by
Gestapo thugs who lock him up and threaten to send him back to Germany. Formally, the low-key lighting on his distraught face as he struggles
to escape ("I don't want to go back") signals a very noirish moment akin
to the similar scene in *The Red Menace*, as I discussed in the introduction.
Later in the movie, after the bumbling spies confess but before they are
convicted, the narrative focuses on a sequence of obscurely motivated
scenes centered on various figures in relation to U.S. citizenship rights and
statutes: a sick, native-born American of German extraction (a former spy
and a reluctant potential witness for the prosecution) kidnapped and
brought aboard a ship (significantly named *The Bismarck*) heading back
to Europe, and a German-born hairdresser (as in the actual case) being
held in custody in the United States, against the protestations of an
attorney representing the German consulate. These technicalities add
little to the plot, in fact detract from its coherence, but they are crucial for

2 The terror of
nonbelonging,
from *Confessions
of a Nazi Spy*

foregrounding the sheer terror of nonbelonging, which eventually catches up with Kassel himself, who desperately flails against the Gestapo officers, improbably released on bail: "I can't go back . . . I will not go back to Germany" (see figure 2). Abandoned by his Nazi countrymen and hunted by the U.S. government, Kassel has nowhere to turn.

The surprising thing about these "I won't go back" moments when trapped characters unsuccessfully insist on their status as U.S. citizens is that the agency of deportation is not the U.S. government but rather the Gestapo, whose members are depicted in *Confessions* as common criminals along the lines of familiar Hollywood gangsters of the 1930s like Little Caesar. Beyond deviating from the facts, the movie's invention of Gestapo agents on U.S. soil begs the question of why they do not simply bump off betrayers like Kassel rather than wait around to send them back home to face their presumed deaths. Second, the mere existence of the Gestapo in America must give us pause. Not content with exposing a United States ridden with Nazis and Nazi sympathizers, the film takes the extra, unlikely step of imagining the enemy's own dreaded internal security apparatus operating with impunity inside U.S. borders. Here the Gestapo functions as the uncanny shadow of the nation-state's own security apparatus featured in the movie, the FBI. Yet while this covert twinning serves to show the contrast between Nazi tactics and American ones, I wonder if there is not some unintended seepage between the two kinds of police procedure, with the lingering implication that fighting totalitarian regimes and securing safety in a time of peril may demand some voluntary abridgement of rights on the part of U.S. citizens.[33]

Such a case is suggested during the prosecuting attorney Kellogg's summation to the jury, who as in many other Hollywood motion pictures directly come to stand in for the film's viewers. In a movie filled with impassioned speeches, his is perhaps the most intense, a tour de force of conspiratorial terror that echoes and amplifies the urgent voices of Renard and the film's newsreel announcer. As in the earlier marching propaganda scene showing swastikas spreading across a map of the United States, here Litvak again masterfully links in a montage sequence dire warnings with striking visuals: charts in court showing links between the GAB and Nazi leaders, scenes of goose stepping German soldiers invading one European country after another, and perhaps most important, a flurry of newspaper headlines insisting over and over again that these invasions were facilitated by homegrown "fifth columnists" and deceitful "Trojan Horses." *The Trojan Horse in America*, in fact, was the title of a book Dies wrote in 1940 instructing U.S. citizens how to detect and guard against communists and communist activity (with some pages devoted to Nazis as well).[34] In keeping with the film's fixation on propaganda, the U.S. attorney's address to the court hardly touches on the facts of the crime (for which a handful of spies are anticlimactically convicted), but instead whips his audience into a frenzy of fear and hysteria, as if he has been infected by the GAB's own brand of demagoguery.

Presumably to acknowledge that it has gone too far, the movie's final scene between Kellogg and Renard takes place in a local diner, the quintessential midcentury setting to dramatize traditional American virtues and normalcy. The effect is to pull back sharply from this tone of impending doom to affirm a kind of quiet trust in U.S. democracy and unifying common sense. To reassure us presumably that "it can't happen here" (directly after implying that it could if we do not watch out), an indignant waiter serving coffee to a customer casually observes about the case that "this ain't Europe."[35] *Confessions* then closes with a swell of patriotic music accompanying the newsreel announcer's celebration of "the voice of the people," a commonplace phrase or shorthand for progressive New Deal collectivism that belies the dread of the enemy within that has been so nervously on display throughout the entire narrative.

In his concluding chat with his friend the U.S. attorney, the FBI agent

Renard expresses surprise and dismay at the espionage case. How could such a thing occur in the United States? In an unnaturally calm voice, he likens the episode to the experience of living in a "madhouse," to a sense of being "absolutely insane," causing you to "doubt your own sanity." Current events abroad and at home are "unreal" and "fantastic," he continues, as if we were living in the midst of an "absurd nightmare": prescient comments indeed months before Hitler invaded Poland to throw Europe and then Russia (and subsequently the United States and the rest of the globe) into years of turmoil and millions of deaths.

The absurd "nightmare" that Renard alludes to in *Confessions* as a metaphor for a world in crisis and confusion is fully realized in *Stranger on the Third Floor*. This nightmare constitutes the intense experience of an individual who is not an agent of the state but its victim. In other words, the movie is not about subversion but is subversive. *Stranger* was a low-budget, quickly made B movie released in August 1940, only three months after the rerelease of *Confessions*. Produced by RKO, it was directed by Ingster, shot by Nicholas Musuraca (who would go on to photograph *Out of the Past*), with art direction by Van Nest Polglase (who subsequently worked on *Citizen Kane*), and written by Frank Partos (the subsequent author of *The Snake Pit*), with the uncredited help of Nathanael West.[36] Perhaps only such a remarkable group of individuals could make such an extraordinary sixty-four-minute film, and because it is a far denser and more self-conscious work of art than *Confessions*, with a deeper and wider range of affects, it will require a more sustained formal analysis.

Like *Confessions*, the movie opens with a shadowy silhouette. But rather than introduce a newsreel announcer to give the narrative an air of documentary authenticity about international affairs, this shadow lurking in the background of the opening credits shows the figure of a man spied through an apartment window successively smoking a cigarette, composing at a typewriter, and talking on the phone—all solitary activities yet with social dimensions that suggest how the film will be probing the margins between private and public space. Negotiating these spaces is the film's protagonist, a writer whose work as a journalist puts him at the intersection of personal artistic expression and a more collective, communal rendering of events deemed newsworthy to others.

Stranger's plot opens where *Confessions* closes—in an urban diner (actually a drugstore counter), where the New York crime reporter Michael

Ward (John McGuire) and his fiancée Jane (Margaret Tallichet) meet for breakfast, not having any other more private place to share a meal, to discuss their new prospects for marriage and for increased intimacy. Poised (in 1940) between the end of the Depression and the start of a new era of domestic consumerism, Michael extols the virtues of their future kitchen, complete with "an electric stove, a refrigerator, and a washing machine." The couple can finally afford to get married because Michael has gotten a raise for both writing the headline story and for serving as the key witness against a small-time boyish ex-con, Joe Briggs (Elisha Cook Jr.), accused of slashing the throat of the immigrant café owner Nick. The tearful account Briggs gives in court is a familiar 1930s story—he is unemployed, working-class, destitute, belligerent, accepting thirty cents from Michael for a meal, and later returning to the diner to repay the loan when the reporter spies him at the cash register standing over the murder victim.

The quick trial features an oblivious judge and a jury member nodding asleep, a disengaged defense attorney who offers no defense, passionate cries of innocence from a distraught Briggs once the verdict is read ("I didn't do it!"), and a jaded crew of fellow journalists (straight out of Ben Hecht and Charles MacArthur's stage play *The Front Page*) who sarcastically applaud Michael with gallows humor for his professional good luck. But from the start Jane herself expresses a "funny feeling" about the youth's guilt, sentenced to death because of the expert eyewitness testimony of the reporter, who is, after all, as the prosecuting attorney reminds the jury, a trained observer. Leaving the courtroom in anguish and uncertainty, Jane later exclaims to Michael over the phone: "He'll be with us for the rest of our lives. I'll always hear his voice."

So in a complex, deft rendering of well-established social roles, these first few scenes present an indifferent, uncaring justice system no longer moved by New Deal pathos, a cynical news media, an ambitious young man trying to further his career and love life (intimately intertwined), and his soon-to-be wife, morally sensitive and haunted by the thought that her intended husband will be directly to blame for the state-sanctioned murder of an innocent young man. Michael brusquely tries to brush off Jane's misgivings in typically masculine fashion, saying "you're just upset" and insisting that all he did was accurately testify about what he saw at the crime scene—which is perfectly true. But stopping at a bar for a drink with a jaded colleague (Martin, played by Cliff Clark), Michael, too, begins to wonder if she is right, to wonder if he is indeed "personally responsible" for the impending execution of Briggs that conveniently has given him his first big career break, more money, and the promise of marriage. Advancing at the expense of Briggs, Michael may in fact seem complicit in the youth's sentence of death. Yet I would argue otherwise that the reporter's feelings of guilt are all the more potent and unshakeable precisely for being so unmotivated, the sign of an empty formality in the very structure of the law: he knows he has done nothing wrong, but he cannot accept his own innocence.[37]

The brilliance of the director Ingster is to give the narrative's rapidly entangling emotions—guilt, ambition, professional duty, sexual desire—an equally charged condensing of sight and sound arguably unprecedented in the history of American cinema. From the first shot of the courtroom, the mise-en-scène has been filled with angular expressionist shadows cutting across backgrounds and bodies: witnesses on the stand, corridors, the jury, Michael in the pressroom, Jane sitting by the phone. These visuals now begin to take on an even sharper uncanniness in an eerie sequence that tracks Michael in solitude as he heads for home. A midrange shot of the reporter in the hallway peering through a door is followed by a shot of the now empty, shadow-filled courtroom, including an ominous, skewed scales of justice on the wall. Suddenly the soundtrack fills with Briggs's desperate denials, as if to confirm Jane's fear that "I'll always hear his voice." The camera then cuts to a close-up of Michael, who starts talking to himself, asking, "What's the matter with me?" Ingster next presents a conventional tracking shot of Michael walking down the street, pedestrians in the background, but with that interior monologue still running, interrupted at one point by the distraught voice of Jane echoing in his head, compounding his doubt and confusion.

With "what's the matter with me?" we have entered noir territory—and for the first time in film history, I would argue, although of course it is risky, if not downright foolhardy, to indulge in such pronouncements. Before following up on my claims, let me finish describing the rest of this striking sequence. Still self-interrogating, Michael pauses on the sidewalk in front of the scene of the crime, a new sign on the café window indicating "Jack's" diner instead of "Nick's." Indulging in the same sort of cynicism that infected his fellow reporters, Michael muses "business as usual," disgusted that the murder has already been forgotten, and turns to cross the road. But the dark street is now almost empty, with only a few pedestrians receding far into the darkness. And so on the front stoop of his apartment he suddenly encounters sitting in the shadows the silent figure of the Stranger (Peter Lorre, sporting a long, white silk aviator scarf), whose slight boyish stature clearly resembles that of the condemned criminal Briggs. The answer to "What's the matter with me," we understand, might very well be, "Michael, you are no longer yourself, you are (a) strange(r) in your own house."

Doppelgängers were certainly nothing new in the cinema of the 1920s and 1930s, especially in Hollywood horror movies and German expressionist film, and even the scene's compounded mirroring (the Stranger and Briggs; Michael and the Stranger) does not fully account for its power, which depends on the relentless internal monologue we have been hearing. Talking to oneself is inherently a kind of doubling, a self-alienation that sets up the movie's anguish to come. Even more so than a film like *Detour*, made five years later at the end of the war, here it is a first-person voice that spookily shapes and inhabits the narrative, making it border on insanity.[38] More intense and pointed than the emotional cuing offered by soundtrack music alone, Michael's accompanying inner voice serves to bind and fold together discrete shots within a tightly focused subjectivity at once persistent (it will not go away) and unstable (it does not understand itself). This constant self-questioning here functions to collapse boundaries, blurring distinctions between inside and outside, as we enter with Michael a kind of dream state so typical of many noirs in years to come.

Announced by Michael's self-address to "me," the film's noirish inward turn is also a move outside, to the kind of world in crisis depicted in *Confessions*. If the movie is somewhat ahead of its time in negotiating complex psychoanalytic themes, its brand of Freudianism, we shall see, is more akin to Frankfurt School theory than to typical 1940s mainstream Hollywood versions that also deal with guilt and sexuality such as *Double Indemnity* (discussed in the following chapter). After passing the Stranger on the threshold of his apartment, Michael climbs the dark, shadowy stairway to his room, muttering as he moves from public to private space, "what a gloomy dump," and asking (as a kind of joke?) for a bigger lamp. His call for stronger lighting is a self-reflexive remark that directs attention to the film's unusual visual design, whose baroque style (in advance of

Citizen Kane) would anticipate noir cinematography and composition for the following two decades.[39] As if to comment on the vexed relation between inner and outer that I have been discussing, the phrase "what a gloomy dump" also underscores an important issue raised by Dana Polan about noir in the 1940s more generally. Contrasting these films to German expressionist cinema, which seems similar visually, Polan argues that settings in wartime American movies rarely reflect the inner psychic turmoil of characters, who remain existentially detached from their barren surroundings.[40]

But at this point in the film it is difficult to decide if the gloom Michael detects on the stairs is an external projection of his increasing despair (characteristic of German expressionism) or if his despair and contempt result from his increasing awareness of the moral corruption enveloping him, since shadows have been falling and following him everywhere since the opening courtroom scene, when he still felt pretty chipper about his chances. Is the gloom his or New York's or that of America's? Reaching the third floor, Michael in disgust walks past his sleeping neighbor, whose snores recall those of one of the snoozing jurors in the courtroom. This noise surreally and loudly lingers on the soundtrack to be registered by Michael even after he enters his claustrophobic studio.[41] The snoring not only sutures shots by crossing between two bounded spaces—the neighbor's apartment and Michael's—but more pointedly suggests a kind of interpenetration of the two men's subjectivities, so that this neighbor intrudes on Michael's thoughts even when the reporter is alone in his own room. Here in this grim space, after briefly regarding himself in a mirror, still talking to himself as he wearily prepares for bed, Michael is tormented by three flashback scenes (rendered by extreme close-up, low-key lighting, a camera zoom-in, and a dissolve). Each is more intense than the previous one, and they are followed by an extended nightmare sequence; taken together, this quartet of memories and fantasies organize the rest of the movie, so that Michael's initial guilt at helping to condemn Briggs turns into a far more peculiar set of feelings running from fear and rage to humiliation.

The source of this intensity is "that snoring animal next door," Michael's neighbor Albert Meng, whose name and bespectacled appearance are sufficiently ambiguous to suggest an oriental lineage as well as a German one. In fact, even though he speaks with no accent, Meng most closely resembles the character of Mr. Moto, the Japanese master spy and detective that Lorre himself played in a series of movies in the late 1930s. How and why Meng (Charles Halton) functions as an assimilated combination of two Axis enemies (Germany and Japan) is the crux of my political reading of the movie, particularly in relation to *Confessions*.[42]

In all three flashbacks, Meng plays the figure of censoring authority for Michael. Remembering how he first met him, the reporter flashes back to a scene of writing, in which the landlady and Meng push into his room and accuse him of making too much noise on the typewriter. Here is another extremely self-reflexive moment, for the suppression of writing not only refers back to Michael's role of journalist (recall the opening credits silhouette) but also to artistic creation more generally, including the making of movies. That Michael is typing late at night makes it all the more plausible that he may be writing a work of fiction, not a news story. In any case, beyond endangering his livelihood (one key source of his masculinity), Meng threatens the journalist's ability to report the news, the freedom of the press. Given my previous discussion of *Confessions*—its preoccupation with propaganda in the context of various laws aimed at curbing speech for the sake of national security—Meng's intrusion resonates profoundly.

The film's second flashback will push Meng's regulation of expression into increasingly disturbing territory. As Michael revives from his unpleasant initial reverie, lurking on the third floor he spots again the mute Stranger, who has moved from outside the building to inside, closer to Michael's personal space. Seeing the Stranger's luminous, babyish white hand emerge from the shadows, he chases him down the stairs (with a towel around his neck that mirrors the Stranger's trademark flowing scarf).[43] Outside on the empty street, Michael loses sight of him, reflecting, "What an evil face; he and Meng make a swell team," as he makes his way back up to his room. When Michael tries to communicate through his thin apartment wall with Meng, now eerily silent (much like the Stranger), he suddenly fears that his tormentor may be dead, killed by the intruder. The Stranger is somehow tangled up in Michael's own animosity against the interfering censor, combined with his lingering guilt about Briggs.

What follows is another flashback trigged by a large knife Michael picks up in his apartment, a lethal object less benign than a typewriter. As the camera dissolves on a close-up of Michael, we are transported via a deft storefront window shot to the scene of the crime, Nick's café, where he recalls again being interrupted one day by Meng. The memory begins with Michael and his newspaper colleague Martin playfully making fun of Nick's heavy Greek accent. Meng enters, looks disapprovingly at a pair of attractive young women, and then begins to chide the reporter for drinking coffee rather than milk.[44] Reacting to Meng's peculiar ways, Martin asks, "Who is that citizen? . . . He looks like his mind could stand a little laundering"—a remark that sets off an astonishing outburst from the mild-mannered Michael as he fiddles with his steak knife: "Did you ever want to kill a man? . . . He's not a man, but a worm, the kind you want to jump on with heavy boots. It would be a real pleasure to cut his throat." Years before George Orwell's dystopian novel *Nineteen Eighty-Four* (1949) and more than a full decade before the term *brainwashing* entered the American lexicon during the Korean War (1951–53), *Stranger* puts the concept of mind laundering into play.[45]

How do we explain the excessive virulence of Michael's reply? The overtly political resonance of the dialogue—references to citizens, the laundering of minds, and heavy boots—suggests that the offending superego has extended beyond the realm of the guilt-ridden individual psyche to occupy the collective domain of a state intent on regulating thought crime: "It was just talk . . . you can't convict a man on that," Michael tries to reassure himself as he returns from memory to the present. And while thought crime might seem to be the exclusive province of totalitarian regimes like Nazi Germany in 1940, U.S. laws like the Smith Act, which worked to blur the line between words ("just talk") and deeds (crimes), suggest otherwise. Michael's early pangs of remorse during the opening trial scene—guilt all the more powerful for being unwarranted—have grown and expanded during these flashbacks into an emerging security crisis in which the distinction between subversive ideas or desires (wanting to kill Meng) and illicit action (murdering Meng) collapse in an overarching dread of un-American enemies.

In Michael's third memory he goes beyond paranoia to perversely incriminate himself in Meng's death, as yet unconfirmed and only a suspicion. Searching for a motive for his own intense hatred, he finds it in sex—perhaps the most sacred and last refuge of privacy that a citizen has. The reverie centers on Jane's first entrance into the reporter's studio after a rainy walk in the park, as she expresses her desire for Michael in about as

3 Meng the informer, from *Stranger on the Third Floor*

explicit terms as possible given Hollywood Production Code censorship: "I've always wanted to see your room." The scene is heavily laden with sexual tension, as Michael removes Jane's wet stockings and begins toweling her exposed legs. Suddenly as he starts to laugh in nervous anticipation, there is a sharp series of echoing raps at the door. Meng and the landlady burst into the room and accuse him of breaking the rules against having women visitors. Vowing to call the police, Meng denies pleasure by disrupting the couple's desire. Flying into a rage, the humiliated reporter begins to strangle and threaten the dreaded censor. "Obscene old fool," Michael shouts at him. Just before the disgraced couple leaves the room and descends the stairs, the frustrated lover mutters to Jane, "he's always spying on me"—a remark that once again turns the castrating father figure into a functionary of the state (see figure 3). This intense watching is at once political and personal, a kind of voyeurism that we ourselves have been participating in from the movie's opening credits, which appeared over the dark figure of the reporter framed by his apartment window, a composition subsequently reinforced by our peering into the café window during Michael's second reverie.[46]

To put it simply, Meng's surveillance marks him as an informer. Such figures were crucial for maintaining law and order, Jeremy Bentham insisted in the early nineteenth century, in perfect keeping with the invisible omniscience at the center of his proposed Panopticon. Bentham defends the practice by analogy, so that "the informer is a servant of the government, employed in opposing the internal enemies of the state, as the solider is a servant employed in opposing its external foes." Substituting the bland word *inspection* for the more highly charged term *espionage*, to which "a stigma is attached," Bentham argues that society's widespread "prejudice" against state-sanctioned intelligence gathering is unwarranted, stemming from a "confusion of ideas" between the "judicial" and the "private informer," that is, between one who denounces a crime openly in a "court of justice" and one who "secretly insinuates accusations against his enemies."[47] But this clear-cut distinction between public and private in Bentham's blithe utilitarian analysis, between "justice" and personal animus, is precisely what Ingster's film blurs in the character of Meng—a nosy neighbor whose prying into Michael's affairs extends well beyond idle curiosity. And when we triangulate the relation between the Reporter and the Informer with the Stranger (to draw out the allegorical implications of the narrative by way of those capital letters), then it is fair to ask who poses the greater danger, the mysterious interloper (undetected by all except the journalist until the end) or the authoritarian German Asian, ambiguously either overseeing internal threats against the homeland or else working for a foreign enemy.

Up to this point in the film, Meng's spying could be read as a commentary on the Nazi police state, but Michael's subsequent nightmare, revisiting the court of law that opened the film, phantasmagorically upsets that reading by relocating the Gestapo in the United States. This striking seven-minute montage sequence is very difficult to describe, but I will briefly try. Reiterating the line, "What's the matter with me?" (by now the movie's refrain), Michael, slumped in a chair, covers his face with his hand (paralleling the Stranger's) and falls asleep, entering his nightmare by ironically hearing the call to "wake up," suggesting how this dream is more "real" than reality. A Kafkaesque scene of interrogation ensues, made up of scrambled, free-floating, and distorted images from the earlier trial, with Michael now replacing Briggs as the guilty criminal and the German/Japanese Meng replacing the Greek immigrant Nick as the murder victim: extreme close-ups of the reporter's agitated face protesting his innocence, as well as the faces of his accusers; jagged skyscrapers looming over Jane screaming in disbelief; his colleagues reading monstrously blown-up "MURDER!" headlines; twirling newspapers filling the screen (a feverish rendition of the headline montage in *Confessions*); Michael violently shak-

4 Fascist American justice, from *Stranger on the Third Floor*

ing Jane to echo Briggs ("I didn't do it"), while a prison guard darkly hovers over them; Briggs's defense attorney hysterically laughing at Michael, who sits dwarfed in a cavernous cell. All these images are composed in stark, exaggerated chiaroscuro light and shadow, in surreal scale, dramatizing how a vast visual design dominates and controls the minute individuals trapped within.

And then we shift from the prison to the courtroom, a setting out of *The Cabinet of Dr. Caligari* (1920), with witnesses shot in extremely titled camera angles, overhead and low; Michael trying to rouse jurors fast asleep (all twelve); a judge who constantly shouts him down; and a stern prosecuting attorney whose objection at one key moment in the proceedings takes the form of a Nazi salute (see figure 4). The scene momentarily changes to what seems to be a theater auditorium, where the Stranger is seen climbing over seats toward the front, before we return to the courtroom verdict and sentencing, the judge now transformed via Michael's nightmare vision into the sinister scales of (in)justice we saw earlier in the film. Then we witness the condemned man's slow march to the electric chair, cast as a grotesquely magnified shadow, accompanied by the crazed taunts of Briggs behind bars. The nightmare closes with the sudden appearance of Meng, still chiding the reporter for drinking coffee, as Michael wakes up drenched in sweat to his own screaming "he's alive." It should come as no surprise now that immediately after he regains consciousness, Michael goes into Meng's room to confirm that the informer has indeed been permanently silenced by way of a slashed throat, as if dreaming it made it so: a thought turns into a crime, confirming once again the antisedition reasoning of the Smith Act.

It is hard to unpack this entire extraordinary sequence, but I am most intrigued by two fleeting shots that only make sense when given a specific political context. In terms of visual style, this is German expressionism 101 transposed to a New York setting, with camera techniques, mise-en-scène, and composition right out of Fritz Lang, such as an execution death march that closely resembles the zombie shuffle of factory workers in the opening scenes of *Metropolis* (1927). In terms of submerged content, we must begin with the most disturbing image in this fantasy of paranoid persecution, the district attorney briefly gesturing Sieg Heil. Patterns of shadow resembling swastikas projected on the courtroom wall during Michael's show trial match his salute. What shows up in *Confessions* as a charged sign of GAB foreignness is here transposed to the very center of the American justice system. In the Litvak film the courtroom is a cherished civic space and the very spot where law and order is restored near the conclusion. As if to mock this restoration, even the district attorney in *Stranger* (played by Charles Waldron) closely resembles the speechifying prosecutor Kellogg in *Confessions* (Henry O'Neill), both well-known Hollywood character actors frequently cast as upright authority figures such as lawyers and judges throughout the 1930s. It is difficult for me to think of any prior American movie treating the justice system so subversively, even in a dream; evidence might be faulty and juries misled or misguided, but the law itself ultimately prevails in classic Hollywood narrative. While films such as Lang's *Fury* (1936) and *You Only Live Once* (1937) depict mob behavior and false accusation, the U.S. court as an institution is largely exempt from the kind of wholesale structural assault implied in the cinematic fantasy directed by Ingster. The administration of justice helps contain the domestic Nazi threat brewing in *Confessions*, but in *Stranger*, the machinery of law *is* the nightmare.[48]

From jaded journalists to the informer Meng's censoring presence to the district attorney's menacing authoritarianism, dread and distrust of government pervade the movie. And lest we think that Michael is made to pay for the crimes of his uncanny double, the Stranger, only in his dreams, I would argue that his turmoil is more than the psychic projection of a guilty conscience, since the nightmare merely accentuates and amplifies what was latent in Briggs's own trial and continues well after Michael wakes up. Realizing who has committed the two murders, the reporter the next morning reveals the truth to the district attorney as he shaves himself in front of a mirror, recapitulating the ghastly modus operandi of the throat-slashing Stranger. But the prosecutor dismisses him as crazy: "I hope you didn't dream him [the Stranger] up too," to which Michael sarcastically replies: "Congratulations. You'll be governor yet." Extending beyond the solitary Gestapo figure of Meng (now silenced), totalitarianism has become firmly entrenched in U.S. politics and law; while the film offers no solution to address such a bleak prospect, it does struggle to achieve some sort of equilibrium after the nightmare. Normalcy returns only by a sacrificial purging of the mute Stranger from the state itself: to save Michael and Briggs, the Stranger must be pursued and prosecuted, leading to a kind of deportation panic resembling those instances of consternation troubling *Confessions*.

In another more direct way, however, the nightmare does quickly come to a close; when the reporter is arrested and locked up for Meng's murder, this time for real, he departs the movie until its conclusion and therefore no longer subjectively dictates the narrative's sight and sound via his incessant monologue.[49] But if neither Michael nor the law can rid the nation of the un-American danger within, who will be the agent of the Stranger's purging? Interesting enough, particularly for implications of gender, it is the innocuous Jane. Once Michael shuts up, Jane takes over. Her quest in the end to prove her fiancé's innocence by identifying and locating the mysterious Stranger (seen by nobody but Michael up to now) brings us back to the sunlit, social world. Canvassing the neighborhood for help, Jane reaches out to a community of postmen, grocers, housewives, and café owners (including immigrants, more or less assimilated), people largely missing from the moment Michael thought to himself, "What's the matter with me?," and walked across that dark, lonely street.

And what of the Stranger, where does he fit in this world? Here a precursor text to Freud's essay on the uncanny proves helpful: Georg Simmel's "The Stranger" of 1908, a short discussion of a distinct social type marked by a spatial dialectic of nearness and remoteness while interacting with others.[50] Simmel distinguishes between an alien and a stranger, who as a participating "member of the group itself," functions as an "inner enemy," an "element whose membership within the group involves both being outside it and confronting it." The classic example for Simmel is the history of European Jews, and here I cannot resist saying something briefly about the actor Lorre, who was born Laszlo Lowenstein, fled Nazi Germany in 1933, two years after playing a child murderer in Lang's *M*, and began in the mid-1930s playing terrorists, spies, and foreign villains in an assortment of movies, including Alfred Hitchcock's *The Man Who Knew Too Much* (1935) and eight films in the Mr. Moto series.[51] When *Stranger* was made in 1940, he was not yet a naturalized U.S. citizen—a fact whose significance will become apparent shortly. Drawing on Simmel, we can appreciate the fluidity of Lorre's roles as the stranger in the movie—first as a stand-in for the boyish victim Briggs, then as an accomplice or dark twin of Meng (recall Michael's "swell team" remark), and third and most important, as the protagonist's own uncanny double, allowing the reporter to realize his darkest desires.[52]

Insofar as the Stranger helps realize the repressed desires of others, he plays another sort of role in the movie, one more artistic than overtly criminal, that emerges briefly during the nightmare trial sequence, when he inexplicably shows up in what appears to be a theater climbing over seats as if to orchestrate the action onstage. Even given the jumbled illogic of a dream, this abrupt shift in setting from courtroom to auditorium can be accounted for only in relation to the film's wider political implications. The deliberately inserted shot of the Stranger in a theater, ostentatiously flourishing his white scarf (what subsequently gives him away to Jane), fits the old-fashioned stereotype of a Hollywood movie director, say Erich von Stroheim. Reinforced by the two scenes of Michael composing at his typewriter (including when the opening credits list the movie's screenwriter), this notion of the Stranger as director suggests how he might not simply be passively stuck in Michael's nightmare but more actively shaping or guiding it. The courtroom momentarily becomes a movie house, with the Stranger responsible for the flickering shadows projected within (and with silhouetted Michael getting credit for writing the script), so that Meng's final appearance as the Gestapo informer next door also points to the repressive function of the Production Code Administration set up to police Hollywood morality, to regulate expression.[53] Coming from different directions, polemics and fantasy, the narratives of both *Stranger* and *Confessions* blur any easy distinction between aesthetics and politics, which converge in the well-nigh unstoppable power of propaganda—words and images—to sway citizens. I have shown how *Stranger* begins in public spaces (a diner followed by a courtroom), exactly where *Confessions* ends (a courtroom, then a diner). But in thematic terms *Stranger* ends where *Confessions* begins, in the fear of a spreading stain of un-Americanness that must be excised from the nation.

Hence the final encounter between Jane and the Stranger at the scene of the crime, Nick's (now Jack's) café—an exchange as remarkable as the nightmare sequence. First a luminous white disembodied hand reaching across the counter, and then the Stranger's initial act of speaking, made possible, we presume, by the silencing of Michael and Meng: a heavily (German) accented request for two hamburgers, raw, to which the immigrant café owner responds in jest how his customer must enjoy "the taste of blood"; as if in parody of a Lorre movie, the joke here (on us) is that what appears mysterious and sinister quickly turns out to be mundane, even sentimental. Exiting the diner, the Stranger takes the meat to feed a stray dog on the sidewalk—a creature as homeless as he, as he pathetically admits to Jane while worrying that the dog will get a "tummy ache" if it eats too quickly. Evil intruder, cinema director, Gestapo silencer, Wandering Jew, impossibly sad, kindhearted soul—the Stranger's overdetermined identity in the narrative takes one last turn as Jane boldly begins to confront him with his crimes as the two walk down the same dark street on which Michael had started asking "what's the matter with me." By contrast, the Stranger's string of questions to Jane is less inward directed and more openly paranoid: "Why are you looking at me like that?"; "Why are you following me?"; "How do I know I can trust you?"; and most important, "Did they send you to take me back?" When Jane asks, "Who?," the Stranger replies, "Don't you know? The people who lock you up."

And so the deportation panic starts. When Jane reassures him that "they" would not send a woman, the Stranger smiles in agreement, acknowledging (in a gesture to conventional Freudianism) that "the only person who was ever kind to me was a woman. She's dead now." From mommy's boy (two full decades before Hitchcock's *Psycho*), the conversation turns to "they":

5 "I'll not go back!":
Deportation panic
in *Stranger on the
Third Floor*

J: Why do they want to lock you up?

S: So they can hurt me. They put you in a shirt with long sleeves [he demonstrates] and they pour ice water on you.

J: Oh, that's terrible. Did Nick want to send you back to them?

S: Yes, he did. How do you know?

J: Did Meng try to do it too?

S: Meng? Who is Meng?

J: You know, the man up there in the house.

S: Oh, that man. He said he was going to report me. I had to kill him. What's the matter?

A struggle ensues, with the Stranger, now happily and safely (for us) identified as an escaped lunatic from an insane asylum, afraid of getting caught, trying to strangle Jane, declaring, "You live there, with them," while hysterically insisting over and over, "I'll not go back" (see figure 5). This line echoes the GAB leader Kassel's frantic cries in *Confessions*. Hit by a truck while chasing Jane across the street, the dying man admits his crimes to a policeman conveniently arriving on the scene. His last words are, "Yes, but I'm not going back."

Near the end of *Confessions*, the FBI agent Renard compares events in Europe on the verge of war to a "nightmare" and a "madhouse"; in *Stranger*, the nightmare is Michael's and the madhouse would seem to belong to the Stranger, who offers his own confession to conclude the movie. Nightmare and madhouse turn out to be two sides of the same coin, inner turmoil externalized (the mode of expressionism), as well as political trauma internalized (the emergence of film noir). What feels throughout like a random menace, a proto–serial killer loose on the streets, ends up being given a specific motivation. Yet the Stranger is no Nazi spy like Kassel, but rather a suspicious inner enemy who murders the informer Meng (a different sort of "reporter" than Michael) to avoid being sent back.[54] After his various incarnations in the film, friendly and hostile, rational and irrational, creative and criminal, he remains an uncanny embodiment of estrangement at home that simply refuses to go away. Nor is he apprehended by the law; rather, he falls victim to a random accident, the first in a long line of fatalistic twists that would become film noir orthodoxy (or theology) for years to come. But more important than how he dies is why he dies. On the surface the movie conceives of insanity and torture as dwelling in a foreign land, but Renard's closing words in the Litvak film would encourage us to reverse the equation—that insanity stands as a metaphor for the Stranger's radical condition of nonbelonging at a moment of global crisis.[55] In the name of national security that insidious threat must be cast out from the state.

White-Collar Murder

Double Indemnity

Work is hardly the stuff of noir. Here Michael Ward's
standing as a professional news reporter in *Stranger on
the Third Floor* represents something of a lost cause or
false lead for subsequent dark films, whose protagonists primarily indulge in more leisurely pursuits. Vivian Sobchack wonderfully calls this mode of activity
"lounge time," although hitchhiking, gambling, en-
tertaining, drinking, smoking, driving, and especially
detection (not to mention revenge, betrayal, theft, and
homicide) often require exertion and sophisticated
skill sets beyond the motive and matter of financial
remuneration. Work space is similarly hard to find in
these uncanny crime narratives, whose urban mise-en-
scène is more often made up of streets, bars, and
boarding houses than of shining modern office build-
ings. Of course in many detection noirs, starting with
The Maltese Falcon (1941), the private eye's first encounter with his enigmatic client takes place in his
office, but quickly thereafter he is forced to pursue the
case in less familiar, more ominous surroundings.[1]

Earning an honest living would also seem to have little to do with issues of citizenship as I have started to pose them in this study, especially for middle-class salaried workers employed in the commercial and service sectors (as opposed to less assimilated immigrants laboring in factories who at midcentury still might have needed lessons in how to follow the American way of life). So it is a bit striking that one of the earliest and most canonical dark films, immediately recognized as "noir" by the French in the aftermath of the war, should for long stretches take place in a bland suite of offices and feature a glib salesman and his claims investigator colleague engaged in intense competition. Their rivalry generates ugly emotions shaped by the codes of white-collar bureaucracy and recorded by a business transcription device that parallels the movie camera in its capacity to capture the agon of the workplace. While in James M. Cain's source novel of 1935, insurance is mainly the occasion and context to spin out a clever murder scheme, in Billy Wilder's movie version of 1944 it becomes the center of attention, with implications for questions of national belonging as well. Wilder's film thus shares with Ingster's *Stranger* a deep distrust of authoritarian structures, though this time governmental agency is not located in the U.S. press or justice system, as in the earlier noir, but in the modern corporation.

Double Indemnity enacts a series of couplings, doublings, and scenes of triangulated desire of a dizzying, Shakespearean complexity. The framing, intermittent retrospective voice-over narration of the insurance salesman Walter Neff (Fred MacMurray), grievously wounded, spoken into an office Dictaphone late at night, introduces us to an entangled set of relations and emotions that would come to define film noir conventions for a decade to come: a sadistic-erotic affair with the ravenous, conniving, bored, and lonely housewife, Phyllis Dietrichson (Barbara Stanwyck); their co-conspiracy to murder her husband (Tom Powers), who figures as a father standing in an Oedipal relation to the younger lover, Neff; another sort of father-mentor for Neff, the insurance claims manager Barton Keyes (Edward G. Robinson), who investigates the murder and fraud; and the subsequent tension generated between Phyllis and Keyes as rivals for Walter's affection. It is these various couplings and triangles that constitute the affective dynamics of identification and alienation driving Neff's narration, ostensibly about the twin temptations of sex and money.

The film also presents a number of subplots that shadow or double these primary relations: a covert liaison between Phyllis's stepdaughter, Lola (Jean Heather), and her boyfriend, Nino Zachette (Byron Barr); Lola's fairy-tale hatred of her stepmother; Neff's growing attraction to Lola; and, seemingly more peripheral still, the antagonism between Keyes and the president of the Pacific All-Risk Insurance Company, Mr. Norton (Richard Gaines), whom Keyes regards as a weak, flawed boss. Many readings of *Double Indemnity* focus on the affair between Neff and the femme fatale Phyllis. But looking especially at the first half of the film, I will be arguing that the primary relation is between Neff and Keyes, an intricate combination of personal and professional admiration and contestation that suggests how midcentury American corporate culture (and its discontents) constitutes not simply the backdrop for the film but its heart—a preoccupation that Wilder would return to later in his career.[2] When Neff first refers to his Dictaphone recording as an "office memorandum" concerning business operations, explicitly rejecting the term *confession*, I take him at his word. While his voice-over narration is certainly a running commentary pushing against the dictates of conscience, the film's Freudian schematics derive less fundamentally from personal interplay, Oedipal or otherwise, than from the dynamics of the insurance game.[3]

To arrive at the movie's corporate center, we begin with a minor but important scene early on that introduces us to Keyes and the work he brusquely performs as an insurance claims manager. Leaving his first erotically charged meeting with Phyllis, Neff in his retrospective narration, addressed always to Keyes (and himself), moves from the seductive but dangerous, darkened, and domestic space of the Dietrichson house to the apparently more benign space of his company, where he returns that same afternoon to pick up his mail. As we watch him joyfully driving back from Los Feliz, Neff surmises (via his voice-over musing) that Keyes might have known from the start what he himself did not—that murder was in the air. Already Keyes has assumed for Neff the virtual role of an overseeing and ominous superego.[4] In other words, the sort of sinister function Albert Meng had in *Stranger*, shadowing the protagonist's inner directed speech, is given in Wilder's film a more outer-directed object of address, so that Neff's narration is less a self-questioning monologue than a plea for approval or understanding aimed at a particular audience, Keyes, who comes to assume the (company) role of interrogating Neff's claims. This first, pivotal transition between Phyllis's gloomy home and Keyes's sunnier office is made as Neff enters a building filled with dozens of employees busy at desks lined up on the ground floor. As the camera looks across this mundane bureaucratic activity toward the second-floor balcony of the administrators' offices, the narrating voice fades away with a direct question or injunction to the claims manager ("remember, Keyes?") to recall how he had asked Neff to review an insurance case with him.

Here in the workplace we witness a minidrama of fraud and punishment that closely resembles Neff's own crime story as he comes to tell it. Keyes is quizzing Sam Gorlopis, a Greek immigrant described as a "big, dumb bruiser" in the screenplay, about a claim on a truck policy that Neff had sold him.[5] Dramatically exposing the immigrant's claim as phony, the result of a fire Gorlopis himself started, Keyes proudly announces the unmediated, intuitive method of detection that inspires him: the memorable "little man" in the pit of his stomach that goads his suspicions about such fake accidents. Leaning on a file cabinet, Neff silently listens to this amusing self-explanation that the manager has presumably repeated many times before. But after Gorlopis leaves the office in shame (and without collecting a dime), Neff is forced on the defensive about his own role in the fraud when Keyes immediately begins to rail against the company and its "dimwitted amateurs" who would take on such bad risks and sell these kinds of policies.

Although Keyes exempts Neff from his withering criticism, shifting his blame to other "fast-talking salesmen" who (unlike Neff) do not exercise caution with potentially shady characters such as the Greek, their exchange exposes a crucial conflict between their professional roles: one earns his living by selling (with a 20 percent commission) as many policies as possible, while the other saves the company money by stopping payouts, invalidating all the phony claims made on these policies. What sales makes and takes, the superintending claims investigator cancels and withholds, so that "they won't throw more money out of the window than they take in at the door." Anticipating the film's closing line, the scene ends with Neff affectionately lighting Keyes's cigar as he says "I love you, too" to the irascible claims manager. But already here we note an uneasy edge to this loving esteem, which is mixed with resentment and fear provoked by Keyes's obsessive oversight that in so conscientiously striving to maximize company profits inevitably cramps Neff's effusive style. And insofar as the salesman is always selling himself (especially sexually to Phyllis), Keyes in effect threatens to stifle Neff's very being.

I will consider shortly this friction between corporate roles as it develops throughout the movie. But for now I want to return to the immigrant's fraud, particularly Keyes's response to it as witnessed by Neff, who first opens the manager's door to find himself on the same side of the room as Gorlopis. One seated, one standing, both men stare at the imposing figure of the accusing claims manager, shot from the back, with a chart about insurance "surrender rates" looming in the background (see figure 6).[6] This is our first look at Keyes. Beyond triggering an instance of self-satisfied professional triumph for the manager, his badgering becomes the occasion for patronizing humiliation when the befuddled immigrant is humorously instructed by Keyes how to work the doorknob as he leaves the office, buffoonishly grinning. Eric Lott shrewdly calls this moment "a mock naturalization lesson" intended to initiate a primitive, heavily accented foreigner into the more sophisticated ways of U.S. citizens.[7] The Greek's shaky national claims are matched by his equally dubious social class as well; he is clearly a desperate blue-collar criminal out of his league, even cruder and more incompetent than the "amateur" company salesmen Keyes excoriates after this "boy" (as Keyes belittles him) signs a legal waiver and is dismissed. This act of signing off is mirrored a few scenes later when Mr. Dietrichson inadvertently affixes his signature to the double indemnity policy and thereby effectively seals his own death warrant.

The triangulated shot composition that opens this initial business meeting is revealing: watching Keyes relentlessly expose and bully the immigrant—putting him in his place—produces for Neff (and for us) a kind of doubling, both a sameness and difference, between the hapless working-class Gorlopis and the bourgeois salesman.[8] Neff, after all, has already been compelled to think about accident insurance earlier that afternoon during his playful but risky flirtation with Phyllis. Neff is surely no foreigner, and in fact from the beginning plays a clearly recognizable American type: the self-confident, glib, ingratiating huckster. And yet Neff's insider status masks a more profound nonbelonging or disenfranchisement in relation to his employment that puts him on the side of the immigrant, not on the side of Keyes. It is this deep-seated resentment at work that inspires Neff to try

6 Neff and Gorlopis
under the sway of
Keyes, from *Double
Indemnity*

his luck with Phyllis. Nurturing seeds that have already been planted by the
femme fatale in the pair's initial interaction, this episode with Gorlopis
serves as Neff's warning to take a different tack, from the inside, against the
superego (and super egotistical) surveillance and taunts of the claims
manager. To succeed as a white-collar criminal, rather than to kill for sex or
for money, remains Neff's primary if psychologically obscure motive, as we
can appreciate by looking closely at his relationship with Keyes.

Neff's first voice-over gloss about (and to) Keyes is a bit puzzling. After
joking "I love you, too," Neff's inner monologue, cued by Miklós Rózsa's
brilliant score,[9] resumes to offer this explanation: "I really did, too, you old
crab, always yelling your fat head off, always sore at everyone. But you
never fooled me with your song and dance, not for a second. I kind of
knew that behind the cigar ashes on your vest you had a heart as big as a
house." Both at the moment of retrospective narrating and at the moment
of the narrated scene, Neff's direct second-person address presumes to see
through the claim manager's performance, through his gruff exterior, to
the generous soul within. But given Keyes's mocking, unsympathetic treatment of the immigrant, we can appreciate how Neff has hedged his bets
with that awkward modifier "kind of," since Keyes has given little to
indicate such warmth beneath. It could be argued that although Keyes
threatens to bring in the cops, he does let the Greek go, indicating that
Keyes is less interested in legal remedies than in professionally satisfying
ones. Yet he does not even bother to inquire into the immigrant's family or

financial situation—clearly dire circumstances compelling the man to torch his own truck.[10] So for Neff to emerge from this scene of interrogation to praise the manager's heart implies a curious blindness when it comes to assessing Keyes.

This consistent pattern of sentimental misrecognition stands in contrast to his representations of Phyllis, whose motives Neff clearly finds suspect from the beginning. The famous opening scene of flirtation has attracted enormous critical attention for the masterful way in which Wilder constructs shots (Phyllis descending the staircase; close-ups of her ankle bracelet, and so on) that quickly establish his protagonist's subjective point of view—a robustly heterosexual gaze aimed at comprehending, enjoying, and containing the alluring femme fatale, who responds in kind. And in this sense the fatal visual allure of Phyllis (seen from below at the top of the stairs, fully frontal, barely covered) is matched by Neff's poetic running soliloquy about her seductive fatality (e.g., the intoxicating smell of honeysuckle). When the couple is filmed interacting, their words and images also closely align, with Wilder preferring conventional shot–reverse shot close-ups that perfectly match their intimate conversation, such as their opening witty banter in which Neff is playfully punished by the motorcycle cop Phyllis for driving too fast. Of course after the two lovers hatch their murder plan and are compelled to meet secretly in public to trade information, as in the tense scenes in Jerry's Market, both before and after the killing, the glances between the two become more furtive.

But in the case of Neff and Keyes we have a more unsettling disjunction between word and image. While he remains the incessant addressee of Neff's speech, both on and off screen, Keyes is rarely the bearer of Neff's look until the film's end. Instead of eliciting or sharing gazes, Neff increasingly tends to avert his eyes in the presence of Keyes, or tries to see past or through him to avoid detection—precisely the fate of the guilty immigrant Gorpolis. Most often exchanges between the two are shot midrange, both in the frame at the same time, with the intimate gesture of lighting Keyes's cigar frequently the focus of attention instead of sustained looking. Keyes himself often seems so absorbed in figuring out the clever fraud (how, why, who) that he barely registers his surroundings, let alone the close regard of his colleague. This lack of reciprocity of recognition, I would argue, suggests how Neff's take on Keyes is often oddly skewed.

Shortly after praising Keyes's "heart as big as a house," Neff introduces another sort of house, not in any domestic context (the ostensible sphere of Phyllis), but again in relation to the insurance company he works for. This is yet another indication of how personal space and the office place symbolically interpenetrate and grow more difficult to keep distinct as Neff's story progresses. In the movie's first dissolve back to the opening scene of retrospective Dictaphone narration, Neff suddenly shifts from his feelings for Phyllis to his feelings about his job: "So we just sat there, and she started crying softly, like the rain on the window, and we didn't say anything. Maybe she had stopped thinking about it, but I hadn't. I couldn't. Because it was all tied up with something I had been thinking about for years, since long before I ever ran into Phyllis Dietrichson. Because, you know how it is, Keyes, in this business you can't sleep for trying to figure out the tricks they could pull on you. You're like the guy behind the roulette wheel, watching the customers to make sure they don't crook the house. And then one night, you get to thinking how you could crook the house yourself. And do it smart. Because you've got that wheel right under your hands."

This crucial passage verbally reinforces the film's earlier composition pairing the scheming salesman and the alien immigrant (a lesser version) with the intimidating figure of the claims manager poised between the two criminals, blue collar and white. In Cain's source novel, Huff (as the protagonist is called) refers to his long-standing desire to "crook the wheel," an impulse that predates his meeting Phyllis, whom he describes as "a plant out there to put down my bet."[11] Explaining the importance of this passage, Cain himself stressed that the femme fatale is not a root cause but only a triggering mechanism or mere ploy for the salesman's plot, which he has been contemplating and planning for years.[12] In this regard Neff's attraction to Phyllis may be less motivated by libido per se than by a deeper sort of identification: how her discontent speaks to his own and emboldens him to take action. Wilder and Raymond Chandler in their revision of the original follow it very carefully, but they substitute the word *house* for *wheel*, thereby moving the focus away from gambling, that is, from taking on fate (as in the traditional wheel of fortune), to a more specific target: the corporate house that employs the salesman. Pacific All-Risk Insurance is literally a dynastic house, because the current president, Mr. Norton, "was raised in the insurance business," presumably the son of the company's former "big boss," Norton the elder. Cain's novel makes this relation explicit, indicating that "Old Man" Norton actually founded the business. Hence the significance of Keyes's open contempt for Norton the younger, whose "front office" distance from the nitty-gritty world of claims stands in stark contrast to the commonsense, intuitive leadership his father had once given the company.

In his excellent discussion of the Cain novel, John Irwin deftly compares the Norton father-son relation with the relation between Keyes and Huff to show how the claims manager and the salesman hold fundamentally different attitudes toward authority.[13] Associating himself with Norton the elder, Keyes (the father) rails against the younger Norton's incompetence, just as he rails against the slackness of fast-talking salesmen, but he does so because he so fiercely believes in the insurance business that he has dedicated his life to. The middle-aged bachelor is a responsible company man through and through. Positioned, if mainly by formal default, in relation to the smug, woefully obtuse Norton the younger, Huff (the son) bears allegiance to no organization, in fact to nothing outside his own pleasure principle, which is linked ultimately to a willful self-destruction that Irwin shows derives from Edgar Allan Poe's "The Imp of the Perverse." And as in Poe's first-person murder tales, appreciation of the perfect crime requires acts of self-betrayal. The same set of conclusions rings true for the movie. Neff comes from a long line of self-destructive American losers. But while for Cain and for Poe this perversity simply looms as an inexplicable black abyss, Wilder and Chandler channel it more pointedly toward the corporation.[14]

We need to further examine this revision, which foregrounds the centrality of Keyes, by returning for a moment to the "crook the house" passage. As I have mentioned, it occurs during the film's first return to the scene of narration. But precisely where and when it occurs in the movie is striking indeed. As Phyllis and Neff are about to enjoy intimacy for the first time in the privacy of his dark apartment, signaled by their reclining together on the sofa, the camera pulls back from the couch to shift to and then zoom in on Neff at his office Dictaphone, recalling his desire to defraud his company. When he finishes his monologue, the scene returns to Neff and Phyllis on the sofa, he now smoking a cigarette and she applying lipstick, a clear Hollywood code for consummation that would circumvent Hayes censorship. Unlike the film's five subsequent cuts to

Neff's act of retrospective recording, this one is not transitional between different narrative sequences, but rather disrupts the middle of a crucial point in the plot—the very moment of her adultery.

Noticing this strange withdrawal (literalized visually) from impending sex, followed by a cut to business, and then back to consummated sex, Hugh Manon offers a Lacanian reading of Neff's fetishizing of Phyllis, arguing that the salesman is driven by lack, not greed or lust.[15] Manon emphasizes the endless self-imposed deferrals of desire and contact on the part of Neff, pointing out, for instance, that while the murder plot for Phyllis is well-motivated and linear (their famous "straight down the line," a seemingly mutual refrain), Neff tends to operate via repetition-compulsive loops or circles (hence his references to gaming wheels). Manon also calls attention to the equally odd, surprising moment near the end of the film when Neff, breathing heavily, surreptitiously listens to Keyes's own Dictaphone recording, a confidential office memo to Norton that marks the only time we hear the manager's disembodied voice instead of Neff's. In a single, painfully long close-up, the salesman's face drops in obvious disappointment to learn that Keyes has rejected him as a suspect in favor of Lola's boyfriend, Nino. As the one instance when Neff briefly gains the upper hand by accessing the investigator's secrets, this occasion should not trigger sadness but rather joy and relief—even the screenplay indicates that Neff feels "deeply moved" by Keyes's faith in him.[16]

Manon's focus on loss usefully illuminates the differences between the femme fatale and her coconspirator, who does appear to court failure, particularly after the crime is committed. But this particular psychoanalytic slant tends to slight the powerful claims on Neff made by the manager Keyes and his company, which Manon implies is merely a convenient coverup (for lack) characteristic of film noir in general. Yet I am suggesting that we read the compulsion to defraud not as a displacement or distraction but as a more primary assertion on the salesman's part. What exactly Neff is asserting himself against, by way of the admittedly extravagant means of murder, remains to be seen.

Business is therefore not simply an excuse for coitus interruptus, but rather the reason Neff decides to gamble with Phyllis in the first place. The movie's initial reference to "right down the line," in fact, occurs not in the context of the criminal plot the two will hatch, but rather during their very first meeting, when Neff lays out his bill of goods: "Fire, earthquake, theft, public liability, group insurance, industrial stuff, and so on, right down the line." Here *line* defines the essence of Neff as salesman prior to his fatal entanglement with Phyllis—the line of products he sells and the lines of patter he deploys to sell them. In this regard his "crook the house" speech is unexpected in another way; by presuming he has the wheel under his own hands, protecting the assets of the company against fraud, rather than selling policies, Neff momentarily plays the part of a claims investigator. The salesman's criminal fantasy is thus double, working in two stages: first, to usurp by identification the role of the negating manager whom he loves/hates, and second, to defy and destroy that figure of authority and law by cheating the company whose principles he represents. First imitation, then destruction. Many commentators loosely refer to Keyes as Neff's "boss," as somebody whom the salesman works under or for, but he most decidedly is not. They work in two separate departments whose goals conflict, as the film critic Parker Tyler was the first to recognize some sixty years ago.[17]

The two in fact express competing feelings about risk, which is the foundation of the insurance business. To persuade people to buy life or accident insurance, the salesman must overcome their resistance to imagining their own deaths. He does so by presenting insurance as a protection against the threat of bodily harm (hence the "indemnity"), when in truth all such insurance can do is compensate retroactively for contingencies that remain beyond human control. In the case of Mr. Dietrichson, the sale is easy because it is made on the sly without his knowledge, so that the wife in effect replaces him as Neff's willing client, a shift entailing its own temptations and dangers. We have a double displacement: Phyllis now becomes the salesman's new (sexual) client, persuaded to buy into his criminal plot, which in turn demands that the salesman literally impersonate her hobbled husband as the centerpiece of the murder scheme itself, although of course in gradually inventing the scheme over years, Neff has more fundamentally identified with Keyes's work as a company detective. No accident, the deliberate death of Mr. Dietrichson, doubly displaced, will be offset by the wager the lovers Neff and Phyllis take by trying to cash in on it.

Risk for the insurance salesman is associated with protection (for clients) and potential pleasure and gain (for himself). But for the insurance claims manager, risk must be contained and nullified by way of statistical probabilities. Converting random chance into actuarial tables and numbers, Keyes seeks to turn the salesman's all-risk speculation into no risk at all. Despite the manager's boasts about the intuitive "little man" inside, he is thus guided as much or more by the potency of rational and rationalized calculation. While the source novel's paeans to statistics are sometimes recited by Neff to Phyllis as part of his aim to educate her about insurance fraud in relation to his clever murder plot, Wilder and Chandler saw that this sort of logic made more sense coming solely from the claims investigator. In this regard the movie's major celebration of numbers, significantly enough, is a passionate outburst directed by Keyes at the ineptitude of the company president Norton (junior), who has stupidly surmised in front of Phyllis that her husband killed himself to allow his wife to collect on his policy. After she indignantly leaves the office, Keyes berates his pompous boss in front of Neff: "Come on, you never read an actuarial table in your life, have you? I've got ten volumes on suicide alone. Suicide by race, by color, by occupation, by sex, by seasons of the year, by time of day. Suicide, how committed: by poisons, by firearms, by drowning, by leaps. Suicide by poison, subdivided by types of poison, such as corrosive, irritant, systemic, gaseous, narcotic, alkaloid, protein, and so forth. Suicide by leaps, subdivided by leaps from high places, under the wheels of trains, under the wheels of trucks, under the feet of horses, from steamboats. But Mr. Norton, of all the cases on record there's not one single case of suicide by leap from the rear end of a moving train."

It is important to stress that in a crime narrative in which the police remain so completely and conspicuously absent, Keyes's attempt to statistically defeat chance serves primarily a policing function. To protect profits, to make sure more money comes in than gets paid out, as he puts it, the insurance company is more highly motivated to investigate and solve crimes than the state is; as Keyes tersely remarks about the cops, "it's not their dough." The company clearly has the financial resources and the wherewithal to put the scheming lovers under surveillance, whereas the police presumably do not. Even in dialogue, the presence of the state is so diminished as to be almost nonexistent throughout the movie, except for a handful of fleeting references: Phyllis's opening flirtation as a motorcycle officer, a passing threat aimed at the foreign cheat Gorlopis, Neff asking Keyes what the police think about Dietrichson's death, as well as a closing mention of a "police job" by Keyes when he calls an ambulance for Neff.

That is why the movie's alternative ending featuring Neff in a gas chamber strikes me as so inappropriate: there is no reason to introduce suddenly an otherwise absent state authority, when the claims manager has always already been assuming this function.[18] Virtually sui generis in film noir, Keyes is neither a self-employed private eye, that is, the familiar figure of a gun for hire, nor an officer of the law (rogue or otherwise), but a salaried employee paid by a company to detect a range of social transgressions that fall under the umbrella crime of fraud.[19]

There is actually another, very brief mention of the police in the movie that Keyes makes during another one of his impassioned speeches glorifying the insurance business. Invented from scratch by Wilder and Chandler, this crucial scene is not in the Cain novel. Walking into Neff's office right after Neff has expressed in his voice-over doubts about going through with the crime (now that the husband has unexpectedly broken his leg), Keyes makes a strong pitch for Neff to take a pay cut and become his "assistant." Paralleling the opening scenes of seduction between Neff and Phylllis, this talk, too, works as a kind of wooing, with Keyes tempting Neff to abandon his current position as a "peddler," "glad-hander," and "backslapper": "You're too good to be a salesman." To which Neff snappily replies, "Nobody's too good to be a salesman"—a highly ambiguous retort that either defends the job of sales and/or denigrates himself for practicing it. Insisting romantically that the cases he investigates are "packed" with "twisted dreams," Keyes continues, gesticulating broadly, with his most lyric, most compelling, most inflated self-description: "A claims man, Walter, is a doctor and a bloodhound and a cop and a judge and a jury and a father confessor, all in one."

Here is what seems to be the moral crisis of the film: Neff's last opportunity to save himself from the machinery of fate assuming total control over him and his plot, as he recounts it. And suddenly the phone rings, another kind of coitus interruptus between office and personal space, as the camera cuts back and forth between Phyllis, explaining her husband can still travel (on crutches), and Neff, pretending to talk to "Margie," while Keyes rudely looks on and refuses to grant Neff his privacy. Once he quickly hangs up, Neff's conversation with Keyes about the subject of marriage remains the most revealing moment in the film regarding the manager's personal life. But to be more accurate, what their exchange underscores is that Keyes has no such life, that long ago his

7 Oedipal visual
schematics in
Double Indemnity

suspicious "little man" had investigated a potential wife as if she had filed a bogus claim (on him). In this way he has let his professional duty seep into and ruin any chance he ever had for an intimate relationship.

This might make us feel sorry for Keyes as a kind of tragic figure, but it is difficult to imagine the basis for his sacrifice, which remains outside the scope of the movie. Even to infer some sort of past tragedy afflicting Keyes is a dubious prospect, especially given his sketchy, generic understanding of "dames" ("I bet she drinks from the bottle"), including his own fiancée. And this tendency is less an indication of the bachelor's homosexual inclinations, I would argue, than a sign that he is wedded to his company: the corporate version of the nun as bride of Christ. And so for Neff to save himself by becoming Keyes's protégé would exact too great a price. After decisively rejecting Keyes's offer to improve his station (and self), he shows the investigator the door, as Keyes had done for Gorlopis. The claims manager leaves with an insult: "I guess I was all wet. You're not smarter, Walter. You're just a little taller."

This parting phallic crack, coupled with Keyes's pointed earlier reference to "father confessor," squarely pits Keyes and Neff as Oedipal rivals, with office politics (sales versus claims) as the arena of competition, interrupted by the femme fatale's urgent voice on the phone. After the murder, "Papa" Keyes (as he actually calls himself at one point) returns her favor by unexpectedly invading Neff's personal space to (almost) catch the two lovers together standing right outside his apartment. In this famous and most emblematic shot, Wilder neatly visualizes the Oedipal triangle at its most suspenseful (see figure 7). Yet there are other moving images in the film, particularly those of Neff in isolation, that resist such schematic signification, that work more by affect than by configured allegory. As I have been suggesting, the movie, as Chandler and Wilder deliberately rewrote it from Cain's novel, draws heavily and explicitly on the popularizing of Freud that was quite common in Hollywood during the 1940s. Wilder, after all, even professed to have tried to interview Freud during the 1920s in Vienna, where he worked as a journalist.[20] Killing the father (Mr. Dietrichson) primarily to get back at another (Keyes) may be one story, a tale that in fact comports closely with Neff's own narrated understanding of his motives. But this is not the film's whole story.

If *Double Indemnity*'s obvious Oedipal dynamics cannot fully account for the salesman's urge to "crook the house," how can we? I suppose it is time for me to put my cards on the table, since I have been deferring and circling around (in Neff fashion) an explanation for so long. In stressing the insurance business as the heart of the matter, my references to "white-collar crime" might have seemed loosely colloquial. But the term *white-collar crime* is actually historically very precise. This concept was introduced into social sciences vocabulary late in 1939, roughly three years after Cain published his novel, and roughly three before Chandler and Wilder during the war began transforming it into a movie (set in 1938).

Delivered as a presidential address to the American Sociological Society, and subsequently published in the *American Sociological Review* (in February 1940), Edwin H. Sutherland's essay "White-Collar Criminality" marks a decisive shift away from Depression-era explanations for criminal behavior that tended to emphasize and totalize environmental factors such as social class, wretched living conditions, and poverty. Rejecting such sociopathic theories, Sutherland turned to corporate fraud (e.g., stock manipulation, the misrepresentation of asset values, bribery, and embezzlement) to suggest how breaking the law was learned behavior driven primarily (and self-evidently) by greed. For Sutherland these crimes, rarely punished or even acknowledged as such, fundamentally "violate trust and therefore create distrust, which lowers social morale and produces social disorganization on a large scale," a scale far greater than that of conventional "lower-class" crimes such as burglary and robbery.[21] More interested in consequences than causes, Sutherland is not especially illuminating about what exactly motivates white-collar criminals. He is also imprecise in failing to distinguish between crimes committed by heads of corporations (whom he compares to "robber barons") and those committed by employees lower down the rung who cheat their own companies (as in embezzlement). But his fresh analysis did open up new ways to think about criminality beyond early New Deal social determinism, including, in the happy phrase of his followers, "crimes against bureaucracy."[22]

By the 1950s a host of American social scientists would come to regard these middle-class crimes as one kind of reaction against a burgeoning and stultifying corporate culture itself. Given Wilder's immersion in the Hollywood studio system since the 1930s, and Chandler's own dodgy career as an oil company executive (like the insolvent Mr. Dietrichson) in the 1920s, it is not so surprising that the movie's screenwriters in revising Cain's novel to highlight the business friction between Neff and Keyes would anticipate a slew of influential studies about "work and its discontents," to borrow the title of a long essay by Daniel Bell published in 1956.[23] Other popular studies in this vein included books by David Riesman (*The Lonely Crowd*, 1951), C. Wright Mills (*White-Collar: The American Middle Classes*, 1951), and William Whyte (*The Organization Man*, 1956). Focusing on the problems of cold war prosperity, these social critics drew attention to social isolation and conformity as the noxious side effects of an increasingly rationalized labor force subject to new and subtle forms of management and domination, with "overt coercion," Bell argued, being replaced by "psychological persuasion."[24]

The gruff, eccentric mannerisms of the insurance claims manager, his florid disdain for formality, and the seeming self-sufficiency of the salesman, his easygoing attitude in the workplace, belie a more tense and rigid relation between the two employees, one marked by anomie and fear on Neff's part, and by surveillance and suspicion on Keyes's. Of course both also express mutual fondness for one another, Keyes for Neff's selling (and sexual) prowess, and Neff for the manager's unyielding (celibate) vigilance, which resembles (a "kind of") caring. But as I have been arguing, their reciprocal admiration for what they each lack is tainted with darker emotions, so that what they profess to love in the other are the very things they hate and resent, a perversity that helps us appreciate how Neff's long-standing impulse to "crook the house" may stem from a disaffection that extends beyond their father-son roles.

Noticing this disenchantment, commentators typically point to the outsider status of Cain (an Easterner), Chandler (raised in England), and Wilder (an émigré from Vienna and Berlin) in relation to California. Critics are especially quick to emphasize Wilder's Weimar roots. Yet the movie's pessimism is more specifically aimed at labor in the highly structured modern corporation, as another Weimar journalist and master of irony helps us appreciate. After publishing a series of critiques examining the distractions of mass culture (including movies and movie audiences) in the newspaper *Frankfurter Zeitung*, Siegfried Kracauer turned his attention in 1930 to Germany's new middle-class workers, whom he called *die Angestellten* (translated as "the salaried masses"). Modifying and updating Marx's notion of alienation, Kracauer argued that "the mass of salaried employees differ from the worker proletariat in that they are spiritually homeless." Kracauer does not directly discuss how employees like Neff might convert their feelings of estrangement into criminal action. But his analysis of how business is pursued "as an end in itself" does shed light on the behavior of the claims manager Keyes, whose belief in the supremacy of enterprise turns him into "the servant of his work, just as the King of Prussia was the servant of the state." And if it might seem that this intimate association between the corporation and the state is strictly a feature of European bureaucracy, Kracauer actually suggests that American modernity is the source of this newfound allegiance to the corporation.[25]

What American sociologists began systematically noting about middle-class employees at midcentury had clearly been brewing for some time, both in the United States and in Europe. The erosion of social trust Sutherland attributed to white-collar crime paralleled other dramatic changes occurring well before the war, as registered by the movie's source novel. Some critics have intriguingly read Cain's *Double Indemnity* (1936) and its predecessor *The Postman Always Rings Twice* (1934) as hard-boiled parables about New Deal liberalism, with their complex insurance fraud plots dramatizing anxieties attending the state's takeover, under FDR, of the task of providing for each citizen's social security.[26] Acting as a gigantic insurance corporation, state bureaucracy in this view came to recreate its citizenry as a conglomeration of statistical profiles in ways that tended to attenuate individual political and personal agency. This historical process accelerated toward the end of the decade and during the militarization of the U.S. economy in the Second War, as a set of civic affiliations increasingly gave way to more abstract patterns of association, what one scholar has called "Taylored citizenship."[27] Although the significance of state institutions in Cain's first two novels is certainly debatable, this line of reasoning usefully suggests how his crime narratives centrally raise important questions about national belonging, disenfranchisement, and communal bonds of affection and trust, or a lack thereof.

As an excursion into Cain's first novel about insurance fraud will show, *The Postman Always Rings Twice* most explicitly articulates such a politics of dispossession. At the dawn of the New Deal a rootless drifter named Frank Chambers finds work in a "roadside sandwich joint, like a million others in California," has an affair with the owner's wife, Cora, with whom he conspires to kill the owner, Nick, to collect on his life insurance.[28] The lovers are arrested for the crime but get off thanks to a clever lawyer, only to end up in a car accident in which Cora dies and Frank is found guilty of her murder: hence the poetic justice of the "twice" in the title of the story (like the "double" in Cain's subsequent novel), a first-person tale that Frank recounts while awaiting execution, confident that in dying he will be reunited with Cora, "wherever it is"—the final words of the novel.

Frank's uncertainty about where he and Cora belong is not limited to the afterlife. From the start, with unerring precision, Cain marks off his characters' "zone of anomie," to borrow Giorgio Agamben's resonant phrase.[29] In the novel's memorable laconic opening sentence, "they threw me off the hay truck," onto which Frank had swung "down at the border" after spending "three weeks in Tia Juana"(3). A locale for sexual license, Mexico throughout the novel serves as a plausible alternative to a life of confinement and failure in America. To enter the United States is to cross over into the narrative's uncanny space, a geopolitical boundary Cain pointedly emphasizes at two other times when Frank tries to escape the diner, first by catching a "truck to Mexicali" (31) following the pair's initial failed attempt at murder (foiled by an electrocuted cat), and then during his more extended dalliance with another woman after the murder has occurred. In this baffling and surreal interlude, Frank and his new pickup, Madge, discuss plans to hunt wild cats in a phantasmagoric Nicaragua while spending a few days holed up across the border in a hotel in Ensenada, which Frank describes as "all Mex, and you feel like you left the U. S. A. a million miles away" (94). Frank is more at home in Mexico than the United States, which seems more hostile to him.

Frank is unable to rest easy in his own country. This unease is immediately established when he first arrives at the diner, which combines a "lunchroom part" (the business) and "a house part" (the domestic space), where he stays with Nick and Cora. Throughout his narrative Frank identifies the owner not by name but by ethnicity, "the Greek," and it is precisely Nick's status as Greek that powerfully draws Cora and Frank together. Although Frank is attracted to "sulky" Cora as soon as he sees her, it is their shared difference from the Greek—and their resentment of him as a successful, assimilated businessman—that unites them and fires their passion. In their very first exchange, the dark-haired Cora accuses Frank of thinking she's "Mex," even though "I'm just as white as you are" (7), as she compulsively reiterates three times, insisting that she does not come "from around here" but from Iowa. To dwell in Mex (Frank's intermittent desire) is one thing, to be Mex (Cora's constant dread), another. Later fondly calling Cora "his little white bird" (8), Nick accentuates his wife's racial insecurity. But the issue is not origins, looks, or nationality, as Frank quickly intuits: "It was being married to that Greek that made her feel she wasn't white, and she was even afraid I would begin calling her Mrs. Papadakis" (7). Here "Greek" and "Mex" occupy the same category of nonwhiteness, a concept that Frank and Cora will struggle, unsuccessfully, to define and set against their own uncertain sense of what it means to be American.

Although the novel's opening fixation on race that prompts a kind of guilt by association might seem mainly to register a strain of nativism especially virulent in California during the 1920s and early 1930s, there is more to it than that. In the film's MGM version of 1946, bent on glamour (casting Lana Turner as Cora) rather than uncanniness, the character of Nick was somewhat ludicrously turned into a Canadian, presumably to avoid offending sensibilities (and censors), while the clever but manipulative Jewish defense attorney Katz was given a more Anglo-sounding name. This completely misses the point, since Cain's bold stroke is to show in the novel how Papadakis and Katz, foreign business and law, completely run the show. In his gleefully conniving machinations exploiting insurance company policies, in fact, Katz saves the couple by fusing law and business, even if he compels the now passive lovers to turn against each other and even if they never fully understand what he has done. The result is to render Frank and Cora powerless despite, or rather because of, their privileged status as "clean," pure-bred citizens. Hence the irony of Frank's early mocking advice urging Nick to gain customers by changing his restaurant's sign: "A place is no better than its sign" (10), he announces, helping the Greek draw "a new sign for himself," with properly spelled words in "red, white, and blue Neon letters" and "a Greek flag and an American flag" (12).

"A little soft greasy guy with black kinky hair" (16), as Cora crudely calls him, the Greek nonetheless is more American than Frank, who can teach others the material tokens of belonging (a sense of place) but remains always an aimless "bum," an outsider in his own home. Sending Nick to Los Angeles (twenty miles away) to fetch his sign allows Frank and Cora to satisfy their intense lust ("'Bite me! Bite me!'"), the first of many episodes in which the husband's eagerness for profit enables their affair to develop (11). But for Cain the sexual relation between Frank and Cora, however powerful, is essentially theological or transcendent only momentarily, taking place out of space and time—"it was like being in church" (17), as Frank describes it, and thereby unable to offer them any firm social grounding to counter their feelings of anomie. Killing Nick does not release them to enjoy their pleasure either, since Katz and the law quickly descend as a bewildering alien force dictating their behavior. While Cora after her acquittal at least tries to make good on her plans to "be something" (16) by improving the diner (a theme Cain would return to in his novel *Mildred Pierce*), Frank is exempt from believing in such domestic upward mobility that combines the traditional woman's sphere (the home) with commerce. Turning the diner into a beer garden would "entertain people" (88), Cora understands, serving mainly as a substitute for her own failed movie career in Hollywood.

Ultimately the only way that Frank and Cora can together repossess their domain is to make a family. When Cora near the end reveals to Frank that she is pregnant, she treats this "new life for us both" as a form of providential compensation: "Because we took a life . . . now we're going to give one back" (109). Yet the equation is not so simple. The dead Greek must be replaced by a white baby, as an earlier scene between Frank and Cora makes perfectly clear. "Fix'm up red, a white, a blue"—after the first murder attempt, a jovial Nick in his garbled English convinces a reluctant Frank to return to Twin Oaks to work for him and his wife again. Seeing Cora "pale as milk" in the kitchen with a knife in her hand, Frank agrees with his suicidal lover that there is not "any other way out for us" but to kill his boss once she tells him that Nick wants to have a "greasy Greek child" (38). Although of course by law such a child born on U.S. soil would automatically be a citizen, the repulsed Cora feels outrage. Americanness, in this view, as Werner Sollors has claimed, is construed primarily by "prohibiting black-white heterosexual couples from forming families and withholding legitimacy from their descendants."[30] For Sollors it is this long-standing ban against interracial progeny that makes the United States so historically and culturally exceptional.

But Frank's and Cora's desperate effort to reaffirm their Americanness in the context of this exceptional prohibition has already been foreclosed by laws that locate citizenship on the side of the Greek, not of the couple. Narrating his return to Twin Oaks, Frank calls it "the worst flop of a home-coming you ever saw in your life" (37). Directly before the scene in the kitchen, Cora first greets him by saying, "You're quite a stranger around here" (34), a telling barb that is immediately followed by Nick showing Frank a big scrapbook filled with newspaper clippings about his "acciden-tal" fractured skull (the first attempt at murder). A record of Nick's life to be passed down to his children, this cherished scrapbook also contains "his naturalization certificate, and then his wedding certificate, and then his license to do business in Los Angeles" (35), along with patriotic deco-rations such as eagles and flags. The lovers' feelings of belonging exist only in an uncertain symbolic register (whiteness), but Nick is all-American and has the papers to prove it. On seeing these tangible signs documenting Nick's success, Frank's resentment boils over, leading to one of the bit-terest moments in the novel. Reminded that he is more of an outsider than the Greek, Frank with a mixture of disdain and envy proposes to Nick that over the clippings he draw "a cat with red, white, and blue fire coming out of its tail" and paste a "buzzard over the Los Angeles County license" (35).

Racial and ethnic identification in this way define and fuel the couple's disaffection, their un-Americanness. In his subsequent insurance novel, *Double Indemnity*, Cain would clean up his criminal protagonists, making them respectable, middle in class and white in collar as well as in race. He would also shift their objects of antipathy from a self-employed immigrant businessman and a shrewd Jewish lawyer to an uncaring husband and a grumpy claims manager loyal to his company but otherwise uninflected. In this sense Cain's second novel seems more concerned with corporate citizenship than with national citizenship. With the exception of a Filipino houseboy (cut in Wilder's film) and the Italian Sachetti (a college student), the novel's characters are homogeneous. There is not even a blue-collar deceiver to trigger the distrust of Keyes, only a nondescript "fellow" who torches his truck. With little basis for difference, Cain preoccupies himself with the procedural details of the crime, which in the novel's closing his first-person narrator Huff turns into poetic allegory, as his lover, dressed as Death, approaches him in preparation for a double suicide: "She looks like what came aboard the ship to shoot dice for souls in the Rime of the Ancient Mariner" (215). In adapting the novel for the screen, Wilder and Chandler pushed the narrative in two directions, high-lighting the professional/personal rivalry between Keyes and Neff, but also giving the narrative a bit of an ethnic edge, as in Cain's *Postman*. The movie restores the oafish Greek immigrant by way of Gorlopis, for example, and inserts some African Americans in minor but key roles to prop up by contrast the white-collar criminal's whiteness.[31]

However compelling a cultural context, midcentury U.S. citizenship, in all of its sociological and political ramifications, still seems an inadequate explanation for the saleman's deadly crimes. After all, white-collar resentment is a long way from double murder. But if we pull back and probe a bit further the Oedipal overlay offered by Wilder and Chandler, we can see how the film's father-son interplay points toward contested authority of a more impersonal and abstract sort. Here Keyes and his actuarial mentality remain central, as Joan Copjec has suggested. In her very dense, wide-ranging reading of *Double Indemnity* and film noir, Copjec situates the struggle between Keyes and Neff in relation to classic detective fiction, with Keyes the suspicious detective understanding the world and the case as operating by statistical laws, and Neff the noir monad perversely gambling against those laws of probability in a last-ditch effort to satisfy pleasure and to preserve his privacy.[32]

In this psychoanalytic (Lacanian) view, Keyes works by desire (to solve the crime and expose the killer) and Neff by drives (to commit the fraud and defy the investigator). Pushing the arguments about New Deal liberalism that I have briefly discussed back a century, Copjec is particularly good in the first half of her essay at showing how the growing preoccupation with recording and enumeration in the social sciences during the early 1800s accompanied the rise of the nation-state, effectively allowing concepts of universal citizenship to emerge: the classification of people along nonempirical principles of abstract identity. A citizen is made by being counted as such. Accelerating toward the end of the century, this "avalanche of printed numbers," as Ian Hacking has described it, diminished the significance of individuals and discrete events in favor of averages, trends, and norms.[33] By this process, modern America was constituted as a set of "statistical communities," to borrow the historian Daniel Boorstin's resonant phrase, a perspective that is the basis for the insurance business as embodied by the ever-vigilant claims manager.[34]

In fact, if we shift from a psychoanalytic perspective to a Foucauldian one, then insurance, in functioning as a "technology of risk," carries profound political implications for being calculable, collective, and capitalized. Tracing the development of accident insurance from mid-nineteenth-century British railway companies to French enterprises later in the century that competed with the state for the right to secure its subjects, Daniel Defert shows how this calculus of probabilities introduced a new "way to manage populations which conceives them as homogeneous series, established in purely scientific terms rather than by empirical modes of solidarity such as trade, a family or a neighbourhood." These modern modes entailed "a new set of rules for supervising the behaviour of individuals: a system of extra-judicial rules grounded not in traditional moral or social imperatives, but in technical modes of knowledge." Based on contract rather than affiliation, "under the auspices of insurance," Defert concludes, "an immense opportunity opened up for the state to introduce itself as an intimate, regular presence in the existence of its citizens," at the same time that these citizens still enjoyed the freedom to pursue self-interested liberal individualism.[35] But by violating this mutuality of contract, the insurance defrauder (something Defert does not consider) rejects the state's offer of security. In this precise sense Neff's resistance becomes an act of sedition, treating Keyes as an overbearing father to be bested, rather than as a benign guarantor of governmentality, which is how he primarily sees himself.

Neff's subversive plan suggests how such rationalized principles do not fully apply in the new postwar world of noir, as Copjec helps us appreciate. She points out, for instance, how Neff is tripped up by Keyes following the murder when the investigator's nagging inner "little man" questions why Mr. Dietrichson never bothered to file an accident claim after breaking his leg. This flash of intuition leads him to conclude that the man on the train was not Phyllis's husband. The irony (paradox, really) here is that it is the classical detective who probes his own foundational belief that persons are interchangeable by category, whereas it is the noir schemer who by impersonating Mr. Dietrichson on crutches (a prosthesis for unstable masculinity) tries but fails to achieve such a seamless identity exchange with another. This paradox is further complicated by its position in the narrative: Keyes divulges his intuitive flash after barging into Neff's private space, the only time we see him in Neff's apartment, with Phyllis soon to appear in the hallway.

To reject Keyes is to deny his way of constructing the world as an amalgam of numbers; to risk defrauding your company by the extreme measure of murder is to escape any bureaucratic classification that the claims investigator (as an extension of the state) might find for you. But the problem for Neff is that to maintain an elusive exception outside the system of Keyes's categories, he must first learn to think like him. In Sutherland's sociological terms, the white-collar criminal imitates superiors (inventing a perfect plot that only somebody like Keyes could appreciate) to destroy social trust. As we have seen, Chandler and Wilder developed and enhanced *Double Indemnity*'s family romance, situating Neff in a web of relations that shape his identity: wayward son (for Keyes), surrogate husband (Mr. and Mrs. Dietrichson), and perhaps even sympathetic father (Lola). But drawing on Lacan's complex rendering of "not-identical-to-itself" (against Gottlob Frege's set theory), Copjec helps us understand the alienation and nonbelonging of Neff that underlies his glib sociability. She acutely notes, for example, that for all of the incessant addresses to Keyes as the explicit recipient of Neff's voice-over remarks, Wilder repeatedly returns to the scene of narration: the salesman alone talking into the Dictaphone trying to explain himself. These shots emphasize his radical isolation, not his communion with others. Face-to-face conversation gives way to a unilateral commentary mediated by inanimate technology, a monologue otherwise untethered to the film's moving images that it seeks to suture, accompanied by Rózsa's haunting music.

8 The machinery of fate, from *Double Indemnity*

The third such scene of narration is particularly revealing: a close-up of Neff's sweating, pained face taken from a different angle than the others, so that we can see the spinning wheel of the Dictaphone cylinder during Neff's monologue (see figure 8). At first glance it might seem as if the spinning wheel visually and allegorically confirms Neff's sense of being entrapped by a machinery of fate, the tangle scheme that will take the lovers "straight down the line" to their inevitable deaths. But the shot points to a kind of separation or disengagement between the salesman and this machinery. Rather than signifying fate's entanglement, the shot leaves us with a more uncanny feeling for and of Neff suffering his traumatic wounding in solitude. In this regard I would also point to the brief scene earlier on when Neff tries to clear his head of the femme fatale by going bowling alone. Here some fifty years avant la lettre, Wilder literalizes the metaphor that Robert Putnam would invoke to describe Americans' loss of civic association and ties of community.[36]

Copjec allows us to see how Neff's drive to crook the house is linked to his defense of subjectivity at all costs against others. But her ambitious Lacanian analysis is sometimes marred by overly broad and reductive generalizations about film noir based on a relatively small sample of movies. And her predilection for abstraction sometimes leads her to factual inaccuracies, such as when she claims that "throughout the film, Phyllis and Keyes have a 'revolving door' relationship: they do not and cannot occupy the same space."[37] This is simply not true—during the crucial confrontation in Mr. Norton's office, the femme fatale and the investigator are directly introduced to one another, when all three main figures are gathered together by the company president as he proposes his foolish suicide solution. This factual error points to a larger blind spot in Copjec's analysis, her tendency to schematize characters as abstract functions. Her interest in Keyes, for instance, remains purely theoretical: insofar as he embodies some sort of perfect ideal of ratiocination, the older man cannot for Copjec be contaminated by noir sexuality. Yet as I have been arguing all along, Keyes's remorseless detection is not for its own sake, but in the service of making money for his company, which is why he dutifully shows up when his boss calls him and Neff into his office to confront Phyllis. Giving the contest between salesman and manager strictly a philosophical turn, Copjec overlooks the corporate context, the specific professional roles assigned to them and authorized by the insurance company.

But to err on the side of philosophy is preferable to erring in another direction, on the side of psychological realism. Rather than assume that Keyes stands purely for principles of detection, most commentators grant the claims investigator a fully fledged personality. This is Neff's own misreading of Keyes, that beneath his abrasive façade he possesses a "heart as big as a house." This sort of misconstruction by critics obviously takes its cue from Neff's narration. But I also suspect that E. G. Robinson's brilliant, beguiling performance is partly responsible. By the logic of Hollywood narrative, an actor succeeds by endowing a character with depth and life, an inner authenticity. In the case of the crusty claims manager, this means pushing his affective range to the limit, from anger to tenderness, with a kind of honest, blunt, lovable charm at the core of Robinson's energetic interpretation. Every time I show the movie, students inevitably laugh at his commanding browbeating of the immigrant Gorlopis, who himself is so entranced by the investigator's mockery that he, too, grins sheepishly when instructed how to turn the doorknob.

Yet if we simply *read* Keyes, detach the lines that Wilder and Chandler wrote for him from Robinson's scene-stealing performance of them, we begin to see how troubling a figure he is. From start to finish his only concern is his job and his company, whose inept boss and fast-talking salesmen make Keyes work even harder to monitor and prosecute claims; the "little man" dwelling in his gut is less an essence of his personality projected outward than an internalization of his duties as an investigator that he undertakes with such gusto. The care he shows Neff may resemble a father-son bond, but in the end it turns more on his desire to recruit the younger man into his way of statistical thinking, a domain in which nobody is immune from surveillance and classification (including the one possibility he ever had for a private relationship). Lively and amusing, Keyes is hollow: remove the suspicious little man that animates him, and nothing is left. By playing up the little man's impulsive quirkiness, Robinson manages to make the bureaucratic look idiosyncratic.

If Robinson's gift as an actor is to endow an exuberant but single-minded character with the illusion of depth, Barbara Stanwyck's performance as Phyllis Dietrichson is even more brilliant, giving richness to a static character who seems to be limited strictly to a seductive and / or demonic function. Near the end of her analysis of *Double Indemnity*, Copjec somewhat dismissively claims that "the femme fatale remains a two-dimensional figure with no hidden sides; the deception is *only* upfront."[38] While such a broad assertion strikes me as rather reductive and dubious for film noir in general, it would seem to hold true for Phyllis, especially given the way that Neff's narration repeatedly foregrounds her self-conscious artifice: forgetting it is the maid's day off; playing the role of the devoted wife seeing her husband off on the train; cloaked in widow's weeds indignantly reacting to Mr. Norton's false accusations; and pretending to shop at Jerry's Market, disguised (absurdly) in dark sunglasses. Not to mention the infamous, blindingly blonde wig Wilder treated as a sexual prop, the feminine counterpoint (along with her anklet) to the prosthetic crutches that both her husband and Neff lean on to bolster their wounded masculinity.

Enjoyed and then disparaged by Neff as he rapidly grows disenchanted, Phyllis's ostentatious theatricality has led most commentators to either dismiss or ignore her last lines, when after wounding Neff she professes suddenly to love him, despite their mutual rottenness. Like almost every other scene in the movie, Phyllis's murder attempt is filmed from Neff's subjective point of view: a midrange shot of him taking the bullet (our own surprise partly mitigated by having seen her plant the gun), followed by a tracking shot behind and over his shoulder that shows Phyllis holding the weapon in her hand as he strides toward her. Unable or unwilling to pull the trigger a second time (the femme fatale always shoots twice?), Phyllis by these lines seals her doom, as the salesman suddenly becomes an unconvinced consumer. Responding, "I'm sorry, baby, I'm not buying," he coldheartedly shoots her when they embrace for a final kiss.

Neff's intimate killing of Phyllis culminates a pattern of erotic sadism toward her that begins with his very invention of the scheme to defraud the company. Immediately after his "crook the house" speech, that is, immediately after the pair's initial act of adultery, Neff promises to help Phyllis murder her husband: "We're going to do it together. We're going to do it right. And I'm the guy who knows how." This pseudo–marriage vow is matched by an equally fierce gripping of his coconspirator, who responds to his violence with a pained, "Walter, you're hurting me"—a line that shows up in an array of films noirs.[39] This noir sadism toward the femme fatale is less surprising in itself than the way it is so closely linked to Neff's desire to cheat All-Risk and best the claims manager, suggesting yet again how his relation with Keyes drives his reactions to Phyllis. Both Keyes and Neff in fact share a disdain for the particularity of women, manifested by the claim manager's generic remarks about "dames" like "Margie" and the ease with which the salesman after the murder replaces the stepdaughter Lola for Phyllis as the object of his affection.

It might seem that this swerve from Phyllis to Lola sharpens the contrast between "bad" and "good" females and therefore signals Neff's growing moral apprehension about his crime. But I would argue otherwise that Lola mainly serves as just another (interchangeable) version of her stepmother, somewhat more sincere and innocent but no less given to theatrical display: just turn off the sound and watch one of her staged crying jags. While her story about Phyllis as a nurse causing the death of her mother ostensibly helps turn Neff against the femme fatale, this is just the excuse Neff needs to abandon a lover he has despised all along; not only is there no independent corroboration of Lola's tale, but in carefully revising Cain's source novel, which explicitly demonizes Phyllis as a serial killer of children, Wilder and Chandler intended viewers (if not Neff himself) to regard Lola's story with some doubt, even downright suspicion.

The same holds true for the role of Nino, who near the end of the narrative becomes the target of the company's investigation; following the lead of Keyes, imagining Nino as Phyllis's latest conquest and coconspirator, Neff can confirm his worst misgivings about her. Confronting Phyllis about Nino, Neff simply aligns himself with the claims manager ("what's good enough for Keyes is good enough for me"), while refusing over her objections to relinquish control of his narration: "Save it. I'm telling this." By the colloquial economic metaphor "save it," Chandler and Wilder effectively suggest Neff's growing resistance to his lover's continuing offers of sexual expenditure. As far as the devious woman is concerned, the stories of Keyes and Neff have merged, a sign that here at least Neff has succeeded in "trying to think with your brains, Keyes," as he earlier had vowed. In the two men's version of events (true or not, Neff says he does not care), Lola's boyfriend muddles the film's previously neat Oedipal dynamics by introducing the possibility of cross-generational liaisons. This is certainly the implication of the company surveillance team that spots him at Phyllis's five nights in a row, as Keyes notes in his own confidential Dictaphone memo (causing Neff some obvious distress). But Nino may also be a measure of Neff's increasing paranoia, his eagerness, believing he is being played for a sucker, to jettison Phyllis for the sake of some misplaced regret: hence his slightly ludicrous attempt at nobility, right after brutally killing the femme fatale, by trying to make things right between Nino and Lola instead of pinning the murders on Nino, as he had initially planned.

If Neff is quick to discard Phyllis, the reverse is not true. That is why her final, fleeting profession of love rings true, despite all her obvious self-serving treachery. Her repeated injunctions to her lover after the murder to keep "straight down the line" indicate her desire to remain together as a couple at all costs. Even before the murder she complains to Neff about "a wall between us"—*us* and *we* being her preferred pronouns, in contrast to Neff's inclination to use the first-person singular. Conforming to Keyes's statistical view of the world, Neff regards women as a transposable category, but men for this femme fatale are not, which is why she wants to stay with Neff after killing her husband, in effect honoring that second marriage vow he has made.

One scene makes this especially clear. Fake shopping at Jerry's and reacting to Neff's desire to stay apart, Phyllis paints the difference between Mr. Dietrichson and Neff in stark terms: "I loved you, Walter. And I hated him. But I wasn't going to do anything about it, not until I met you. It was you had the plan. I only wanted him dead." When the salesman paranoidly interprets this as an accusation, she takes off her sunglasses and replies: "And nobody's pulling out. We went into it together, and we're coming out at the end together." Of course we can read these lines as expressing the evil woman's desperate but steely need to drag down the man with her, but beneath the cold delivery, Stanwyck manages to convey a genuine pathos and poignancy, aided by the moving Rózsa score. If Neff refuses or is unable to fully see her after she removes her disguise to risk vulnerability, we need a clearer perspective than his own to comprehend the femme fatale.

In fact, a strong case can and has been made that the only character in the film to attain any sort of tragic recognition is Phyllis. Drawing on Stanley Cavell's influential analysis of Shakespearean tragedy, as well as on Jacques Lacan, Elisabeth Bronfen points to close-ups in the movie, such as the scene in Jerry's, that focus on Phyllis as a conscious, ethical agent who understands the consequences of her deadly choices even if she may not be entirely in control of them.[40] These powerful images of Stanwyck's expressive face remain independent from Neff's framing (and coercive) narration, as we can appreciate most clearly during the moment of Mr. Dietrechson's murder in a car. One of two extended sequences that take us outside Neff's epistemological scope (the other being Phyllis stashing a gun under her chair in preparation to shoot him), the murder takes place offscreen, while the camera lingers on Phyllis in the driver's seat, faintly, silently smiling while Neff from behind breaks her husband's neck (see figure 9). In recounting this crucial turning point precisely halfway through the film, Neff could not possibly see what is registered by Wilder's more objective camera. The director and the actress, not the narrator, here manage our view of Phyllis for a change.

In this regard it is illuminating to contrast Phyllis's direct, unmediated look at the camera during the murder with a subsequent one by Neff that seems to be similar but actually works quite differently. This is the instance near the end when he turns from his all-night speaking into the Dictaphone (seemingly neutral technology like the movie camera that records Phyllis smiling) to suddenly discover that Keyes has been watching and listening to him for some time from the office doorway (see figure 10). Keyes here has been tipped by the company janitor, not by his little man. As Sianne Ngai cogently shows, this unsettling succession of images creates enormous unease for the viewer as well as for Neff, who is now captured, both in the visual field and by the policing of Keyes.[41] Shifting from the close-up of Neff to the midrange figure of the investigator, we realize after the fact that Neff's gaze into the camera was not impartial but

9 The look of death: The husband's murder, from *Double Indemnity*

rather registered Keyes's subjective act of looking—the moment at which his relentless surveillance finally overtakes Neff and turns him into his own object of vision. With the sudden intrusion of Keyes, the entire movie's frame of retrospective narration collapses, as the detective moves from Neff's isolated recounting of the past into a space they both momentarily occupy in the present before the film draws to a close.

In so replacing the source novel's murky double suicide with this concluding restoration of law, Wilder and Chandler would seem to satisfy the censoring logic of the Production Code Administration, for which no crime could go unpunished. Ngai sees Keyes as the film's sole representative of social order, but in that case, why should this direct association between the director's camera and the claims manager's monitoring feel so uncomfortable? The abrupt displacement in viewer identification from Neff to Keyes certainly produces a jarring effect, but why does it feel so coercive and creepy to be put in the domineering position of Keyes? Like nearly all critics (including James Naremore), Ngai assumes that Keyes acts as a figure of moral authority.[42] Authority, yes, but in what sense "moral"? He shows no interest in the Greek immigrant's reasons for burning his truck, and no concern at all for the death of Mr. Dietrichson beyond how it will "cost us [the company] money," which is "always wrong," as he pointedly declares, consistently casting moral issues (right and wrong) in strictly financial terms. And in finally catching Neff, Keyes seems remarkably unmoved by his colleague's betrayal.

10 The look of death: Neff watching Keyes watching, from *Double Indemnity*

Critics are fond of pointing to their ending exchange—"closer than that, Walter" and "I love you too"—as a sign of mutual tenderness, but I would emphasize instead what the claims manager refuses to give the salesman during their last encounter. In the film's perversity along the lines of Poe, getting caught is all the first-person protagonist ever really desires (and perhaps this is yet another reason why Neff is disappointed to hear Keyes suspect Nino). Watching Keyes observe (and hear) him, Neff with a strange mixture of triumph, admiration, and disdain at the detective's failure predicts "the big speech" that will chastise (but also appreciate) him for his sins. Again and for the last time, hoping against hope that Keyes has some ethical stake in the proceedings, the salesman sentimentally misreads the manager. Yet all Keyes can offer is a statement of fact: "You're all washed up, Walter." What Neff (the wayward son) expects and wants, Keyes is unable to provide; once the ingenious crime is solved, or more accurately, overheard, he no longer has any function, certainly not the one of "father confessor" that he had earlier romantically claimed for claims. There is no romance or reconciliation here, only death.

Taking a page from Fritz Lang, in fact, Wilder films Neff's direct gaze into the camera as a look of and at death. As Tom Gunning has argued in his impressive, exhaustive analysis of Lang's films, the direct look at the camera is frequently an enunciative gesture that signifies fatality.[43] In Cain's novel it is the femme fatale who fantastically dresses up in "a scarlet shroud" (124, 215) to play that allegorical part, but the screen version gives the role to the numbers man Keyes. As a witty, minor aside, Richard

Schickel describes the wounded Neff's lengthy Dictaphone recording as "talking himself to death" (50), a gradual process that becomes literal—talking *to* Death—the instant the investigator breaks into the narration to learn what we already know.[44] To the extent that we are positioned as Keyes, then, we are being addressed (both by speech and sight) as the impending source of Neff's demise, which is why this moment is so unnerving. Who needs a gas chamber (the ending as originally filmed) when Keyes alone will do? A "loyal agent of industrial rationality," as Naremore has accurately described him, Keyes is incapable of the redemptive emotions (horror, regret, and/or sympathy) that Neff and Naremore and scores of troubled viewers (complicit in the manager's policing surveillance) have strained for the past sixty years to bestow on him.[45] Like the insurance salesman's clients, talked into life and accident policies despite their aversion to imagining death, that is what we must finally acknowledge we have bought in the figure of Keyes.

And so Neff vanquishes the femme fatale only to fall prey to a stronger, more powerful lethal force embodied by the claims investigator when he suddenly comes on the scene of narration. Of course the ultimate triumph of such lethality is a commonplace in almost all films noirs, and in equating Keyes with Death, I seem to have pushed my analysis of nonbelonging to a more absolute and extreme existential state that extends well beyond national or corporate citizenship. But this equation, I would insist, is less allegorical and more historical than it might seem, tied as it is to a specific time and place: the mid-twentieth-century corporate United States and the birth of white-collar crime as a distinct category of social transgression. If nobody in the movie understands why they do what they do (except, perhaps, Phyllis), we still can.

THREE

Cuba, Gangsters, Vets, and Other Outcasts of the Islands

The Chase and *Key Largo*

The intrinsic basic quality of Havana is a deadly magic.
—Helen Lawrenson, 1955

He rendered great service to the United States.
—Inscription on Lucky Luciano's New York City tomb

From a trio of émigré directors (Litvak, Ingster, Wilder) charting peculiar features of the American home front (spies, strangers, company men), we turn to two native-born directors, Arthur Ripley and John Huston, who take noir abroad, specifically Cuba in this chapter. For both of these filmmakers, moving outside the confines of the nation is directly related to the deeply felt impact of the Second World War. Movies made in the United States from Edison's actualities in the 1890s onward have depicted their compatriots working and adventuring around the globe. But it was not until the experience of hundreds of thousands of U.S. soldiers fighting across Europe, North Africa, and the South Pacific that citizens en masse came in contact with many different foreign lands. Numerous survivors brought back to the United States a profound sense of the foreign, still carried within, even well after the war ended: a surfeit of dark feelings, or an emotional war surplus, as I mention in my introduction.

Film noir scholars have noted how the trope of the disenchanted veteran plays a key role in defining the cycle, with most discussions centering on the psychic turmoil experienced by these ex-GIs trying to readjust to postwar life.[1] In almost all these movies the repatriated vet is compelled to relive his combat trauma on the mean streets of the United States. In *The Crooked Way* (1949), for instance, the climactic shootout between an amnesiac war hero and his criminal nemesis actually takes place in a warehouse filled with leftover military equipment. Battling the enemy now within (country and self) becomes the central way for these vets to regain a semblance of American normalcy. In this regard, the decorated soldier who risked dying overseas to save democracy has a symbiotic relationship with the cowardly gangster who stayed at home. Mirroring one another, both suffer from a twisted masculinity—unnatural, excessive, and/or overly aggressive.

The Chase (1946) and *Key Largo* (1948) stand a bit apart from these other noirs for having their protagonists work through their wounds by returning more directly to menacing alien spaces. The demobilized solider in effect becomes remobilized to yet another foreign land. This is Havana in the case of *The Chase*, and in the case of Huston's film, an island off the U.S. mainland, where a former army major full of sorrow, mourning the loss of one of his men, must take up arms against a deported mobster who is seeking to reenter his homeland after exile in Cuba. In both films, it is this striking triangulation between Cuba, the civilian gangster, and the maladjusted war veteran that constitutes the drama of the narrative, giving the soldier's psychological alienation a specific geopolitical logic as well.

Before looking closely at the movies themselves, it is important to consider more broadly the long-standing, tangled relations between the United States and Cuba. Here I am indebted to the pioneering work of the historian Louis A. Pérez Jr., who in a series of books over the past two decades has probed the "ties of singular intimacy" between the United States and the small island situated less than two hundred miles to the south across the Straits of Florida. Given this closeness and the countries' respective sizes, it is no surprise that Cuba has been profoundly shaped, economically and culturally, by the looming presence of the United States since the early nineteenth century. But Pérez makes a far more interesting case when he shows how the United States has been just as profoundly influenced by Cuba and Cubans, especially on the key question of home-land security.

It is clear that the Spanish-American War of 1898 helped give the United States a sense of itself as a world power, "transform[ing] the substance of Cuban sovereignty into an extension of the U.S. national system" by virtue of the Platt Amendment (1901). It is equally clear that the Cuban Revolution (1959) led by Fidel Castro compelled the United States to confront its worst cold war fears about a communist presence in the Western Hemisphere. Yet Pérez is also adept at showing in detail how during the relatively calm period between war and revolution, Cuba continued to exert a powerful sway on U.S. American politics and culture, and vice versa.[2] As Cuban markets were inundated by all kinds of U.S. products in the first half of the twentieth century, including Hollywood movies, Americans in turn were saturated with images of Cuba that defined it as an exotic land of pleasure, vice, and license (sexual and criminal) conveniently located within easy reach of the United States. It matters little that this cultural imaginary depicting Cuba as the adult playground of the United States was largely promulgated by Americans themselves, or that the brothels, mobsters, and casinos of Havana hardly figured in the experience of ordinary Cubans, as long as this "deadly magic" could be evoked by atmospheric noirs such as *The Chase*.

The Chase is actually the third in a series of low-budget B movies from the 1940s directed by Arthur Ripley that feature remote island settings and phantasmagorically explore the trauma of war. Each stranger and more surreal than the last, this trilogy of films might be called Ripley's believe-it-or-not, since these cinematic islands are less romantic than uncanny, claustrophobic spaces of dread and entrapment. Made only two months after FDR's Executive Order 9066, the first of the trio, *Prisoner of Japan* (1942) can in fact be fruitfully read as a kind of dark commentary on the internment of Japanese Americans at home. The plot follows the efforts of U.S. naval officers trying to stop Japanese radio transmitters operating from a secret communications center on the South Pacific island of Nukuloa. But the narrative quickly deviates from conventional war films by concerning itself mostly with a pair of American civilians who are trying to escape the island. Just as Japanese American citizens were confined in concentration camps for security reasons, so too, the pacifist, alcoholic, and cynical astronomer David Bowman (Alan Baxter) and the feisty nurse Toni Chase (Gertrude Michael) are held on the island against their wills by a brutal Japanese spy master. To defeat their captor and his spy operation, David and Toni in the end are sacrificed: calling for a navy ship to destroy the control room in which they have barricaded themselves, the doomed couple declares their love as the island blows up. As Dana Polan has persuasively argued about this and other wartime movies, normative Hollywood romance must be displaced and absorbed by military power for the greater good, but here in such a strange and disturbing manner that it is difficult to imagine how this grim conclusion could inspire any sort of patriotic reaction. There is no way out for the Americans to get off the island and return home, only the destruction of the island itself.[3]

Ripley's subsequent movie *Voice in the Wind* (1944) makes *Prisoner of Japan* look like a walk in the park. The film opens with a prologue urging us to sympathize with war refugees who failed in their attempts to come to the United States and instead have washed ashore on obscure islands like the French Caribbean Guadalupe. Here we find the crazy "El Hombre," a former Czech concert pianist (played by Francis Lederer, the spy in *Confessions of a Nazi Spy*) who has been tortured by occupying Nazis for publicly performing Smetana's nationalist piece "The Moldau," we discover in flashback. His sick wife is also on the island, even though neither spouse knows the other is there. Deranged, El Hombre sets fire to a fishing boat owned by a pair of Italian brothers who have falsely promised to take refugees to the United States. Just as the tormented pianist regains his memory, he is shot by one of the brothers, who in turn is killed by the other brother (himself stabbed). The fatally wounded El Hombre (now in his right mind) reaches his wife just as she expires, and then he collapses on top of her, Romeo and Juliet style. Even by the gloomy standards of French poetic realist cinema of the 1930s, on which the film is clearly based (doleful foghorns and all), this narrative is extremely intense and bleak; as in *Prisoner of Japan*, nobody succeeds in leaving the island, except by death.

Based on the Cornell Woolrich novel *The Black Path of Fear* (1944), Ripley's following movie, *The Chase* (1946), depicts the eerie experience of the unemployed drifter Chuck Scott (Robert Cummings) who is hired as a chauffeur by the sadistic Miami gangster Eddie Roman (Steve Cochran). Every night Eddie's mistreated wife, Lorna (the French émigré actress Michèle Morgan), asks "Scotty" (as Eddie has nicknamed him) to drive her to a spot on the beach where she stares out across the Straits of Florida, longing to escape her abusive husband. The two quickly fall in love and develop a plan to flee on the ship ss *Cuba* to Havana and beyond, but minutes after arriving in the foreign country she is mysteriously stabbed to death and he is charged by the local police with the murder— this is staple Woolrich fare with its ominous atmosphere of nightmarish paranoia. In fact, along with *Stranger on the Third Floor* (1940), *Detour* (1945), and *Fear in the Night* (1947, also based on a Woolrich story), *The Chase* is among the most oneiric of films noir, to use one of the key terms Raymond Borde and Etienne Chaumeton introduced in the 1950s to define the cycle.[4]

The movie differs from Woolrich's first-person narrative in two crucial, related aspects: first, in the film the protagonist is a troubled, pill-popping navy veteran, and second (spoiler alert!), Chuck's pursuit and persecution in Havana turn out quite literally to have been a dream, a feverish hallucination triggered by his sudden collapse into unconsciousness as he is preparing to leave the United States with Lorna. So instead of a crime mystery centered on how the gangster Roman managed to reach beyond the United States to exact revenge on his abused wife, as in the novel, we have a clinical case of post-traumatic stress disorder (PTSD). Chuck's pathological state, we retrospectively understand, is signaled the moment he hears Spanish spoken all around him in Havana, so that, as in *Stranger*, his delirium is likened to dwelling in a foreign country. A ringing phone in his room, shot in luminous close-up (like the surreally magnified coffee cup in *Detour*), arouses him from this imaginary sojourn in a disorienting and alien land, anything but a tourist jaunt that has run a full thirty minutes on the screen.

Reminiscent of the "it-was-all-just-a-dream" ending of *The Cabinet of Dr. Caligari* (1920), Chuck's sweat-drenched awakening from the nightmare of Cuba is actually far less conservative and conclusive. What may look like a cheap gimmick dramatizes rather sharply the moment the ex-soldier "returns" to the reality of the United States, a space he had departed, it would seem, only in his head: a wish fulfillment gone bad. Back on U.S. territory, in the third and perhaps most interesting section of the movie, Chuck seeks help for his "shock case" by visiting the commander of the U.S. naval hospital in Miami. The commander, a doctor who had also previously cared for Chuck, "technically" identifies his problem as an "anxiety neurosis," reassuring the decorated veteran (who is wearing a chauffeur's suit and cap resembling a military uniform) that his condition is not as terrible as the diagnosis sounds. Dismissing Chuck's story about Cuba as "dream stuff," the commander takes the soldier to the Florida Club (in contrast with La Habana, just in case we have forgotten where we are) for some drinks to "relieve tension."

Beyond the dubiousness of using alcohol as a medical treatment for PTSD, the nightclub scene grows even more unlikely when the doctor (but not Chuck, who is sitting alone at the bar) runs into Roman. The gangster has locked up his wife (who is still waiting for Chuck to take her to Cuba) to enjoy a night out with his peculiar little henchman, Gino (Peter Lorre). Why would a commander of a navy hospital exchange friendly banter with a common mobster? With one oddity piling on top of another in this presumably objective rendering of home life, "Doc" Davidson was Roman's personal physician before he joined the navy. Their meeting suggests, however briefly, a disturbing complicity between the civilian criminal who sat out the war and a military officer who quickly rose in the ranks while treating decorated heroes like Chuck, soldiers who actually fought and suffered abroad. Thinking he is escaping the clutches of a villain to fulfill his romantic desire, Chuck vividly relives this combat trauma during the second section of the film, the harrowing interlude he imagines taking place in Havana.

The island of Cuba represents alien territory, one menacing and confining, but arguably no more so than Miami, as Chuck's return to normalcy after his hallucination suggests. From the opening of the movie, in fact, his experience appears pretty damn strange. The first image of Chuck—grubby, down-and-out, homeless, his face pressed hungrily against a diner window—evokes a Great Depression ethos more than a postwar one. But once he enters Roman's world—he has found the mobster's wallet on the street and returned it to him—the veteran's economic desperation gives way to a far more curious sort of ordeal. Handsome and dapper, Roman is also violent, domineering, and (no surprise) misogynistic, viciously hitting a manicurist for messing up his nails (more on nails and gangsters shortly), keeping his wife under lock and key, preferring the male company of creepy Gino (more on the queerness of gangsters in the 1940s shortly), fatally siccing a mad dog on a reluctant business associate, and drawing both Gino (as passenger) and Chuck (as driver) into his private death-wish fantasy by pushing his sedan (via a hidden backseat pedal) to lethal speeds. That is what kills him and Gino in the end.

Yet perhaps Roman's oddest and most oppressive feature resides in his house, a baroque, shadow-filled mise-en-scène cluttered with ancient Roman statues, busts, and other garish works of art. These signify not simply the bad taste of a thug but rather the spoils of a tyrant who functions as a kind of an amalgamation of Hermann Goering and Benito Mussolini. *The Chase* was completed three days before Goering killed himself on October 15, 1946. As I discuss in chapter 1, the association between fascists and gangsters was a common, long-standing one that began in the early 1930s. Seeing the movie in late 1946, as Axis war criminals were being tried and executed, audiences watching the sadistic machinations of an Italian gangster and his German-accented sidekick would need little stretch of the imagination to be reminded of current events across the globe. And so even before the ex-GI Chuck feverishly fantasizes himself in Cuba battling an invisible enemy, he has already thrust himself into a war scenario by walking into Roman's mansion.

In his room anticipating his escape on the SS *Cuba* with Lorna, Chuck to the accompaniment of lush piano music skims a promotional brochure titled *Island of Romance*. Not exactly, as it turns out. The problems begin as soon as they leave the ship. Transported from the Cuba docks by a strange, sad guide driving a horse carriage, surrounded by a host of Spanish voices (untranslated), the couple enters a crowded bar whose neon sign announces "La Habana." The city is meant to be only a brief stopover on the way to South America. But in the steamy bar Lorna suddenly collapses, stabbed to death in Chuck's arms. What follows is a series of loosely connected episodes of confusion and pursuit filmed with some of the murkiest compositions found in urban noir (or elsewhere). Earlier in the Miami and ship scenes, Ripley and his cinematographer Franz Planer had given us surreal shots of eyes peering through peepholes and heads masked by oval portholes, but in the Havana scenes, all is darkness.

These enigmatic, inky vignettes are almost impossible to see, let alone comprehend: interrogation by local police; a visit to a curio shop run by a gypsy woman named Chin to clear up some uncertainty about the apparent murder weapon (a Chinese jade-handled knife); Chuck's escape from the shop and concealment by a mysterious crying woman, deep in mourning, who tells the "Americano" that she hates cops; his search for a missing photograph and negative that records, two decades in advance of Michelangelo Antonioni's *Blow Up* (1966), the commission of the crime; the corpse of the photographer; Chuck's return to the shop, where Gino (showing up out of nowhere) burns the incriminating evidence—a flash snapshot that documents a man throwing a knife; and finally, illuminated only by a few dim candles, Chuck's demise at the hands of Gino. All this displaced violence and aggression (including Lorna's murderer captured on film) conjures up the bewilderment and trauma of combat, which closes, in an extreme visualization of third-person disassociation, with Chuck witnessing his own dead body being tossed down a trapdoor as a bell begins to ring (cut to a close-up of the telephone) ... and he wakes up.

The bridge between this nocturnal Cuban fantasy and Chuck's earlier time in Florida is of course the sinister Gino. Reprising a role he would continue to play, for better or for worse, Lorre functions as the very embodiment of uncanniness in the movie, just as he had in *Stranger*—the return of the repressed foreigner, the man without a country. A proxy for his gangster boss who remains at home, Lorre enters the war veteran's nightmare to negotiate the difference between Cuba and the United States. And yet his sudden appearance in Chuck's delirious dream is actually reassuring, because it establishes a logical connection between Havana and Miami and helps explain how Lorna was murdered.

Even if this sequence remains one of the most fantastic in all of noir, it is still heavily grounded in a clear historical reality, once we come to discover that this is not Gino's first time on the island. The continuity between Miami and Havana in the end is simply a matter of business. As he is about to kill the devious Madame Chin for attempting blackmail, Gino cryptically alludes to sneaking contraband into the United States, insisting that "same as last time," "we run the stuff across." As Woolrich's novel more fully elaborates, the mobster Roman makes his money by smuggling drugs into America, and indeed throughout the 1930s Havana was home to a large ring of Chinese drug traffickers smuggling opium into the United States.[5] Cuba in this regard is not some randomly chosen enchanted isle for Ripley to dramatize his protagonist's captivity and alienation, but a source of malignancy particularly close to home that helps account for Roman's income, apart from his desire to destroy his disloyal wife when she lands there.

But if the Miami gangster has a specific financial stake in Cuba, what about the war veteran? It might seem that his destination with Lorna simply signifies an exotic "island of romance" outside America; as his reading of the travel brochure would indicate, he appears to have no prior familiarity with the country. But a curious comment by Doc Davidson indicates otherwise. Convincing Chuck that his fever dream stemmed from battle shock, his physician points out that "you haven't been to Havana in three or four years, to my knowledge." This places Chuck in Cuba around 1942. What would he be doing there, and how would the naval hospital commander know?

One possible answer is that he was stationed at Guantánamo Bay Naval Base, on the other side of the island. While Guantánamo was not a hot spot during the Second World War, and became a prison only years later, it did experience an armed forces buildup from the early 1940s onward, as the United States sought to bolster its defense of the Panama Canal against enemy incursion. In 1942 alone German submarines sunk more than 250 ships in the Caribbean region. A *New York Times* article from early 1943, for instance, reports a German sub torpedoing a U.S. merchant vessel, whose survivors were taken to Guantánamo.[6] Presumably Chuck suffered his debilitating combat trauma elsewhere, but the doctor's remark suggests how the film registers both an American criminal presence and a military one in Cuba during the war. When Chuck fantasizes meeting up with Gino in Havana, perhaps it is not so crazy after all, since both the anxious vet and the shady crook share some previous material connection with the place.

Although *Key Largo* does not take place in Cuba (even in fantasy), it, too, concerns American gangsters and vets returning from abroad who confront one another on uncertain island terrain. But unlike the oneiric, highly convoluted, and twisted narrative of *The Chase*, the plot of *Key Largo* is uncomplicated and minimal: an aging, banished gangster holds hostage a group in a Florida Keys hotel in the midst of a devastating hurricane. His captives include the owner of the resort, the old man's daughter-in-law, and a disillusioned ex-army officer who must rouse himself to defeat the mobster and his gang. In keeping with its origins as a stage play, there is a lot of (interesting) talk, and the action is mainly confined to the claustrophobic space of the hotel. The complexity of the film stems from its locale, as well as from two simple facts, one having to do with American cinema history, and the other with midcentury geopolitics: the gangster is played by Edward G. Robinson, and his character, Johnny Rocco, is closely patterned after Salvatore Lucania, aka Lucky Luciano, the most influential Mafia crime boss in U.S. history.

Let us begin with the setting. The film credits open with a long, overhead shot of a highway, followed by an explanation scrolling onscreen: "At the southernmost point of the United States are the Florida Keys, a string of small islands held together by a concrete causeway. Largest of these remote coral islands is Key Largo." The written equivalent of a travelogue or police-procedural voice-over, this authoritative text gives way to a shot of a bus driving down the highway, again from an omniscient overhead point of view. But thereafter this comprehensive, linear perspective vanishes, to be replaced by fluid tracking shots and low-angle close-ups for the increasingly tense, sweaty interior scenes. On his way from the U.S. mainland to Key West, Major Frank McCloud (Humphrey Bogart) has stopped off-season (summer) at the Largo Hotel to pay his respects to the invalid father (Lionel Barrymore) and widow, Nora (Lauren Bacall), of George Temple, a fallen comrade who had died in Italy under his command. Immediately these figures are positioned in a global mapping that complicates conventional notions of the domestic and the foreign: even though he has restlessly wandered all across the United States, Frank finds that these "Keys are different than anything I've seen," while Mr. Temple asks the ex-officer if the "plot of ground" in Italy where his son is buried "belongs to us."

The relation of island to nation(s) is essential for the story. Before the Overseas Highway so prominently featured in the credits was finally completed in 1938, the Florida Keys were detached territories connected by a combination of railways, roads, commercial ferries, and boats. As the one farthest removed from the U.S. mainland and a common sailing departure point to Havana, Key West in particular became a haven for authors and intellectuals, not only Americans such as Ernest Hemingway, Wallace Stevens, and Elizabeth Bishop in the 1920s and 1930s but also Cubans at the end of the nineteenth century. One of them was José Martí, who first visited Key West the same year (1891) that he produced his seminal essay "Nuestra América" ("Our America"), written while in exile in the United States and published simultaneously in New York City and Mexico City. Many in the United States during this period might have been eager to annex Cuba, but Martí and his émigré followers living in Key West (and there were many) viewed the American island as a "noble" utopian model that could serve as a staging arena for the Cuban independence movement.[7]

As a middle ground between two countries and cultures, the Keys allowed these writers to view their own homelands from a distance. In a notorious letter of 1932 to his friend, the novelist John Dos Passos, for example, Hemingway joked about declaring Key West an independent "South Western Island Republic." He had been a resident for four years at this point, having moved from Europe in 1928. After fantasizing the destruction of bridges and telegraph lines, Hemingway vowed in his letter that on the first night of revolution he would "massacre the catholics and jews," to be followed by "free thinkers, atheists, communists."[8] Six years later, disgusted with FDR's New Deal, Hemingway in 1938 would move to Havana, shortly after penning *To Have and Have Not*, a bitter novel about a mercenary American who uses his fishing boat to smuggle rum and human cargo (Chinese and Cubans) across the Straits of Florida.

As Hemingway's pre–Second World War political and geographical trajectory suggests, the Keys and Cuba were closely aligned locations. And so it should come as no surprise to discover in Huston's movie that the mobster Rocco has come from Cuba to set foot on U.S. territory (Key Largo) for the first time in eight years. His foreign experience parallels Frank's time fighting in Italy. But unlike Frank (traveling south), Rocco arrives by sea, not land, which is the same way he departs. In fact, he is associated with water throughout the film: the first we see him, quite a risk for the fifty-four-year-old actor Robinson, he is sitting naked in a bathtub trying to cool off, smoking a cigar, and swigging a drink (see figure 11).[9] Heading in opposite directions, the ex-soldier and the ex-con cross paths in Key Largo. This unexpected meeting sets up the narrative's primary confrontation about what counts as American—who belongs and who is merely trespassing.

Before considering in greater detail Robinson's casting as a barely disguised Lucky Luciano, we need to add two more elements to complete the movie's conceptual mapping: Indians and a hurricane. Indians are introduced from the beginning of the plot; before Frank's bus pulls up to the hotel, it is stopped on the highway by two local police officers looking for a pair of Seminoles, John Osceola and his brother Tom (played by Jay Silverheels, of *Tonto* fame). Named after a famous Seminole warrior, these two

The exiled gangster's watery return, from *Key Largo*

"boys" have busted out of jail, where they were imprisoned for a rowdy fight in which they tried "to take Florida back to the Indians," as Mr. Temple quips to Frank. Later in the film, we see the fugitive pair pull up to the hotel dock in a small boat, confirming the bus driver's prediction that Indians "always head for home," with Frank completing the thought, "home being Key Largo." They are accompanied by two boatloads of an extended Indian family (men, women, and children) seeking shelter from the "big blow" that is threatening to hit the islands. The patriarch of this clan is Charlie, a "prince of the Seminole nation," who now "sells seashells by the seashore," Nora jests, as she and Frank greet the group arriving ashore. With the exception of Mr. Temple, everyone drawn to the hotel comes from somewhere else: Frank and Nora from the mainland, the Indians from a small outlying key, Rocco and his gang from Cuba.

The hotel functions in the movie as a dislocated microcosm for the country. Learning that the brothers are ready to give themselves up to the police at the urging of Mr. Temple, Nora remarks to Frank that the Indians trust the proprietor: "As far as they're concerned, he's the United States of America." In this mingling of natives and transplanted whites, Huston focuses on the extraordinary face of an elderly Indian matriarch, fondly called "Mama Chobee" by Nora and reputed to be more than a hundred years old, who is carefully framed between the starched white shirts of Bogart and Bacall (see figure 12). She looks like a Great Depression icon out of a Dorothea Lange photograph or like something far more ancient, a

12 The ur-American
framed by Bogart
and Bacall, from
Key Largo

presence predating the nation and national history altogether. As Nora explains, "every Indian around here is a descendant of Mama Chobee." Excluded by Rocco (himself an exile) and cast as criminals by the police (who are initially oblivious to serious gangsters in their midst), these dispossessed Indians serve as touchstones for probing the meanings of U.S. citizenship. Linked to "home" and to taking back Florida, the Seminoles come to represent a third way, the ur-American, unsettling any fixed binary between American and un-American. Against the threat of the despised intruder's uncanny return, the film thus imagines a racialized solution: a vestigial indigenous population more pure than the whitest of whites (such as Nora and Frank) for seeming to have always belonged to the motherland.

A second source of destabilization is the intensifying storm itself, a force of nature closely associated with the Indians. This hurricane replays one that actually pummeled the Upper Keys on Labor Day, 1935, the first and still most intense category-five storm ever to hit the United States.[10] Leaving massive destruction in its wake, when it was over more than four hundred people had died, as Mr. Temple recounts (with somewhat exaggerated numbers) to Rocco and his gang in terrifying detail. Entire island communities were wiped out. Responding to the decimation, Hemingway published an angry letter in the Popular Front magazine *New Masses*, accusing the Roosevelt administration of incompetence.[11] As in the sea fictions of Joseph Conrad and Jack London, the gathering fury of nature in the film functions to collapse conventional cultural categories, boundaries, and associations, indeed, to disintegrate culture altogether, leaving individuals to fend for themselves in a primeval state of existence. This is especially true for the Indians, who are cruelly barred by Rocco from entering the hotel and left to their fates in the wild.

Yet while the hurricane would seem to erase the narrative's deliberate mapping of national affiliations (Cuba, Italy, the Seminole nation, the United States, the island "home" of Largo), it also can be read more figuratively as an evocation of the violence of the Second World War itself, which had also recently wreaked havoc on traditional borders and populations. An intimate enclosure, the hotel serves as a protected haven set against the howling winds outside; but having been infiltrated by Rocco and his gang, the hotel becomes a toxic and potentially fatal space that replays the chaos outside, forcing the ex-major to go through the crucible of battle again.

Rocco, the source of Frank's inner turmoil, is an unwanted interloper threatening the security and safety of the hotel, home, and state. As consummately portrayed by Robinson, the middle-aged gangster is crude, sadistic, volatile, and petulant, obsessed with displaying power over others simply for the sake of power. When goaded by Frank to say what he wants, he can only respond by reiterating "more." *Key Largo* is the third movie in this study starring Robinson, and at the risk of confusing the fictional character with the actor, it makes sense to step back and ask what all three roles have in common: what might a resolute and resourceful FBI interrogator in *Confessions* and a relentless insurance claims investigator in *Double Indemnity* have to do with a ruthless, grasping mobster. Not much, we might conclude at first glance, simply noting the range, versatility, and brilliance of Robinson as a performer who could play anybody. After all, he sometimes even assumed multiple parts in a single picture, including the delightful John Ford comedy *The Whole Town Is Talking* (1935), where he pulled off the feat of impersonating two opposed types at once—a hard-boiled criminal named "Killer" Mannion and his double, the mild-mannered clerk "Jonesy" Jones, who keeps on getting mistaken for the mobster. This meek alter ego, in fact, helped pave the way for the similar victim roles Robinson took up in Fritz Lang's mid-1940s noirs, *The Woman in the Window* (1944) and *Scarlet Street* (1945).

Yet on closer scrutiny, the clever agent Renard, the inspector Barton

Keyes, and the hoodlum Johnny Rocco do share some essential traits. Projecting an aura of authority and control, all three exhibit a curious hold over others, what we might call a manipulation or surveillance effect, seeing without being seen.[12] In all three movies, for instance, even before we meet the Robinson character, we feel his presence, as he listens silently to military intelligence officers worry about espionage in the United States (*Confessions of a Nazi Spy*), is addressed in the second person (offscreen) throughout Neff's voice-over narration (*Double Indemnity*), and via a henchman invisibly issuing commands to his jumpy, alcoholic moll, Gaye Dawn (*Key Largo*). Despite (or because of?) the charismatic power emanating from the actor, we tend to like him, no matter what the role. As I argued in chapter 2, this gruff but endearing exuberance interferes with our capacity (and Neff's as well) to fully appreciate the investigator's sinister side. To be overly schematic, if the federal agent Renard is inside the law and Rocco well outside, Keyes occupies a problematic position somewhere in between, his fatherly solicitude notwithstanding. Although it would be too extreme to suggest that we admire Rocco, one of the vilest villains Robinson ever played, at one pivotal moment (to be discussed shortly) the aging mobster does engage our sympathy.[13]

More to the point, perhaps, is that "Rocco" is quite explicitly a recycling of another immensely popular Robinson portrayal, the charismatic gangster Rico in *Little Caesar* (1931), the Warner Bros. movie that catapulted the actor to fame. So when the director and cowriter Huston in another Warner's movie introduces viewers to a middle-aged Italian criminal trying to stage a comeback, this becomes an obvious homage—self-conscious and self-reflexive, seventeen years later—to Robinson himself and the American gangster film he helped create. *Key Largo* is as much about the actor Robinson, or even more so, than about the character Rocco.

In their valuable introduction to *Mob Culture: Hidden Histories of the American Gangster Film*, the editors Lee Grieveson, Esther Sonnet, and Peter Stanfield rightly criticize the way many cinema scholars construct partial and narrow canons based on a limited number of films, which then serve as the foundation for misleading and inaccurate generalizations. In the case of the gangster genre, the holy trinity commonly consists of *Little Caesar*, *Public Enemy* (1931), and *Scarface: The Shame of a Nation* (1932); from these "classics," influential critics such as Robert Warshow identified a series of characteristic features and narrative structures (such as "rise and fall") from which all else would follow. But as Stanfield points out in his contribution to the volume, for example, Robinson (born Emanuel Goldberg in Romania) played a number of hoodlums prior to *Little Caesar*, and both before and after this particular movie, he impersonated a range of urban ethnicities, from Portuguese to Chinese. To brand him simply as the iconic Little Caesar ignores the richness of cinema institutions, particularly the way in which Hollywood production practices encouraged variety and hybridity to appeal to the tastes of a wide array of viewers.[14]

Yet this seems to me to tell only one half of the story. At the same time that a profit motive might encourage variety, financial success would also seem to demand predictability. This speaks to Hollywood's more conservative inclinations. To put it bluntly, the industrial studio system sought to repeat innovation. Whether we interpret this as a contradiction, a paradox, or a dialectic depends on how generous we might feel. But we cannot assume that film canons are mainly created by academic critics, or even by influential public intellectuals like Warshow. For every studio worker who might have read Warshow's "The Gangster as Tragic Hero," there were a hundred who simply looked at the bottom line and saw that *Little Caesar* was a big hit, the kind of movie that audiences would flock to over and over again, with little variation. A studio in the early sound era might have tried out five different sorts of crime movies (including some featuring women), figured out which kind made the most money (strong ethnic male protagonist), and then sought to duplicate that formula. And the same would hold true in some respects for *Little Caesar*'s breakthrough star Robinson, despite his impressive range as an actor. Punning on the stage and financial meanings of *stock*, Stanley Cavell has noted how Hollywood studios functioned as "an enormous stock company, America's only successful one, its State Theater," whereby "the individuality of stars was defined by their self-identity through repeated incarnations."[15]

In this view, canonicity is construed less by critics in isolation than by the complex interplay among studios, directors, screenwriters, actors, audiences, reviewers, journalists, various other arbiters of taste, and (well after the fact) academic scholars. When the dying Little Caesar asks his immortal question, "Mother mercy, is this the end of Rico?," Huston's answer seems to have been "well, not exactly." Bringing Rico back from exile, so to speak, for an encore performance, now as Rocco, Huston is acknowledging a seminal moment in the history of American cinema, as well as signaling his own intention to join the pantheon of directors, as Andrew Sarris dubbed it.[16] However limited the individual film *Little Caesar* might be when situated amid the dozens of other crime movies made around the same time, it cannot but help define the genre. And even if we admit that genres are simply artificial constructs, especially noir, Hollywood producers, writers, and directors found these constructs useful for shaping filmmaking intentions. In this respect, not all movies are equally influential.[17]

The self-consciousness of the studio and its director casting Robinson as Rocco extends to the characters in *Key Largo* themselves, making it all the more vital to read the film intertextually through the lens of Hollywood gangster history. Yearning for the good old days, Rocco and his gang act, in fact, as if they have ended up in the wrong movie, more comfortable in the 1930s urban world of *Little Caesar* than on an island in the middle of a hurricane. With names like Curly, Angel, and Toots, they are anachronisms in the postwar United States, as their nostalgia for bootlegging suggests. Their desire to bring back Prohibition is something of a running joke in the film: "Next time it will be different," one of the henchmen claims, vowing to avoid the internecine bloodbaths that cut into venue during the early years of the Great Depression. But this refrain about the glories and mistakes of their criminal past also bespeaks a certain kind of wistfulness on Huston's part: they do not (and cannot) make gangster movies as they used to. Why is it so difficult to film a good gangster yarn in 1948? Or to put the question differently, why is it so difficult to be a convincing gangster in 1948?

Clearly the Production Code Administration (PCA) regulation starting in 1934 made it uncomfortable, if not impossible, for Hollywood to follow up on charismatic figures like Little Caesar. During the war PCA restrictions were supplemented by the Office of War Information (OWI), which was concerned about Hollywood depicting demoralizing domestic lawlessness while the United States was engaged in a life-or-death global struggle. If there were gangsters to be portrayed, it could only be Hitler and his ilk. But another movie made in 1948, *I Walk Alone*, neatly suggests another kind of answer. Frankie (Burt Lancaster) and Noll (Kirk Douglas) are a pair of bootleggers who strike a deal to share nightclub profits if one gets caught, and sure enough Frankie gets sent to prison for a long stretch. After his release, feeling like a stranger in a strange land (the new postwar America), he comes to collect his due, but he is told by his brother Dave (Wendell Corey), who works as an accountant for Noll, that the business is too complicated, with too many ownership clauses, boards of directors, incorporated entities, and legalities, to be able to even know what "half" means, let alone actually divide the money. In typical Lancaster fashion, the big lug Frankie goes ballistic, beating his breast, ripping up all the account books, and threatening physical violence, unable to fathom how the ex-bootlegger Noll has turned the illicit smuggling of a tangible product into abstract and complex (shall we say late?) capitalism.

Crime's bureaucratization may not exactly be Rocco's problem, but the nature of gangsterism certainly seems to have changed from the Depression era, when street toughs like Little Caesar reigned, to the Cold War, with a bunch of guys sitting around a hotel lobby waiting for a flabby middle-aged man to get out of his bathtub and do something. Whether we take a narrow or a more expansive sampling of mob movies from the early 1930s, their narratives do tend to depict youth, energy, and ambition centered on immigrants and newcomers, often ethnically marked, trying to climb up the American ladder of success. As a number of scholars have noted, a decade later, by 1940, the protagonists of many gangster movies appear more assimilated into mainstream U.S. culture. Made more than ten years after he directed *Little Caesar*, Mervyn LeRoy's *Johnny Eager* (1942) provides an interesting case in point. The ex-con Johnny (Robert Taylor) may still be eager, but his name is bland as white bread, he speaks with no accent, he has standard, matinée-idol good looks, and he is interested in developing a semirespectable business enterprise (a new dog-racing track) that depends more on bribing corrupt politicians than on shooting people. While his love interest, Lisabeth Bard (Lana Turner), at first seems attracted to him for professional reasons—she is a student majoring in sociology on class assignment (how self-conscious can you get?)—her interest turns personal once she realizes that the unloved man comes from a damaged family, or as his cynical, boozy sidekick Jeff says: "Mr. Freud, take a letter."

This shift in crime and the criminal from public to more private concerns, from sociology to psychology, as *Johnny Eager*'s plot makes explicit, moves the gangster genre in two seemingly disparate directions: toward assimilation and toward the pathological. Yet the directions paradoxically merge. In the context of the early 1940s, especially at the start of the Second World War, assimilation can be achieved only by converting what was formerly social deviance (mainly a function of a bad environment) into a more pervasive but also more individual sort of dysfunction. Every American is now neurotic, including gangsters, who therefore no longer can be viewed as such outsiders. To be in need of psychoanalysis becomes the norm, to have Oedipal troubles is par for the course: Mr. Eager, take a seat.

Part of this growing interest in the pathology of the quotidian stemmed from the widespread popularization of Freud in the United States, another part from the insanity of world war itself, as the agent Renard remarks at the close of *Confessions*.[18] And a third part, I suppose, could be chalked up simply to Hollywood and cold war America's search for new entertainment value. Criminal or otherwise, big business proved a pretty dull subject compared to dysfunctional family dynamics: abusive fathers, castrating mothers, juvenile delinquents. But in relation specifically to the figure of the gangster, I would argue that his maladjustment largely has to do with his failure to go through combat abroad in the company of other men. In her interesting discussion of male homoerotic desire in *Johnny Eager*, Huston's early noir *The Maltese Falcon* (1941), and Stuart Heisler's *The Glass Key* (1942), Gaylyn Studlar shows how homosocial intimacy, submerged and displaced onto violence in gangster movies of the early 1930s, remarkably erupts in crime films a decade later, with *The Maltese Falcon* giving us no fewer than three memorable characters whose masculinity is highly suspect (Gutman, Cairo, and Wilmar). How obtuse could the PCA have been, we might retrospectively wonder? Or perhaps thanks to Freud, as well as to pop diagnoses of various psychosocial maladies troubling the country, homosexuality was becoming something of a cultural commonplace that no longer raised many eyebrows.[19]

In her analysis Studlar demonstrates how Johnny's pathology primarily manifests itself sexually: he prefers his jaded, poetry-spouting, and devoted assistant Jeff (played wonderfully by Van Heflin) to Lisabeth. But although Studlar makes a convincing case for how this "new corporate-style hood" is adept at repressing his true, darker self (sexual and otherwise), she does not situate his relationship with Jeff in the context of the war that had already been raging in Europe for more than two years.[20] The film concludes with a poignant scene between the grieving Jeff and the mortally wounded Johnny cradled tenderly in his embrace—an image straight out of a myriad of combat films that filled American screens since the turn of the century, and intensified when war documentaries and propaganda films started up in the late 1930s. War was the only context in which intense physical affection between two unrelated adult men could be so openly visualized, suggesting how by the early 1940s the crime-film genre and the war-film genre were becoming intertwined.[21]

The bonding between men in these crime films of the 1940s not only both extends and revises how masculinity is represented in earlier gangster movies, as Studlar argues, but also evokes the organized and sanctioned violence of battle. Lacking any genuine partner in arms, the queer gangster on home turf finds a substitute by surrounding himself with fawning henchmen. For the true warrior, by contrast, male-male bonding in war films is often cut short by the untimely death of the fallen comrade. In the domestic case there is an excess of homosociability, while overseas homo- social ties tend to be unrequited and prematurely foreclosed. So while the gangster and the ex-GI share a masculinity that is rendered abnormal or unnatural, the reasons differ. If we recall for a moment the character of Chuck in *The Chase*, we note how the maladjusted veteran frequently suffers from some mysterious psychic injury or loss that interferes with his capacity to enjoy heteronormative romance—his dream of escape to Cuba with Lorna, for instance, turns into a nightmare that conjures up her brutal murder (at once a stabbing and a penetration). Chuck's own wounding corresponds to a sense of self-estrangement, a residual alien anxiety that must be discharged by undergoing additional (imaginary) violence inflicted by Roman's peculiar companion (Lorre, as in *The Mal- tese Falcon*, again marked as both foreign and homosexual). In this regard the two kinds of damaged males, tyrannical crime boss and loner veteran, double one another.

These returning soldiers help create what we might call the noir gang- ster, or "neo-gangster," as Borde and Chaumeton in the 1950s dubbed these postwar cinematic criminals. Here we find a long list of pathologies, not simply a strongly implied intimacy between boss and stooge, as in *The Chase, The Crooked Way* (1949), and *Where the Sidewalk Ends* (1950), but a host of dubious quirks that code these men as queer: fastidiously clipping nails (*The Chase* and *The Crooked Way*), frequenting bathhouses (*T-Men* [1948] and *Where the Sidewalk Ends*), setting people on fire (*Raw Deal* [1948], where pyromania gives the cinematographer John Alton an occasion to work his magic with lighting effects), and, perhaps most extreme, burying a head in mommy's breast (*White Heat* [1949]). Manic as ever, Jimmy Cagney in *White Heat* reprises his persona as public enemy number one, now with a hysterical mother complex ("Made it, Ma! Top of the world!"). Unlike Robinson in *Key Largo*, however, he acts without a hint of self-consciousness that at age fifty he might be past his prime. The screenwriter Ben Hecht was particularly clever at coming up with bizarre fetish objects for these psychopathic criminals to prosthetically fondle, such as a bulky hearing device (*Ride the Pink Horse* [1947]) or a nasal inhaler (*Where the Sidewalk Ends*). And this warped masculinity goes hand in hand with the traumatized behavior of the ex-soldiers they frequently encounter and fight.

The striking thing about *Key Largo* is that the writers Huston and Richard Brooks actively reject this prevailing postwar tendency to pathologize both gangster and veteran.[22] There is nothing especially sick or perverse about Rocco, beyond his cruel treatment of the aging (and so ironically named) Gaye Dawn, played by Claire Trevor in an Oscar-winning performance—sadly familiar misogyny which is consistent with early thirties gangster movies. But queer criminals? Been there, done that, Huston appears to be saying in *Key Largo*. The same holds true for Rocco's foil, Frank, who seems mildly diffident, reluctant to act (a not-so-young Hamlet), but otherwise relatively normal for a field officer who has suffered the loss of men under his command. As Borde and Chaumeton astutely recognized, this film's bad guys "through some highly acute psychological touches defy the then-current model."[23] The French critics do not elaborate on these touches, but presumably they mean the way that Rocco and his gang repeatedly register the fact that they are over the hill, that they have been eclipsed and rendered obsolete by a new era of American crime. In this regard Huston's unusual take on the middle-aged gangster is as much historical as it is psychological; the Second World War comes into account not simply as a predictable and convenient source of trauma, as in many other noirs, but more broadly and centrally as part of the movie's complex transnational mapping.

The importance of the Second World War is most apparent when we compare the film to its literary source. In Maxwell Anderson's stage play *Key Largo* (1939), the protagonist King McCloud is a disgraced veteran of the Abraham Lincoln Brigade fighting in the Spanish Civil War who in the play's prologue abandons his fellow Americans on a hillside in Spain to return to the United States. He has concluded that the war is not worth dying for, and indeed, his comrades are killed by Franco's victorious fascist forces. Wracked with guilt, the deserter McCloud travels to Key Largo, where he meets the widow of one of his comrades and fights a gang of small-time gamblers holding hotel guests hostage. But at this point the movie begins sharply departing from the play, which imagines McCloud redeeming himself only by perishing at the hands of the gangsters, whose boss is nicknamed "Mussolini" by his crew. So both the historical context and the outcome for McCloud differ. Clearly, Anderson's is a drama about lost causes, not only the Spanish Civil War and the fatal sacrifice of the (non)hero but also New Deal idealism itself, as McCloud's turgid lines near the close of the drama suggest:

> We jump first at the door
> with Christ upon it, hanging on the cross,
> then the door with Lenin, legislating heaven,
> then the emblem of social security, representing
> eighteen dollars a week, good luck or bad,
> jobs or no jobs [24]

Akin to Hemingway's severe reaction against FDR, *Key Largo* the play likewise dwells on the failures of progressivism, positing as an alternative only a conservative withdrawal into individual self-sacrifice. But even the crooks in the play are too petty to pose any serious danger, leaving us with a strong sense of dissatisfaction in the end.

Presumably Huston also felt dissatisfied, because he drastically altered Anderson's script by giving us a cause worth fighting for (the final defeat of fascism), a true war hero, and a menacing criminal who represents a serious threat to nation and home and who therefore needs to be vigorously dispatched. Huston' narrative runs against the grain of most postwar noirs because it is relatively affirmative in the midst of burgeoning disillusionment among cold war liberals.[25] That is why Huston and Brooks resist the temptation to delve into the ills of solid U.S. citizens. Indeed, how cynical could Frank be if he is willing for the sake of the widow and the father to nobly credit George Temple with his own bravery in battle, as Nora herself realizes late in the film? He professes self-centered indifference ("One Rocco more or less isn't worth dying for") and seems to back down during an armed standoff with the gangster that proves fatal to another would-be rescuer (one of the policemen). But Frank, we understand, just as Nora does, ultimately will not shrink from doing the right thing in defying Rocco when the time is due.

Huston's refusal to pathologize Frank is all the more noteworthy when we consider the series of increasingly dark fictional narratives and documentaries he directed during the war. *Across the Pacific* (1942), an espionage thriller starring Bogart as a man who foils Japanese plans to destroy the Panama Canal, was followed by a trio of documentaries made for the U.S. Army Signal Corps, starting with *Report from the Aleutians* (1943). This was followed by *The Battle of San Pietro* (1945), which featured Huston's own voice-over narration and graphic shots through hand-held cameras of U.S. soldiers in action bitterly struggling against a "hidden enemy" to take back a heavily fortified hilltop town of strategic military significance. Filmed in the Italian region where George Temple in *Key Largo* is said to have fallen, the documentary spares little, showing body bags, mangled corpses, the digging of graves, and the mourning faces of distraught villagers. And finally, Huston made *Let There Be Light* (1946), the most extraordinary of his wartime films, chronicling GIs in a U.S. military hospital undergoing therapy for extreme nervous anxiety or PTSD. In his moving, somber treatment, Huston focuses on these patients as they recount their harrowing war experiences and attempt to explain their own disabilities. Their suffering and recovery is traced from hospital admission to discharge, most powerfully with anguished shot/reverse shot close-ups of them muttering, sobbing, trembling, stammering, and twitching.[26] The "unceasing fear and apprehension" that haunts these soldiers, as the narrator Walter Huston describes it, makes Frank's indecision about whether to fight Rocco pale by comparison, especially given Bogart's understated, stoic performance in a very familiar (dare we say tired?) role, that of the reluctant savior.[27]

Unable or unwilling to (re)make Depression-era gangster movies; reprising, but only halfheartedly, Bogart's familiar tough guy/good guy routine of the 1940s (*Across the Pacific, Casablanca, To Have and Have Not*); declining to use the Second World War simply as a convenient source to portray postwar trauma—Huston in *Key Largo* brilliantly hits on a way to valorize cold war heroics while retaining the uncanniness of noir. The key is the actor Robinson, not as a retro Little Caesar but as a thinly veiled version of the more contemporary mobster Lucky Luciano trying to return from exile abroad, rather than from the annals of cinema history.

Named by *Time* as one of the "hundred most important people of the century," the only criminal so honored, Luciano is credited for no less than "reinvent[ing] the Mafia." His "vision" was to replace "traditional Sicilian strong-arm methods with a corporate structure, a board of directors and systematic infiltration of legitimate enterprise." By 1936 he had single-handedly "modernized the Mafia, shaping it into a smoothly run national crime syndicate focused on the bottom line."[28] This rationalizing of crime into an efficient business operation curiously parallels similar consolidations that took place around the same time (the early to mid-1930s) in the FBI (thanks to Hoover, with the support of FDR) and the Hollywood studio system. In this regard, Luciano's fictional counterpart Rocco remains old school by contrast, as we discover late in the movie when he reveals his "high-class merchandise" from Cuba merely to be counterfeit money (not even drugs?) that he sells to a fellow old-school gangster, "Ziggy," who comes to meet him from the U.S. mainland. Rocco picks Key Largo, we surmise, because he can evade customs borders by arriving and returning by boat. Yet as he eagerly explains to Ziggy, it "won't be long now," a remark that clearly indicates his design to regain his former grandeur back in the United States.

But what is he doing in Cuba in the first place? Here is where the close resemblance to Luciano becomes significant. Targeted by the New York City special prosecutor Thomas E. Dewey, Luciano in June 1936 was found guilty of running a prostitution ring and sentenced to thirty to fifty years in prison.[29] A decade later he was deported to his birthplace, Italy, from where he soon made his way to Cuba with the help of a passport stamped with multiple entry visas for a number of Latin American countries. In late December 1946 at Havana's Hotel Nacional, he presided over a notorious convocation of crime bosses, including Meyer Lansky, gathered to discuss how to divvy up profits from narcotics trafficking and resort casinos in Cuba and Las Vegas, as well as whether or not to whack Bugsy Siegel. (Frank Sinatra was the headline entertainer for the group.) Hoover was rather in denial about organized crime until the (Estes)

Kefauver senate committee hearings of 1950–51, but the Federal Bureau of Narcotics (FBN) was not, and when the FBN director Harry J. Anslinger got wind of Luciano's presence in Cuba, he hired Hotel Nacional employees as informants and put pressure on the Cuban government to expel Luciano, despite the fact that the gangster was well connected to various Cuban authorities, including the chief of the secret police. Anslinger's strong-arm tactics included an embargo prohibiting the export of medicine to Cuba, with the FBN claiming that Luciano would commandeer and sell these drugs on the black market. Even though the decision was clearly for Cuban officials to make, U.S. political and economic pressure mounted to ship Luciano back to Italy.[30]

In a well-publicized news campaign, Luciano battled against deportation, even while admitting to reporters that "I don't want to be in any place where I'm not wanted." In late February 1947, in an agreement with Cuba, the United States lifted its embargo, while the Columbian government cancelled Luciano's visa, saying it was barring "undesirable elements." Three weeks later, Luciano was deported back to Italy on a Turkish cargo ship, insisting that he would reenter the United States "when its current government is no longer in power," a vow to return that Rocco echoes in *Key Largo*.[31] Luciano was counting on Dewey defeating Harry Truman in the upcoming presidential elections of 1948. Even though Dewey as New York City district attorney had sent him up in 1936, he did not object a decade later, now as governor of New York, to springing him right after the end of the war. Luciano's thirty-year sentence was cut short, we need to know, because he aided the U.S. government in its fight against fascism, not only by identifying fifth-column sympathizers on the New York City docks who might be spying for German U-boats prowling the Atlantic coast but, even more improbably, by helping U.S. naval intelligence prepare for the invasion of Sicily in 1943. This covert cooperation between gangsters and the U.S. military surely ranks among the most remarkable wartime collaborations, one that gained Luciano freedom, but also exile, for his patriotic troubles.[32]

Although it is unclear how and when folks like Huston learned about this problematic alliance (like Frank, Huston was a major in the army, after all), something akin to Luciano's resentment is expressed by Rocco early in the movie, immediately after the gangster gets out of the tub and first greets his captives. This is arguably the most crucial moment in the film.

Referring to himself in the third person, Rocco lists his former exploits: "When Rocco talked, everybody shut up and listened"; "nobody was as big as Rocco"; and so on in elegiac self-praise, to which Frank ironically contributes: "He was more than a king, he was an emperor." The veteran even goes so far as to welcome the gangster back, issuing a mock apology that "America is sorry for what it did to you." No wonder, then, that "the one and only" Rocco feels so bitter about his current state of exile, abandoned by those public officials, he explains a bit later, whom he helped put in power: "I made them just like a tailor makes a suit of clothes." Rocco certainly has a point in exposing this complicity between the government and convicted gangsters, hundreds of whom were sent back to Italy after the war.[33] While his comment ostensibly refers to municipal corruption, another even more indignant remark raises the stakes from the local to the national and the international: "After living in the USA for more than thirty years, they called me an undesirable alien. Me, Johnny Rocco! Like I was a dirty Red or something!"

In a script that largely lacks moral ambiguity or confusion, this resonant line cuts a number of ways. From Hoover's earliest years in the Justice Department, as I have discussed previously, deportation was a political instrument freely deployed by the government to expel unwanted residents of foreign birth who challenged mainstream values and beliefs (such as the anarchist Emma Goldman, kicked out during the Red Scare of 1919). Beginning in the immediate aftermath of the First World War, this practice continued during the Cold War. As the attorney general, Tom Clark, declared in January 1948, when *Key Largo* was being filmed: "Those who do not believe in the ideology of the United States, shall not be allowed to stay in the United States."[34] So Rocco by his comparison is proclaiming his loyalty to the United States, his credentials as a good citizen in opposition to dirty un-Americans. For the assimilated mobster (over thirty years living comfortably at home here) to be treated as if he were a communist is a slap in the face. Closely tied to the deportation panic I discussed in relation to *Stranger*, *Key Largo* nearly a decade later gives us the next step, exile anger.

There are several turns of the screw to consider. Rocco rejects any association lumping Mafia members and communists together as foreign criminals who do not belong in the country. But his justification for citizenship is dubious, based on his outraged feeling that he had not gotten his due for his contributions to the state. In the movie these contributions amount to bribery and corruption, suggesting a highly ironic juxtaposition between two sorts of undesirables, one complicit with the government, and the other not. And yet if we substitute Luciano for Rocco, the screw turns again, for in that case the gangster would have a more compelling reason for feeling betrayed, since he actively aided the U.S. war effort. In fact, since Frank and George Temple fought in the Italian campaign, as the film repeatedly emphasizes, we could go further and suggest that the information that the American Mafia gave the U.S. military for its invasion of Italy helped Frank and his comrades achieve victory. This puts us full circle. Frank must begrudgingly draw on his experience as a "soldier," the name that Rocco and his stooges repeatedly invoke while taunting him, to ultimately defeat the gang, but perhaps Rocco has helped forge that very identity. Frank quotes (without attribution) FDR's eloquent determination to "cleanse the world of ancient evils, ancient ills" (January 6, 1942, message to Congress), while Rocco breaks into untranslated Italian at one point, but perhaps there is more of a connection between the American war hero and the alien criminal than either cares to admit or understand.

There are three further turns of the screw. Less the sign of American ethnicity than of true otherness, Rocco's Italian evokes the gangster's postwar present in exile as much as his roots in the past. In the spring of 1948, as *Key Largo* was completing production and with Luciano already back in Rome, Italy was holding general elections that would determine the future direction of the nation, whose domestic affairs became a crucial test for U.S. foreign policy. Faced with the likely prospect of victory by the Communist Party, a situation *Time* magazine called "the brink of catastrophe," the U.S. government pulled out all the stops, orchestrating a letter-writing campaign between Americans of Italian extraction and families back home and suggesting that all members of the Communist Party in Italy would be banned from immigrating to the United States.[35] Although Luciano's specific role remains unclear, the Italian Mafia actively joined U.S. efforts to ensure the defeat of the Italian communists. And so Rocco's crack about a "dirty Red" in 1948 would have resonated across the Atlantic as well as throughout the cold war United States.

The second twist concerns gender, specifically the crucial role that a washed-up wreck of a woman plays in defeating Rocco. The action of *Key Largo* takes place in a confined space largely devoid of distinguishing cultural features. The blankness of the hotel, the storm, and the sea allows Huston to impose on these spaces the film's nuanced global mapping, but it gives Gaye Dawn little to go on during her confrontations with her former lover Rocco. Those encounters center on a pair of excruciating scenes, among the most abject in all of Hollywood cinema, not just of film noir. In the first episode of debasement, disgusted with his ex's constant pleas for booze, Rocco insists that Gaye Dawn sing for her (liquid) supper. In front of the hotel's hostages (kind of a mock captive nightclub audience), she manages to stumble through a solo rendition of "Moanin' Low" ("I'm feeling sick and sore. . . . / My sweet man I love him so / Though he's mean as can be") without any practice or any accompaniment. Her voice is shot, trembling, awkward, thin, way off key, and painfully sad to listen to, as the reaction close-ups of Rocco and the others make clear. As if she were compelled to strip naked in front of strangers, the pathetic older woman is exposed in all her vulnerability. Once he sees how far she has fallen (a measure of his own decline), Rocco with even greater disgust refuses to give her the drink, until Frank steps in at some risk, makes good on the gangster's promise, and gets slapped for his troubles. It is a difficult scene to watch, one whose abjection of the female carried over from the character Gaye Dawn to the actress Claire Trevor, who may have deserved her Oscar for this role by virtue of what she endured during filming. To achieve authenticity, Huston refused to allow Trevor any musical coaching or rehearsal, suddenly demanding one day on the set that she sing the song in one take.[36]

The second agonizing interaction between Rocco and Gaye Dawn would seem to reiterate the first. As Rocco and his gang are about to depart for Cuba, commandeering a boat to be run by Frank, Gaye Dawn realizes that she is about to be abandoned and throws herself at the gangster, sobbing hysterically and pleading for him to take her along. If anything, this is worse than the singing scene, since her degradation here is voluntary, an act of begging completely bereft of dignity and self-respect, especially considering the way he has just treated her: moanin' low, indeed. Disgusted (once again), Rocco pushes her aside and makes his way to the boat, but not before the moll surreptitiously hands Frank something—Rocco's gun, which she snatched from him in the midst of her clinging, crying routine. So what looks to Rocco (and to us, before Huston shows us the exchange with Frank) like yet another sign of the woman's capacity for abuse turns out to be but a sly simulation of abjection. A gendered noir stereotype—the maltreated woman of dubious repute—is here performed, so that Gaye Dawn triumphs over Rocco not by openly trying to defy him—as does Nora, spitting in his face—but rather by giving him precisely what he expects and sadistically enjoys.[37] Her gesture completely fools Rocco and paves the way for the soldier to vanquish these pretenders to U.S. citizenship. For the gangster, the moll's show of humiliation is literally disarming; once the woman transfers the weapon (phallus) from one man to the other, Frank gains the chance to defeat the enemy alien.[38] Only after Rocco is robbed of his manhood can the nation be properly defended against intruders. Just as Huston updates the American gangster (both the film genre and the historical figure) by imagining the criminal's return from exile, so, too, does he update his female counterpart's comeback. As a man without a country, Rocco dies at sea, but his ex-mistress remains safe and secure at home, where she belongs.

A final twist on this transnational matter of citizenship: I have yet to explain what eventually motivates Frank to fight against Rocco, after the soldier has taken much abuse from the hoodlum early on. The turning point comes after the hurricane passes and the major and the rest of the captives learn that Rocco has told the local head of police that the fugitive Osceola brothers were responsible for the officer's murder, when in fact Rocco himself was to blame. Taking the mobster's word, that he is a guiltless tourist from Milwaukee, the racist sheriff rashly kills the brothers as they try to flee. Huston renders the senseless tragedy offscreen: the audience hears only the sound of shots fired, followed by the sheriff's announcement to the group. But Frank's reaction to these Indian deaths seals the deal: we get a close-up of the signature Bogart jaw clench as he slowly turns to throw Rocco a steely stare. With this gesture, we already know the gangster's goose is cooked, as Frank one by one will finish off the gang on the high seas, with Rocco cowering in the cabin of the fog-shrouded boat, the last to go. It is striking that the veteran shoots the gangster from above, looking down from the roof of the craft, thereby re-establishing the omniscient overhead perspective with which the film began. This time it is indeed, mother mercy, the end of Rocco, left stranded between Cuba and the United States: a satisfying culmination (Hollywood-style) for the narrative's escalating tension between American and un-American, but one whose logic demands that ur-Americans, the indigenous natives barred from Largo Hotel, must be sacrificed to preserve home and nation. What predates the state must vanish for the state to survive the exiled criminal's assault.

In the film he made just before *Key Largo*, the justly acclaimed *Treasure of the Sierra Madre* (1948), Huston briefly included a telling autobiographical flourish. Panhandling in Mexico, the down-and-out gold prospector Fred C. Dobbs (played by Bogart, naturally) runs into a tall man dressed in an elegant white suit. That man is John Huston. Both immediately recognize one another as fellow Americans traveling in a foreign land, and after giving him some money, the elegant stranger tells Dobbs to leave him alone. Long after Dobbs meets his fatal end in the narrative, a victim of his own paranoid greed, this curious encounter between a movie star and his star director lingers. For me it bespeaks a certain self-fashioning on Huston's part as a man of the world, resolutely possessing an American national identity, but conversant and comfortable with other cultures. This self-portrait is fair. Well before he saw combat in Italy, Huston displayed an unusual interest in world politics and history, coauthoring the screenplay for the Warner biopic *Juarez* (1939), for instance, while hanging out at the Santa Monica salon of Salka Viertel, a fertile meeting ground for émigrés and intellectuals. This exposure to refugee sensibility helped at midcentury make Huston, along with Orson Welles, perhaps the most cosmopolitan of U.S.-born directors in Hollywood, American cosmopolitanism being the flip side of a European exile ethos.[39]

But Hollywood studios had their limits, Huston was quick to recognize, and for his next picture following *Key Largo*, the aptly titled *We Were Strangers* (1949), he formed an independent production company and enlisted the aid of Viertel's son Peter as his cowriter. The film continues Huston's intense interest in Cuba, taking us southward from Key Largo to Havana, but also moving us back in time from 1948 to 1933, to a period of political unrest inside the country. The plot centers on a group of revolutionaries determined to overthrow the dictator Gerardo Machado y Morales. In an unlikely twist, the band of subversives (literally underground) is led by an American of Cuban extraction (played by John Garfield) who has returned to his homeland, supported by Cuban exiles in the United States, to help assassinate (by a cemetery bombing) the regime's leaders. Misgivings about killing innocents, a romantic subplot, patriotic quotations from Thomas Jefferson ("resistance to tyrants is obedience to God"), extended scenes of strenuous tunneling, and the ironic death of the American with victory at hand, all add up to a pretty muddled affair that triggered confused responses by reviewers who were unsure whether the film was reactionary (as the *Daily Worker* assumed) or pro-communist (as some in the mainstream press asserted). In any case, the movie proved a flop at the box office, a fact that Huston himself acknowledged in his autobiography, which is mainly intent on recounting his attempts while in Cuba to keep up with the macho exploits of Hemingway.[40]

Yet if Huston happened to read the Havana newspapers in 1948 when he was there filming *We Were Strangers*, he might have learned about a young university student with political aspirations who was just beginning to make a public name for himself. Derided as a mere gangster by his rivals, he was accused on two separate occasions of being involved in assassination attempts, the February killing of a national sports director and, four months later, the fatal shooting of a police officer. Neither of these highly politicized allegations stuck, and later that year he was able to marry and spend three months on his honeymoon visiting Florida and New York City, his first (but not last) time in the United States. It was in New York that he picked up a copy of *Das Kapital*. Perhaps he inscribed his name in the book: Fidel Alejandro Castro Ruz.[41]

FOUR

North from Mexico

Border Incident, Hold Back the Dawn, Secret beyond the Door, and *Out of the Past*

Always the laborer, never the citizen.—Mark Reisler

The previous chapter's discussion of the Florida Keys as offering something of a middle ground between Cuba and the U.S. mainland provided an opportunity to consider how a certain set of dark crime movies after the Second World War helped make visible the geopolitical contours of the nation: who fit in and who did not. While Cuba remained a relatively minor cinematic locale to test the limits of American inclusion and exclusion, another Spanish-speaking country was far richer by virtue of its proximity to Hollywood—Mexico. I think it is fair to say that Mexico in many ways served as American noir's geopolitical unconscious. From roughly 1934, starting with the opening of James M. Cain's novel *The Postman Always Rings Twice,* "south of the border" figured prominently as a symbolic counterspace to the United States.[1] Indulging in a minitaxonomy, by no means meant to be comprehensive, we can distinguish among a variety of functions. First (or rather last), there is Orson Welles's *Touch of Evil* (1958), in a category by itself, the most self-conscious and complex rendering of U.S.-Mexican relations that arguably ended the entire noir cinema cycle, as I will discuss in my postscript.[2] Yet in many earlier noir films, Mexico and its border represents a kind of receding horizon, a safe haven that fugitives never reach, as in *Double Indemnity*, *Where Danger Lives* (1950), and *Gun Crazy* (1950), a terminus that proved fatal, as in *Too Late for Tears* (1949), or else a space for temporary sexual transgression, as in *The Postman*.

In other movies Mexico operates as an exotic or menacing setting for narratives taking place primarily within the country, as in the minimalist *The Hitch-Hiker* (1953) or in the highly convoluted plots of *The Big Steal* (1949) and *His Kind of Woman* (1951), both of which were produced by RKO, starred Robert Mitchum, and verged in mood on the comic. Despite their curious tones (as if Mexico were a funny place), each film bears some interest for my focus on citizenship: *The Big Steal* by virtue of the role of the Mexican state police (played by the silent film star Ramón Navarro) and *His Kind of Woman* by virtue of the figure of the deported gangster wanting to return to the United States, as in *Key Largo*. But neither spends much time exploring just how borders are tested and negotiated, which will be my emphasis in this chapter.[3]

In the first part I take a close look at Anthony Mann's *Border Incident* (1949), an uneasy mixture of noir, police procedural, western, and social problem film that construes its curious hybrid status explicitly in relation to its central narrative and thematic concerns—the illicit smuggling of Mexican migrant workers (braceros) into the United States. This striking movie stands apart from others by virtue of the direction of its traffic in bodies, from south to north, unlike so many other Hollywood noirs that track Americans trying to escape into Mexico. The movie is also unusual for trying to treat Mexicans in their homeland with some seriousness, rather than peripherally as stock characters dispensing occasional folk wisdom to visitors. As I demonstrate, the film offers dual, interrelated crossings, so that its plot, the surreptitious movement of people between nations, parallels its generic mixing or transgressing of boundaries. *Border Incident* is especially important for articulating the condition of stateless-ness or dispossession that forms the crux of my argument, dramatizing the anxieties of a nation-state intent on policing itself against uninvited out-siders at midcentury.

In the second, shorter section I look at a series of films (some not usually categorized as noir) partially set in Mexico that develop marriage or courtship plots involving Americans (and aspiring Americans) who meet as tourists in this alien territory: *Hold Back the Dawn* (1941), *Secret beyond the Door* (1948), and most notably, *Out of the Past* (1947), starring Mitchum yet again. In these cases, "north from Mexico" traces how the couple's interlude outside the confines of the United States affects their sense of national belonging, as well as their relationship on their return.[4]

In underscoring the Mexican-U.S. boundary as noir's conceptual threshold, Mann's film not only anticipates *Touch of Evil*'s more baroque treatment but in some ways offers an even more revealing representation of the dark margins of noir. While Welles presents borders as radically unstable and hallucinatory from the start, Mann suggests how they are built, contested, and undone. From a retrospective, diachronic perspective it is easy to read *Border Incident*'s hybridity in relation to Mann's career, for the film marks an obvious transition from an earlier urban police procedural like *T-Men* (1948) to the director's myriad westerns that were to follow in the 1950s. In terms of plot, *Border Incident* closely reworks *T-Men*, which followed a pair of government treasury agents going undercover to foil a gang of counterfeiters. In *Border Incident* the same screenwriter, John C. Higgins, and his coauthor, George Zuckerman, modified this basic story in two ways, replacing the crime of smuggling bogus bills with the crime of smuggling human cargo, so that *counterfeit* now stands directly for the *illegal* status of these migrants caught between two countries. Second, Higgins divided the undercover action along ostensibly symmetrical national lines, creating a pair of federal agents, one Mexican, Pablo Rodriguez (played by Ricardo Montalban), and one American, Jack Bearnes (played by George Murphy), who have worked together previously along the Texas border. Just as these good guys are paired and split, so, too, are the bad guys, with Mexican *coyotes* doing the dirty work of transport, as well as ambushing and brutally robbing and killing braceros when they try to return home, while Americans, led by the farm boss Owen Parkson (played by Howard Da Silva) and his foremen, receive the workers in the United States and oversee the criminal operation.[5]

The transformation of government T-men into INS agents was seamless and logical enough, as Mann himself subsequently indicated in various interviews.[6] But the reworking of a conventional crime thriller into a narrative about the difficult fate of "Wetbacks," as the film was originally titled, is sufficiently curious to warrant further attention, especially since MGM, the studio that produced *Border Incident*, was better known in the 1940s for glossy musicals than for hard-hitting social dramas. The studio's profile began to change markedly when Dore Schary was hired as the head of production in the summer of 1948.[7] Schary had been at RKO, where he produced *Crossfire* (1947), a movie about a returning veteran victimized by anti-Semitism that was among the first of a cycle of social problem films made by a variety of studios soon after the Second World War.[8] Seeing an opportunity for such serious social realism at MGM, Schary bought the screenplay of *Border Incident* from Eagle-Lion Films and recruited its director Mann and the cinematographer John Alton to complete the film for his new studio. *Border Incident* presumably appealed to the liberal Schary less for its police plot (the depiction of government agents hard at work) than for its representation of a disadvantaged group's oppression. Like two other key social problem pictures released the same year, *Pinky* (1949) and *Lost Boundaries* (1949), Mann's film similarly treats injustice in terms of a kind of passing. But instead of tracing the uncertain racial identity of individuals, *Border Incident* probes a collective nationality left in a state of doubt, as we shall see, once the Mexicans as a group illegally cross into the United States to experience themselves as counterfeit subjects unprotected by any government or law. Although the film is certainly not above racially stereotyping its Mexican villains for comic effect, it is this exploration of citizenship, rather than of the blurred boundaries of race, that makes it so noteworthy.

How Higgins and Zuckerman originally might have come to focus on the plight of these "bootlegged aliens" is worthy pondering.[9] By mutual executive agreement between Mexico and the United States, the Emergency Farm Labor Program (1942–64) was begun soon after the attack on Pearl Harbor to provide much-needed temporary manpower to replace the 1 million rural workers who had quickly moved to factory jobs and into the military. From the start, the guest-worker program was riddled with problems, as these braceros continually had to struggle for the hourly income and living conditions they had been promised. But the arrangement was so lucrative for U.S. agribusiness that even after the war ended the government decided conveniently to extend the ostensible emergency program. Mexico in this regard was at best a reluctant partner, troubled by the systematic mistreatment of the braceros (who sometimes served as strikebreakers and who earned much lower wages than their unionized American counterparts) and by the fact that their permitted seasonal entry into the United States served to encourage and increase the illicit flow of many more undocumented workers across the border.[10] The key here is that the legal braceros were never considered anything but a temporary workforce, sheer bodies of labor (what Michel Foucault called "biopower") with no expectation of achieving status as naturalized U.S. citizens.

A few months before these outside "guests" were permitted into the United States, a second kind of foreign (but internal) presence triggered another sort of emergency mass movement of bodies. On February 19, 1942, FDR signed the Executive Order 9066, which enabled the War Department to detain dangerous or suspicious persons living in militarily sensitive zones. Although it did not specifically call for Japanese Americans to be removed from the Pacific Coast, such quickly was the order's effect, as an entire category of people were identified as "enemy aliens" by ethnicity or race (two-thirds of them Nisei, born in the United States and therefore American citizens) and put into ten so-called relocation centers, or concentration camps. In the eyes of many government officials, this wholesale detention was preferable to other measures, such as the case-by-case tests of allegiance that Hoover recommended. Over 110,000 Americans of Japanese ancestry were sent to other parts of the country and asked to pledge loyalty oaths, with those refusing (about 5,000) ending up jailed in a special "segregation center" in Tule Lake.[11] First-generation Japanese immigrants (Issei) were never allowed to become naturalized U.S. citizens, so that answering in the affirmative when prompted by the infamous question number 28 on the loyalty oath form to renounce their Japanese citizenship effectively turned them into stateless persons.[12]

Because many of these Japanese Americans were farmers, there is an indirect but clear correlation between the two wartime emergencies of 1942, as one group of agricultural workers, provisionally domesticated, helped replace another, now deemed too dangerously un-American to be trusted.[13] That this government-directed movement of braceros (in) and of native sons and daughters (out) took place primarily in Southern California would have hit especially close to home for Hollywood. Even sensible nonhysterics like Walter Lippmann in 1942 viewed West Coast Japanese Americans as a threat to the nation that might lead to "a combined attack from within and without" since, as the mayor of Los Angeles remarked about Japanese Americans, their apparent hard work and agreeable nature made it difficult to "tell who is loyal and who is not."[14] Without a single case of espionage or sabotage tried in court or even documented, the U.S. military was authorized by FDR to keep an "enemy race" detained within the country's own borders. This is precisely the sort of uncanny friend-or-foe paranoia about the nation's safety and integrity that fueled *Confessions of a Nazi Spy* and *Stranger on the Third Floor*.

But in the immediate aftermath of the war, grave misgivings began to be more openly expressed. In 1948 the historian Clinton Rossiter coined the striking phrase *constitutional dictatorship* to describe the extraordinary measures that states historically have taken to accrue power in times of crisis. Emergencies such as war, rebellion, or extreme economic hardship have frequently necessitated dictatorial action that Rossiter in his U.S. examples optimistically assessed as "temporary and self-destructive." Although the burgeoning cold war red menace was perhaps too new a proclaimed security crisis for Rossiter to consider, he did apply his concept to the wartime internment of Japanese Americans. Understanding disloyalty as only a flimsy excuse for racism, Rossiter found the mass evacuation "extremely disturbing" in its long-term implications. Despite acknowledging that contrary to his prior reassurance, by such clearly unconstitutional measures "a considerable degree of permanent change has been worked in the structure and powers of the government of the United States," Rossiter nonetheless concluded his study by perversely asserting, "No sacrifice is too great for our democracy, least of all the temporary sacrifice of democracy itself."[15]

Such rationalizations by even the harshest critics of Executive Order 9066 suggest that most Americans during the 1940s remained largely unmoved by the plight of interned Japanese Americans, and even less by that of incoming Mexican migrants, both legal and illegal. But two events in 1948 did make the news. In February, the Mexican and U.S. governments had signed an agreement suspending the program in Texas because of serious abuses, but nine months later, in late October, U.S. officials, pressured by large-scale farmers fearing the loss of their harvest, "outrageously violated" this agreement (in the words of a *Time* magazine article) by allowing thousands of Mexican workers waiting in Ciudad Juárez to cross the Rio Grande into El Paso. As *Time* reported concerning what would soon become known as the "El Paso Incident," these U.S. immigration agents "thrashed about feebly," first arresting the Mexicans, but then quickly paroling them so that they could go to work.[16] To little avail the Mexican government protested the unilateral U.S. action, which by negating the international agreement for the sake of economic expediency made a mockery of its mutual cooperation with Mexico and compromised the formal distinction between legal and illegal at the heart of the guest-worker program—an undermining of the rule of law that similarly reverberates throughout *Border Incident*.

The second incident of 1948 proves even more intriguing in relation to Mann's film. In May the Los Angeles television station KTLA aired a political documentary made by an affiliate of an American Federation of Labor (AFL) labor union called the Hollywood Film Council and sponsored by the Screen Actors Guild. Titled *Poverty in the Valley of Plenty*, the twenty-minute film described a farmworker strike in Kern County begun the previous fall that included more than a hundred braceros (not directly mentioned in the film), as well as some illegal "wetbacks," who were "smuggled across the Mexican border by headhunters employed by large farm interests," as the documentary's narrator explained while detailing the deplorable sanitary and work conditions in the agriculture industry.[17] The union filmmakers got more than they bargained for, as the DiGiorgio Fruit Corporation sued for defamation, instigating a libel suit against Paramount Television Productions and a year later triggering congressional hearings investigating the Farm Labor Union and the film.[18] Los Angeles newspapers covered both the trial and the hearings, which included the California congressman Richard Nixon, fresh from his HUAC grilling of Alger Hiss.[19] While *Border Incident* clearly grew out of *T-Men* with its overt celebration of governmental authority, this controversial farmworker documentary, as well as the unsettling El Paso Incident, hint at a more subversive, darker undercurrent that runs through Mann's movie as an alternative to its official story line.

Described in the familiar semidocumentary style of police procedurals as a factual composite of real incidents, *Border Incident*'s narrative centers on how two federal agents crack a smuggling ring by going undercover.[20] Pablo pretends he is a Mexican bracero tired of waiting for permits. Along with a group of desperate migrants, including his new friend Juan, he pays to be driven across the Imperial Valley border at night. After watching out for Pablo on the Mexico side, his counterpart Jack then pretends to be a criminal trying to sell forged immigration documents, which Parkson on the U.S. side needs to be able to farm out the braceros as exploited and underpaid labor.

As in *T-Men*, these forged papers take on enormous significance in the absence of any other clearly defined way of distinguishing between legal and illegal, no longer a trait of things (printed money) but rather of people themselves, suggesting deeper ambiguities and confusions about the concept of citizenship itself. Although Jack and Pablo as unimpeachable agents of the state are never personally seduced by the world of crime, their crossing of borders ultimately destabilizes the geopolitical order that they would valiantly uphold. To express this generically, the noir elements of the film gradually overpower its features as a western, a police procedural, or a social problem film, so that the movie's moral binary between good and evil no longer cleanly aligns with its national binary Mexico–United States. Or to put it another way, *Border Incident*'s visual aspects (including Alton's contributions as cinematographer) begin to trump and undercut Higgins's screenplay.

At the film's beginning, imagery and words work neatly together. After a credit sequence that depicts a car speeding along a fence in a murky western landscape (more on this shortly), the film opens, in typical police-procedural fashion, with a third-person narrator deeply intoning, "Here is the All-American Canal," which we view from a sunlit overhead shot that traces the canal's rigidly straight path. This is the same sort of opening John Huston used in *Key Largo*, a surveillance perspective coupled with an equally omniscient voice of authority. As this disembodied *March of Time* narrator continues to explain how this "life-giving artery of water" next to the U.S.-Mexican border "feeds the vast farm empire of the Imperial Valley of Southern California," the overhead camera moves to row after row of rectangular fields and crops that emphasize the perfect order of American agriculture.

Beyond this landscape's "geometric beauty" (as the *New York Times* reviewer Bosley Crowther called it), the film emphasizes how nature here has been engineered and cultivated by deliberate design for great profit: "A half million dollars" a field, as the film's narrator proudly exclaims.[21] Although the canal closely parallels the border, it is important to note that it cannot be the border itself; "all-American," the waterway is wholly contained in U.S. territory and therefore cannot be shared by Mexicans, who fail to reap any of its benefits. In subsequent scenes Alton repeatedly relies on this sort of visual linearity to give the impression of an equal alliance between the United States and "its neighbor to the south," a governmental partnership primarily designed to maintain clear lines of demarcation between them.

Given this national security agenda, it appears a bit paradoxical that the opposition between good and evil ostensibly outweighs the differences between countries, as a Mexican bureaucrat early on suggests: "Since these people [the smugglers] work together to break the law, we will work together to enforce the law." To emphasize this sense of egalitarianism, Alton in successive shots shows U.S. and Mexican federal officials flying in identical sorts of planes to meet one another in Mexicali (or is it Calexico?), positions Pablo and Jack face to face across a rectangular table as two well-dressed counterparts, virtually interchangeable, and in the film's closing shot, displays U.S. and Mexican flags flying side by side as the voice-over narration returns to applaud the "safe and secure" migrants now legally working "under the protection of two great republics." Discounting Pablo's accent, the pair of agents are mirror images of each other, bantering about a pretty girl they both knew, so that gender would seem to transcend national or cultural differences. This formal framing or compositional equivalence represents the film's sanctioned version of Mexican-U.S. parity. Yet the opening overhead shot of the canal suggests otherwise, indicating how the ordered symmetry so central to the logic of police procedurals is itself an entirely American principle (*all-American* signifying the United States alone, not Latin America): a national possession disguised as a universal ideal that earnest, crime-fighting Mexicans can at best only borrow.[22]

Directly on the Mexican side, by contrast, when the introductory voice-over narration stops, we follow at ground level a trio of frightened returning braceros past a pair of border signs (in English and Spanish) and through a flimsy wire fence as they enter a crooked and dark canyon, subsequently called "Valle de Muerte," where they are violently, intimately stabbed in the hearts and thrown into quicksand by coyotes (all but one of the criminals Mexican). First approaching by horseback, figured as a sinister posse of cowboys, these men have been tipped off by an American accomplice, who signals them by a spotlight from a hilltop, an omniscient

13 Blood and soil
in the Valle de
Muerte, from
Border Incident

perspective resembling the opening shot. And so moving from documentary to fictional narrative, the film's second dominant visual trope is established—the murky, treacherous muck of unimproved nature that is a feature of the Mexican borderlands.

Two related points are worth making about this lethal canyon and its elemental ooze. First, if we allow ourselves for a moment to think about film noir as primarily a visual style, then this narrow, threatening landscape becomes a perfect way for the master cinematographer Alton to transpose the urban claustrophobia of noir's more typical dark city streets to the inky shadows of a western setting.[23] Second, this graphic devouring of the braceros by the maw of earth symbolically enacts a kind of birth in reverse, as the sinking, bloodied Mexicans quite literally return to the motherland from whence they came, and where they properly belong (see figure 13). Beyond signaling moral treachery, the deadly quicksand thus more pointedly visualizes and literalizes a long-standing set of customs that traditionally have bestowed nationality on people by virtue of intimate physical contact, "blood and soil." As Giorgio Agamben has argued, what began in Roman law as dual legal criteria for national belonging (jus soli, birth in a certain territory, and jus sanguinis, birth from citizen parents) became by the twentieth century a grander conflated metaphysics culminating in the biopolitical eugenics of Hitler's National Socialist regime.[24] The noirishness of this early blood-and-soil quagmire scene thus establishes an allegorical mode or pattern in the film, with clear implications for the question of citizenship both north and south of the border.[25]

As in the case of the perfectly ordered All-American Canal, this muck is strictly one country's property—Mexico's. Instead of a single boundary shared by two nations, then, we in fact have two distinct border zones, one on each side, each marked exclusively by its own distinct cultural features (culture here translated into amorphous wild nature for the Mexicans). While at first glance we might mistake the canyon's quagmire for the dangerous experiential middle ground of border crossing itself, the film deliberately locates the Valle de Muerte on Mexican territory.[26] This explains why at the film's end, it is only the braceros who can heroically save their fellow countryman Pablo from sinking into the quicksand, not the U.S. immigration officers who arrive on the scene too late. If these officers represent some version of a western's heroic cavalry rescue, as Dana Polan has suggested in his commentary accompanying the DVD, it is striking how ineffectual they are.

Throughout the film, in fact, these forces of law and order remain remarkably inept, even when it comes to patrolling their own side of the border. To cite just one example, the feds are thwarted in their attempt to follow one of Parkson's henchmen who has picked up the package of bogus immigration permits when he steers his motorcycle onto a set of railroad tracks that their police car cannot navigate. Here the linearity that the film has worked so hard to embrace as positive turns out to be the very thing to stymie the agents, who as a group cannot keep up with the more versatile maneuvering of the solitary villain. The instrumentality of the motorcycle may suggest a kind of selfish individualism that in the end causes the cowardly smugglers to betray and turn against one another, unlike the pair of agents who remain steadfast in their resolve. But in this scene at least, one that leads directly to Jack's sacrificial death, such individualism triumphs. More to the point, perhaps, is that in showing the motorcycle first racing on the tracks and then along the furrows of a plowed field (a disturbing image of the machine in the garden),[27] the film develops a third visual pattern that complicates its compositional opposition between the straight canal and the formless muck: over and over, from the beginning credit sequence onward, we see vehicles and persons moving rapidly parallel to fences, walls, and other sorts of lines, which function to contain and rebuff these speeding figures as they attempt to gain access to the other side. In this regard, linearity becomes imprisoning rather than liberating—a barrier that cannot be crossed.

These three visual tropes correspond closely to three different ways in which the film invites us to think about national belonging: as defined by capitalist order (the U.S. agricultural empire symbolized by its "all-American" canal), biological imperatives (organic blood and soil), and administrative structures (fences and crossing permits). United by an overarching concept of the law, these three versions of citizenship would seem to be fixed and mutually reinforcing, but a fourth marker—nationality as a function of culture—at first glance suggests a more fluid set of possibilities. The clearest way to gauge the cultural dimensions of citizenship in the film is to look at the role of clothing. Exchanging his business suit for native garb when he goes undercover, Pablo initially identifies his compatriot Juan as from a neighboring village by the specific kind of sombrero and serape he wears. Lest we think clothing functions as an index of nationality only for colorful ethnic Mexicans, Mann dwells even more on Jack's dress, specifically a fancy, flowered cowboy shirt (a standard icon of westerns) that Juan praises as "beautiful" to Pablo, who agrees that it "gives a man distinction."

This shirt, in fact, soon plays a key part in the movie's plot. Searching for the bogus crossing permits, a trio of Mexican coyotes catches Jack in bed, stripped from the waist up, his white torso exposed, and subsequently torture him, half naked, in signature sadistic Mann style. A coveted object of desire, the shirt is stolen by the villain Cuchillo, played with gusto by Alfonso Bedoya, he of "we don't need no stinkin' badges" fame (*The Treasure of the Sierra Madre*, 1948). When Pablo and Juan later recognize the shirt that Cuchillo is wearing, they know Jack is in trouble. Typecast as a grinning, buffoonish *bandito*, Cuchillo throughout the film is enamored of all things American, fooling with Parkson's cigar lighter (shaped like a little gun) and mistaking a Dictaphone in his office for a television set. The implication here is that although these Mexicans can pretend to be Americans by trying to appropriate national badges (cowboy shirts and technological gadgets), their racial proclivities will ultimately betray them as fakers. Culture may circulate across borders, but national assimilation is still not so easy, at least for the criminals.[28]

In this respect Parkson's own curious get-up is worth mentioning. Unlike the braceros, their cowboy-hatted handlers, or suited federal agents,

Parkson wears a dapper riding outfit or jodhpurs, with breeches and boots that manage to make him look military and effeminate at once, befitting his role as the brains behind the operation who refuses to get his hands dirty. His strange clothing may not be so clearly marked nationally, but viewers seeing the film so soon after the Second World War likely would have been reminded of Nazi officers. This dim Teutonic presence in the movie is reinforced by the fact that Parkson's counterpart on the Mexican side, the man in charge of recruiting and supplying the illegal migrants, is a crafty German named Hugo Wolfgang Ulrich (played by the character actor Sig Ruman), as if to suggest that the Mexican villains did not possess the organizational skills to run the smuggling ring themselves. Neither Mexican nor American, the shadowy figure of the foreign German working on the margins serves as a go-between for the two nations.

Acting as the stationary geographical points of departure and arrival for the braceros, the broker Ulrich in Baja and the boss Parkson in California would seem to help stabilize the border, but once the human traffic between them begins, national belonging becomes an increasingly questionable proposition. The film renders the nighttime migration across the desert as a kind of dark middle passage, with dozens of illegal workers lying jammed like sacks of potatoes in the back of a covered truck that faintly resembles a slave ship, or else a packed train on its way to a concentration camp. When an old man pressed between Pablo and Juan dies in the midst of the journey, his body is unceremoniously dumped on the ground by a coyote, who remarks that he was not paid to "freight corpses." Alton gives the scene an awkward, eerie composition by shooting the body with the head in the foreground and the feet receding in perspective. Unlike the bracercos who are killed in the Valle de Muerte while trying to return home, the old man has died on U.S. territory and therefore is not even accorded the kind of "blood and soil" burial/reverse birth that the quicksand affords the other Mexicans. In the absence of any interment, alienated from the land around them, the remaining men in the truck have recourse to religion, reciting a prayer for the dead in Spanish, the only time that this language is used in the entire movie. Here membership in a transcendental community must substitute for a more secular sort of citizenship; paradoxically affirming the men's Mexicanness by way of Catholicism, the Spanish prayers recall an earlier scene in a church, where Juan tells his wife that he has decided to leave her and their children to find work in the United States despite the obvious danger. One of only four women to appear ever so briefly in the movie, Juan's teary-eyed wife, Maria, allows Mann to conflate God, family, and country under the single sentimental sign of the domestic. But once the braceros abandon their motherland, they must venture into more murky and ambiguous territory.[29]

This dark space of liminality is conveyed most dramatically by the subversive potential of Alton's noir cinematography, especially in contrast, at key moments, to Higgins's ideologically correct script. Take, for instance, the scene in which, after hijacking a truck to attempt to save Jack, Pablo discloses to Juan that he is not a bracero but rather a *federale* working with his American counterpart. In terms of the plot, this revelation is extremely important, signaling how the Mexican undercover agent can finally trust the migrants to help themselves overcome their exploitation. Emphasizing the police-procedural aspects of the film, Polan has argued that there is a subtext of populist politics in *Border Incident*, which imagines the government educating and encouraging the populace to stand up for itself against criminal oppression. Yet as Pablo sincerely explains to Juan that Jack is a "police agent" who is a "friend to all braceros," we are compelled to witness a grotesquely humorous scene of violence played out against the driver's window, as one of Parkson's flunkies tries frantically to reenter his speeding truck (see figure 14). More than a mere comic distraction and completely at odds with the script, this image of wild flailing radically undermines Pablo's heartfelt message of U.S.-Mexican solidarity.[30]

The difficulty with Polan's populist reading, as I see it, is that given the film's structural divisions between Mexico and the United States, there is no single legitimate government to save or people to be saved. As an undercover federal agent working with the FBI and the INS, Pablo enjoys a unique degree of security and immunity, able to cross borders at will because of his special transnational governmental status. He is no ordinary bracero, as Juan intuits. But what about his far more vulnerable countrymen? Precisely because they are illegal and temporary, these workers have no security while in the United States, as Pablo himself admits while trying to teach them about their exploitation: "We're here against the law, so the law can't help us." This is an absolutely crucial remark. The symmetrical reasoning that was invoked earlier to bind the two nations together while their common border is policed ("Since the criminals work

14 A "friend to all braceros," from *Border Incident*

in a circle, we will work in a circle") here functions in similar circular fashion to undo the very authority of government itself.

Ironically, Parkson's vicious foreman, Jeff Amboy (played by the perennial tough guy Charles McGraw), is seized with a similar insight. When Juan complains to him about paltry wages (twenty-five cents an hour) far below those originally promised (seventy-five cents), Amboy angrily shouts back, "You come in here like a crook, break our laws, and expect to be treated like one of us?" The criminal Amboy's invocation of "our laws" is at once laughably absurd (since he is responsible for smuggling the braceros in) and uncannily appropriate. Without recourse to due process or equal protection afforded native-born Americans, Juan and the other smuggled braceros are easily cheated. Although the guest-worker program was originally established by mutual treaty with some built-in safeguards, both Pablo and Amboy follow the visual logic of the film by underscoring not only how the law is in effect strictly (U.S.) American but also that the state can take it or leave it as it sees fit. The result is that these migrants occupy a twilight zone while in the United States, remaining Mexicans by nationality but suffering from a radical geopolitical dislocation and estrangement that parallels the psychic and moral disorientation suffered by noir characters more generally, who typically cross between the domains of the legal/illicit and the rational/irrational. In grimly exposing these figures as displaced counterfeits, *Border Incident* thus nightmarishly dramatizes the instability of U.S. citizenship that noir so frequently probes.

In her wide-ranging recent study of immigration policy in the United States during the mid-twentieth century, Mae M. Ngai calls the illegal alien an "impossible subject"—"a person who cannot be and a problem that cannot be solved."[31] Barred from citizenship and denied fundamental constitutional rights (such as protection under the Fourteenth Amendment), these aliens embody at once "a social reality and a legal impossibility," a condition best epitomized in the film by the dead old man who is dumped on U.S. soil but remains unburied, an unpleasant, exposed leftover that cannot be integrated into the landscape. Emerging from the state's administrative efforts to delimit itself, illegal alienage is neither natural nor stable, Ngai demonstrates, but (like nations and genres) is a made category subject to all sorts of historical contingencies and expediencies. In the case of Mexican migration, that expediency throughout the twentieth century was fundamentally economic: when U.S. business needed cheap labor, these workers were recruited without much concern about their official standing, and even in a binational legal framework like the wartime Emergency Farm Labor Program, braceros came and went according to unilateral action pursued by the United States, as the El Paso Incident made all too clear.[32]

From a social-psychological perspective, being an illegal alien means experiencing oneself in some ways as a nonperson. While there might be certain strategic advantages to operating in a "space of nonexistence," as Susan Bibler Coutin deploys the term to describe the life of undocumented immigrants, this condition clearly constitutes a space of subjugation, with these "shadow" people fearfully dwelling in an "underground" or "netherworld." Subject to immediate loss via sudden deportation (the same fear that drives *Stranger on the Third Floor*, as I discuss in my first chapter), the ties of home, job, and community carry no weight to help anchor selfhood, as Coutin explains: "Unregistered, undocumented, unrecorded, those who lack legal status are nowhere. They do not exist."[33] While this might seem a tad overstated, the psychological effects of statelessness are worth taking seriously, given how many postwar movies trace this psychic disorientation by way of some combination of amnesia, hysteria, and paranoia.[34] In *Border Incident*, Mann gives us only a glimpse of this noirish netherworld occupied by the migrants laboring on Parkson's farm, preferring instead to focus on the stalwart police efforts to rescue them and stabilize each respective nation-state. Yet rescued to what end?

As a kind of afterthought to the plot, we note that the traumatized surviving braceros at the close are indeed repatriated, stuck on the Mexican side (in the Valley of Death), presumably with little hope of going back to the United States for work. But despite its official restoration of order, the film at least manages to divulge, mainly via its unsettling visual rhetoric, how citizenship remains an elusive and dubious prospect once borders are transacted and transgressed.

The movie struggles most mightily against its own darker implications by ultimately insisting on the crossing permits as the defining difference between legal and illegal. But these permits register an utterly empty formalism, what Agamben, drawing on Franz Kafka, deems as sovereignty or Law that carries force without substance, or more accurately, carries force precisely *because* it has no significance.[35] Not only are these documents easily forged (blurring the distinction between illegal and legal) but the very grounds by which they are issued also remains a complete mystery. Early on Alton gives us another long overhead shot of hundreds of braceros on the Mexican side waiting to be given crossing papers, but when Juan excitedly hears his name called, only to discover that it is another "Juan Garcia" who has been deemed legal (a typical noir confusion of identity), we are struck by the seemingly arbitrary nature of the selection process by which only a few of the desperate masses are officially "certified" to cross.

From the Great Depression, when four hundred thousand persons of Mexican descent (many of them already U.S. citizens) were sent back to Mexico, through the Emergency Farm Labor Program, to Operation Wetback in 1954, when immigration officials, fearing a "flood tide" or "invasion" of "hordes of aliens" into the Southwest, in a military sweep suddenly rounded up and deported hundreds of thousands of migrants to clear the way for others with short-term contracts, the U.S. government repeatedly exercised its absolute sovereignty over braceros in seemingly capricious fashion, and in exception to its own principles of rule by law.[36] A high-ranking Mexican official in the film blames criminal border crossing on the fact that his compatriots are "not well-educated" and that as a result certain Americans have unscrupulously taken advantage of them. But those powerful scenes of "too many" fenced-in braceros waiting for "coveted" papers suggests not education but economic reasons as the cause—pressures of supply and demand that return us to the film's opening monologue celebrating the U.S. agricultural empire. In a curious touch of honesty, the narrator admits that this empire is "almost entirely dependent on Mexican labor," a surprising if offhand confession that gives the lie to all the legal formalism overtly working throughout to stabilize the narrative. The United States may own the law, but in financial terms America cannot survive without Mexico.

We see this formalism most graphically undermined in the film's infamous murder of Jack (see figures 15–17). The scene is shocking for several reasons. Not only does Jack's unexpected death shatter the symmetry of the pairing of police agents, but the fact that the white American dies, not the Mexican, clearly complicates *Border Incident*'s national and racial hierarchies. Even more appalling is the way he dies: maimed, bloody, mute, without agency, utterly helpless, like an infant crawling in the mud. The only thing we hear throughout the entire sequence are the mechanized sounds of the tractor driven by Amboy, one of four such scenes (including the motorcycle pursuit and Jack's previous torture) during which human voices are silenced by the noise of machinery. In her excellent analysis of this scene, whose brutality she calls "almost unmatched in American film," Jeanine Basinger notices that the dirt on Jack's frightened face "looks like baby pabulum."[37] But she does not comment on the larger pattern of symbolic nativity and death running throughout the film, how in this scene it is the American hero who is fatally sacrificed in yet another reenactment of blood-and-soil nationalism, reunited with the land (by the custom of jus soli) as if to confirm his U.S. citizenship. Born "all-American," Jack dies one as well.

What makes Jack's ritualized murder so harrowing is Mann's complete destruction of the visual binary that has organized the film up to this point. Looking like something out of a B science fiction movie, the tractor with its otherworldly pair of headlights is pulling a rotating disc, which churns up and cuts across the neatly planted furrows. As Jack is literally ground into the earth, we are reminded of the muck in the Valley of Death that swallows up returning Mexicans at the beginning and end of the film. But the muck here is on the U.S. side of the border, right in the midst of America's vast agricultural empire. Like Pablo and Juan who stare in frozen dread, we are compelled to witness a monstrous machine convert or deconstruct order into elemental chaos, thus reversing or undoing the very logic of the movie western, which so frequently commemorates the

15–17 Death by U.S. agribusiness, from *Border Incident*

advent of civilization. Alternating between shots of the slow-moving tractor and close-ups of Jack's silent horror, the scene closes with Jack's final
glimpse of the underside of the tractor, a purely noir moment of recognition that reveals the terrifying underbelly of the U.S. farm industry itself,
in all its dependence on and ruthless exploitation of Mexican labor.

My gloss on the tractor scene as a pure noir moment exposing the
monstrous underside of the U.S. agricultural empire returns us to the
question of genre with which I opened this study. Throughout I have
tended to invoke the word *noir* both as a noun and as an adjective in ways
that inevitably suggest that the term has some substantive, intrinsic meaning, just as I have similarly referred to "America" and "Mexico" as fixed
entities. But as James Naremore, Steve Neale, and other scholars have
reminded us, *film noir* as coined by the French soon after the Second
World War had absolutely no institutional bearing on American studio
production and marketing during the 1940s (unlike westerns or musicals),
and it only took on critical significance in the United States as a generic
category well after these movies were first released.[38] In this respect it
makes more sense to think of film noir less as a bounded genre than as a
"meta-genre"—a threshold concept, or better yet, a concept or mode that
tests the very permeability and limits of borders.[39] Donald Pease makes
this claim most succinctly: "'Noir' names what cannot be integrated
within a film's narrative."[40] In the case of *Border Incident* (especially in
regard to Alton's cinematography), what cannot be named in terms of
generic narrative, to summarize and oversimplify a bit, is the elemental
muck and chaos that underlies civilization (contra the western), the lack
of any moral compensation for injustice (contra the social problem film),
and most profoundly, the exercise of law based on nothing but the sovereign nation's capacity to invoke at will a state of exception or emergency
(contra the police procedural). These truths do not themselves constitute
the content of *Border Incident*, and they cannot be contained by the
generic label "film noir." But in so powerfully probing boundaries, they do
compel us to consider how cinematic categories are made and remade,
and nations as well.

Mitchell Leisen's *Hold Back the Dawn* (1941) is clearly less noir than
melodrama, a love story with a happy ending that Billy Wilder coscripted
with Charles Brackett a year before he started directing for Paramount. As

we might expect from a Wilder screenplay, the film has enough dark elements of deceit and betrayal, coupled with a kind of urgent despair on the part of the Romanian protagonist and first-person narrator, Georges Iscovescu (played by Charles Boyer), to merit some discussion in my study, especially since the main action takes place in the Mexican border town of Tijuana. The plot (narrated retrospectively) involves the attempts of Iscovescu, a debonair con man, cad and gigolo, to marry his way into the United States after fleeing war-torn Europe. The most compelling scenes center on a depressing Mexican flea-bag hotel, ironically named Esperanza, where Iscovescu and a group of his fellow refugees are holed up, some for many years, as they await word from the Department of Immigration about whether they can enter the United States via its country-by-country quota system established in 1924. Under this law the number of immigrants was limited to 3 percent annually of the number of each nationality already living in the United States. The government is represented in the film by a vigilant but sympathetic inspector (played by Walter Abel) who crosses back and forth between countries to keep track of the fates of various refugees. One boarder is so desperate that she trudges past the town's guarded customs post (more imposing than the barbed wire fence in *Border Incident*) while experiencing severe labor pangs so that her child can be born on U.S. soil.

In another grim irony about this packed Tijuana hotel that has Wilder written all over it, Iscovescu secures a room only because a despondent Jewish German has just hanged himself after repeatedly being denied entrance. This, we may presume, was Wilder's wry comment on his own experience in Mexicali in 1934, where he was forced to renew his short-term visa, waiting along with thousands of other would-be Americans for the United States to fill up quota slots that had been promised but remained woefully vacant. For these foreigners intent on gaining U.S. citizenship, Mexico throughout the 1930s was a key holding or twilight zone, "the end of the earth," Iscovescu calls it. But the most telling scene in the screenplay was too strange and disturbing (too noir?) to make the final cut. As Iscovescu restlessly paces in his room, he addresses a cockroach he spots crawling down the wall: "Where do you think you are going?! You're not a citizen, are you? Where's *your* quota number?!" After which the stateless refugee squashes his insect counterpart.[41]

Unlike Wilder, who quickly smooth-talked his way back into the United

States in 1934, Iscovescu hinges his quest for citizenship on marriage. Inspired by his equally jaded former dancing partner, Anita (Paulette Goddard), who has wed and already divorced a gullible American, Iscovescu sets his sights on the naïve and lonely schoolteacher Emily Brown (Olivia de Havilland), who has brought her Southern California class across the border for Fourth of July festivities, curiously enough. Why would Tijuana be celebrating July 4? Perhaps the transnational observance of Independence Day suggests Mexico's investment in the idea of U.S. democracy, or perhaps a bit more prosaically, this celebration would offer one easy way for U.S. tourists (especially from California) to see themselves from the outside, as it were: nothing like a bullfight to give you some perspective on your own country. In any case, wanting Iscovescu for herself, the vampish Anita at one point warns Emily about Iscovescu's sordid past and his less-than-honorable intentions, in lines that anticipate Phyllis Dietrichson's closing remarks to Walter Neff in *Double Indemnity* regarding their mutual rottenness: "I know what you're thinking—'This woman's a tramp and she's in love with him.' Well, I *am* a tramp, and I *am* in love with him. I'm his sort. I'm dirt, but so is he. We belong together." But predictably, Emily's unconditional devotion begins to gain a greater hold over the opportunistic Iscovescu, who grows less sleazy and more genuinely affectionate for Emily as he gets to know her. To truly love Emily is to earn the right to become a U.S. citizen, it would seem.

Where and how does Mexico figure in this classic confrontation between American innocence and a European cynicism that is deepened, the movie leaves us to infer, by the (unspoken) horrors of Nazism? While it may seem to serve simply as a kind of romantic setting for Iscovescu's and Emily's budding relationship, it actually takes on more crucial significance as a staging ground that enables both Emily and Iscovescu to rehearse and authenticate their Americanness. In both cases Mexico is a space of defamiliarization: celebrating Independence Day with her students outside the country, Emily suspends her usual reticence to free herself to experience passion, while for Iscovescu, Mexico helps alleviate his bitterness and self-contempt. Soon after their quickie marriage, to escape detection by the inspector, Iscovescu takes his wife on a honeymoon outside Tijuana (overflowing with tourists and refugees) to a small village where they are entranced by a more genuine atmosphere of "primitive magic," as Iscovescu recounts this crucial episode. As a kind of parallel to the Fourth of July festivities that signaled Emily's arrival in Mexico, the couple now join in the celebration of a local patron saint overseeing brides and bridegrooms. Blessed in a church alongside Mexican newlyweds, the two begin to talk intimately to one another. Emily the schoolmarm teaches Iscovescu about the greatness of the United States in its capacity to welcome new, pure streams of immigrants (a civics lesson, in effect), while her cosmopolitan husband, who speaks Spanish, among other languages, translates the villagers' traditions and legends into English for Emily. By this process of mutual conversion or translation, the couple bonds in a setting that is neither America nor Europe but somehow manages to suggest the best of both.

Only after uniting with Emily in this transformative space of mediation is Iscovescu entitled to gain U.S. citizenship, but here the movie takes a strange, self-reflexive turn that hints at Wilder's impatience with Hollywood-style romance. Stung by Anita's revelations, Emily returns to Los Angeles, but (naturally) has a car accident and ends up in hospital, allowing Iscovescu to prove (naturally) his true feelings by dramatically breaking through the border to be by her bedside and restore her will to live. (Even though they are legally married, he still has not received his official visa.) This is the one and only time we see Iscovescu actually in the United States apart from the opening frame of his narration. While the hospital might seem a logical (if corny) place to conclude, *Hold Back the Dawn* introduces yet another way to define Americanness. Seeing that Emily will survive, Iscovescu next races to Paramount, where he pitches his story to a studio director, played by the film's actual director Leisen, before he is apprehended by the immigrations inspector and sent back to Mexico. Although he is finally allowed officially to enter the United States, we are left to wonder what in the end has earned him this status as citizen: his love for Emily or his audacious spirit of enterprise.

Once Iscovescu steps across the border legally to be met by his new (and newly recovered) wife, the couple's difficulties are over. But in *Secret beyond the Door* (1948), directed by Fritz Lang, when another pair of Americans, Celia and Mark Lamphere (played by Joan Bennett and Michael Redgrave), leave Mexico after a sudden marriage to return to their homeland, their problems are just beginning. The movie opens with Celia's moody voice-over narration musing on the meaning of dreams amid a portentous image of flowing water. Accompanied by a lush Miklós

Rózsa score, this shot of floating objects is followed by the scene of her wedding in a four-hundred-year-old Mexican church, much like the one in *Hold Back the Dawn* that enabled Iscovescu and Emily to consecrate their relationship. After a brief flashback explaining how the prosperous New Yorker came to Mexico for a "last fling" after the death of her beloved brother and her betrothal to his friend, Celia's narration returns to Mexico, where she is "strangely drawn" to the enigmatic architect Mark. But he is no fortune-hunting foreigner. If anything, his problem is not that he is un-American, but rather that he is too American, his family having lived on a small New England estate since 1698, he tells Emily, a date suspiciously close to the Salem Witch Trials of 1692. And so even before we see his ancestral home, filled with Puritan portraits and grotesque South Sea masks collected by his sea captain forebears, we understand that we are squarely in the realm of nineteenth-century American Gothic, the symbolic terrain of Nathaniel Hawthorne and Herman Melville. That this terrain predates the founding of the United States as a nation-state is underscored by the casting of Redgrave, who is only marginally successful in the movie at suppressing his British accent.

Formally the film marks itself as a gothic romance by way of a woman's voice-over narration, a convention borrowed from the opening of Hitchcock's *Rebecca* (1940), but one that Lang uses in far more sustained and complex ways. Along the lines of *Double Indemnity* and *Detour* (1945), for example, we note curious shifts in tense, so that we are often uncertain about whether we are listening to present feelings about the present, present (retrospective) feelings about the past, or memories about the past.[42] At first hearing, Celia's monologue would therefore seem to evoke the unstable subjectivity of noir. Yet there is a crucial difference, not only in terms of gender (Mann's powerful noir *Raw Deal* [also 1948] being the main instance of a female first-person narrator) but also, more important, because of the focus of her inner speech.[43] If noir is launched in *Stranger on the Third Floor* with the refrain "What's the matter with me?," then the refrain in *Secret beyond the Door* effectively becomes "What's the matter with *him*?" In other words, the woman is not herself erratic but bewildered and disoriented by the behavior of her husband, who remains a mystery, a stranger to her, just as he is a stranger to himself. So we have a typical, traumatized male noir protagonist framed by the gothic monologue of his wife, although Lang complicates this generic distinction as the film progresses by having Celia grow more and more obsessive in her anxiety, repeating her fears to herself over and over again, and by having Mark later at a key point assume the voice-over narration himself.

Secret beyond the Door is one of Lang's most beautiful and evocative films, but certainly not one of his most coherent. Given the fairy-tale plot's confusions and obscurities, it proves helpful to divide it into three stages: the initial meeting of Mark and Celia in Mexico; her subsequent role as mistress of the household overseeing his sinister family mansion, complete with a familiar array of gothic props and types (shadowy hallways, a locked room à la Bluebeard, a surly son from a former wife, a disfigured assistant, and a relatively normal sister); and finally, what I would call Mark's story, the disclosure of his darkest secret, which Celia brings to light by playing the part of a loving amateur therapist. This segment includes a nightmare sequence of self-interrogation akin to Michael's in *Stranger*, including a judge and jury veiled in blackness, as well as the accused criminal's paranoid line of defense provoked by the antisedition logic of the Smith Act (1940): "You can't try a man for his thoughts." That Mark's secret turns out to be spectacularly anticlimactic, arguably trivial (he was locked in a room at age ten by his mother), suggests that Lang might be even less interested than Hitchcock in trying to explain murderous impulses by way of Freud.

It is beyond the scope of this chapter to attempt to fully unravel the narrative's red herrings, its seemingly contradictory fits and starts, which manage to create a rather powerful and eerie atmosphere of foreboding menace despite all the loose ends. Here I point to two thorough interpretations of the movie by a pair of very intelligent film critics, Tom Gunning and Elisabeth Bronfen.[44] Yet for all the excellence of their readings, it is striking to me that neither spends much time considering why nearly one third of the film takes place outside the United States, including its final scene. This is especially surprising given Bronfen's compelling thesis, which argues that *Secret beyond the Door* is about uncanny homecoming. For both Bronfen and Gunning, Mexico functions in the movie mainly as a kind of exotic backdrop to stage sexual desire. Both, for example, call attention to a dramatic knife fight, announced by a scream, between two Mexican men (one bare-chested) vying for a woman in a village square, where Celia first spies Mark staring at her in the crowd just after the knife lands inches from her. As she recounts the scene and as

Lang films the pair's exchange of looks, the fight sparks the "current flowing between us" (as she says) that will quickly lead to her "marrying a stranger," as she confesses in present tense voice-over during the Catholic wedding ceremony. But the violent knife fight is more than a hypnotic fantasy or wish fulfillment or a set-up for the moment near the end when Celia herself screams, thinking Mark has emerged from dark, fog-shrouded woods to strangle her.

Mexico clearly generates a kind of elemental trance state in the movie allowing Mark and Celia by proxy (the knife fight) to break free from repression and to vicariously realize their innermost passions. But to operate as such "a felicitous space" (to borrow Mark's favorite architec-tural theory) that induces identification and projection, the foreign land must first strip away all sense of prior belonging, including national be-longing. This is particularly true for Celia, whom Mark first describes simply as a "wealthy American girl," an insulated identity that must be left behind and blotted out so that "you aren't a bit like you" any longer, he tells her during their intense initial encounter. The assumption is that if Celia had met Mark in the United States, she would not have been so taken by him, certainly not to the point of marrying a complete stranger. Mark for his part emerges from the crowd of native onlookers, not the group of tourists, so that from the start he remains an outsider unmarked clearly as either a foreign visitor or a local. And we never learn what exactly he is doing there in the first place. Unlike in *Hold Back the Dawn*, Lang's Mexico is not simply a slightly defamiliarized ground of mediation foster-ing marriage but rather a source for more profound negation and erasure. It is not a gothic space—after all, there is no haunted house filled with memories or strange family members—but rather the precondition for such uncanniness to grow once the couple returns to the United States.

Hence Celia's persistent references to Mexico after she settles in New England, as if in her search for home ("Where is home?," she pointedly asks on the verge of leaving her husband), she is still carrying around the emotional residue of her un-American experience south of the border. On first passionately greeting Mark in her new residence, for example, she asks him "to collect on that rain check you gave me in Mexico," a sign that their relationship had presumably remained unconsummated there—a sexual threshold yet to be crossed—because of his precipitous departure at the beginning of their honeymoon. Near the very end of the movie, her feelings of rejection come up yet again in relation to Mexico, as she is seized by a sudden insight while attempting to get to the bottom of her husband's trauma: "I locked the door in Mexico—that's when it began!" Traces of Mexico are felt by Mark as well, most dramatically in this same scene, where he falls into his Bluebeard executioner routine by embracing the figure of Don Ignacio. Of all the killers to impersonate among his various felicitous chambers (a world tour of the history of murder, as it were), the architect picks the Latin strangler (technically from Paraguay, but close enough), suggesting how this alien territory remains within. Only after his alienation is exposed and traced to its natural source (the mother) can Mark and Celia return to Mexico, where their relationship initially took root and where the couple can finally enjoy their aborted honeymoon.

The Mexican marriage plots of *Secret beyond the Door* and *Hold Back the Dawn* might require some stretch of the imagination to be considered noirs, but no such straining is needed for Jacques Tourneur's *Out of the Past* (1947). In his suggestive allegorical reading of the film as portraying a law-abiding ex-communist hounded by HUAC about his past criminal associations, Richard Maltby quips, "whatever *film noir* is, *Out of The Past* is undoubtedly *film noir*."[45] The movie's combination of fatalism, failure, femme fatale, and formal features makes this an easy call. And so it might be surprising, if not downright perverse, for me to go against such commonsense consensus by claiming that *Out of the Past* is actually not so typical of noir. Or to be more accurate (and paradoxical), I argue that the film is at once generically definitive and exceptional, and that it is the narrative's interlude set in Mexico that crucially settles this point.

Near the end of the movie, as Jeff Bailey (Robert Mitchum) and Kathie Moffat (Jane Greer) are about to drive headlong to their doom, Jeff (muttering "por nada") proposes a final toast: "We owe it all to Jose Rodriguez." Is he kidding? Rodriguez (Tony Roux) seems to be only a minor figure in the narrative, a Mexican who briefly offers his services as a guide and tries to sell souvenirs to Kathie and Jeff when they first meet at Café La Mar Azul in Acapulco. This meeting has justly been acclaimed for its striking visual composition, but less noted for its telling dialogue.[46] Having been effectively introduced to one another by the Mexican guide, Jeff and Kathie continue on the theme of tourism once Rodriguez leaves their table, Jeff complaining that in ten days he "hasn't talked to anyone who hasn't tried to sell me something" and Kathie suggesting that they next rendezvous in another cantina that plays "American music."

The film's entire Mexican episode (which runs a full seventeen minutes) is in fact fixated on this question of national belonging, defined by the two Americans' sense of themselves as temporary visitors in a foreign land who mutually seek tangible traces of their homeland: listening to a certain kind of music, drinking bourbon in a cantina reminiscent of a Fifty-sixth Street bar in New York City, meeting near a local movie house called the Cine Pico that indirectly conjures up Hollywood imports.[47] Mexico (and Rodriguez) is what binds them together as Americans. Intense sexual attraction and a dreamy, romantic seaside setting are insufficient in themselves to sustain the couple, it would seem. Evoked fondly, these shared recollections of civic association stand apart from the rest of the narrative, which treats the dreaded past as something to escape. Even as Kathie and Jeff find some respite in Mexico from their previous entanglement with the gangster Whit (Kirk Douglas), they nonetheless miss their own country. That is presumably why, when forced to flee once again, they return to San Francisco, rather than go further south to Chile or Guatemala. So what at first glance looks like "fate" customarily ascribed to noir (Jeff's chance encounters with former associates, for example) turns out on closer inspection to derive from a choice freely made by the couple.

This sort of (be)longing—homesickness we could call it—is unprecedented in the movie and very unusual throughout noir: perhaps the only instance in this study would be the poor migrant braceros in *Border Incident*, but even here these emotions are not prominently featured. What makes such yearning especially striking in *Out of the Past* is Jeff's capacity otherwise to feel at home wherever he is. From the opening credits showing a signpost pointing to various destinations, this is a film highly conscious of geography, positioning both viewers and characters in rather specific locations: Bridgeport, New York City, Harlem, Mexico City, Acapulco, San Francisco, Lake Tahoe. Beyond the rarity of majestic outdoor mountain and water scenes in noir—this is the only crime film I know in which a bad guy is killed by a fishing rod—there is something even more exceptional than the settings themselves: the sense Mitchum conveys as Jeff that he is perfectly at ease in all of them (except Mexico, that is).[48] It is not just that Jeff has been in many places, as his devoted girlfriend and fishing partner Ann (Virginia Huston) remarks, but that he is confidently familiar with them all, from a gangster's opulent mansion in Lake Tahoe to an all-black nightclub in Harlem, where Jeff interacts freely with the patrons. He is also perfectly at ease with the mute Kid (Dickie Moore), whose disability causes the gangster Stephanos (Paul Valentine) some discomfort in the opening scene, and in fact we are given to understand how Jeff might actually prefer to communicate in minimalist coded signs than by long-winded speech. Throughout the movie he remains the quintessence of cool, unflappable, and nonchalant, never at a loss for what to do or what to say wherever he might be, the master of the witty one-line comeback. As Whit himself initially recognizes about the secretive man he has hired to bring back Kathie, "you stay inside yourself."

From *Stranger* to *Touch of Evil*, for the noir protagonist an absence of domesticity, a lack of fixity, becomes a source of intense anxiety, paranoia, and disorientation, sometimes even a threat. But not so in *Out of the Past*, which charts a grim lethal course common in noir, in fact central to the cycle, yet without the attendant perturbed emotions we expect to accompany this inevitable doom. No angst-ridden antihero here. Jeff is a stranger without feeling estranged—a fact even more remarkable given his split identity as Bailey/Markum. Whatever his name, he is totally in control: the only time he acts flustered and nervous, spilling a drink on Whit, it turns out to be feigned behavior. Narrating his toxic Mexican affair with the femme fatale Kathie to Ann as they ride up to Lake Tahoe, Jeff puts it simply: "I knew where I was, and what I was doing."

This seems to me at once perfectly accurate and maddeningly evasive. Accurate, because unlike virtually every other noir ever made, *Out of the Past* is simply not about moral or epistemological confusion: when Kathie asks in Acapulco if he believes her story, Jeff memorably replies, kissing her, "Baby, I don't care," just as he only shows a modicum of surprise when she later shoots his former partner in cold blood. Proclaiming "you didn't have to kill him"—the most excited he gets in the entire movie—Jeff then does what he always does, calmly picking up a cigarette to smoke and then moving on to the next place in his life, this time the scenic small town of Bridgeport and his gas station, we presume. But Jeff's line about knowing where and what is evasive insofar as it tells us nothing about why he acts as he does, so that given Mitchum's baffling, cryptic, magnificently close-to-the-vest performance, we can never really understand what Jeff is thinking or feeling behind his inert, inscrutable mask. Why, for instance, does he always seem willing to go along for the ride, so to speak?[49] Even in death (the only thing we can be sure of in the film) we see no revelatory close-up, nothing but his back blankly facing us as his corpse falls out of the car.[50]

If knowledge, belief, and morality are not central concerns, the movie's essential mystery, I would argue, resides in the question of Jeff's tone, his irony and detachment. Assuming from the start that his fate is sealed, Jeff can assert himself only via an ultracool sense of style, an approach to living he famously expresses to Kathie in the Acapulco casino: you cannot win, but "there's a way to lose more slowly." And so I come back to his closing toast, given moments after Kathie has offered the femme fatale's conventional version of events, echoing Phyllis in *Double Indemnity*: "You're no good, and neither am I." Responding to Kathie's desire for the two of them to seek refuge again in Mexico, Jeff cracks his little joke about Rodriguez, but what if we take it seriously here, as an insight masquerading as humor? As in *Hold Back the Dawn* and *Secret beyond the Door*, Mexico would seem to be a place of abandonment and release, where Kathie and Jeff are free from confinement and restriction. Yet in trying to sell them something (guidance, lottery tickets, trinkets), Rodriguez not only brings the couple together but also reminds them of their mutual identity as foreigners. Cast together as American tourists, Jeff and even Kathie, experience an authentic love possible to sustain, albeit temporarily, only in an enchanted un-American utopia. However much its moonlit beaches coincide with conventional Hollywood fantasies of the exotic, this magical Mexico is not simply of Kathie's own deceitful making but shared by the pair.

The paradox, of course, is that Mexico finally makes their doom all the more inevitable, as the convoluted, confusing San Francisco subplot in the movie's second half shows: sans orienting voice-over, set in the present, complete with a second treacherous woman, Meta Carson (played by Rhonda Fleming, who even looks like Greer). Her insertion into the plot suggests that Kathie alone is not captivating enough to ensnare Jeff. The extra femme fatale (a double rather than a foil) implies a kind of interchangeability of role or type, thereby diminishing Kathie's uniqueness, her distinctive sexual hold over Jeff and Whit. As one critic puts in, "post-Acapulco—Kathie herself has moved from the realm of mystery to something more like irony."[51] That dark irony, I would insist, has to do with belonging in and to the United States, for better or (mostly) worse. The couple's leaving behind the romance of Mexico testifies to an inescapable commitment to citizenship that they both willingly embrace with a surprising patriotic sentimentality. They know they must return to their home, even if it means (as it does) that the past will inexorably catch up with them. If the film manifests in its purest noir form a kind of death wish, one especially in the case of Jeff removed from all extrinsic motives, then in fulfilling that impulse to die, Jeff and Kathie remain true Americans to the end.

FIVE

Bad Boy Patriots

This Gun for Hire, Ride the Pink Horse,
and *Pickup on South Street*

Leave my loneliness unbroken!—Edgar Allan Poe, "The Raven"

Spying is just like any other business.—J. Edgar Hoover, 1945

Roughly a year after he coscripted with W. R. Burnett the crime thriller *This Gun for Hire* (1942), Albert Maltz gave a talk before a group of Los Angeles authors titled "The Citizen Writer." Maltz's remarks were fairly pedestrian, focusing on the need for writers to serve as the conscience of their compatriots by engaging in the battle for human dignity and liberty. In the midst of the war (March 10, 1943) these pleas took on more urgency, especially in relation to his repeated references to Nazi Germany. His talk on citizenship ended a bit ominously: "None of us knows what the future will bring."[1] Four and a half years later, Maltz was compelled to realize just what the future had brought—an interrogation before the House on Un-American Activities Committee (HUAC) investigating "Communist Infiltration of the Motion Picture Industry" that led to his blacklisting and jailing for contempt as one of the Hollywood Ten.

Maltz's fate during the early years of the Cold War carries a particularly painful irony when we look back on the script he coauthored for *This Gun for Hire*. The screenplay is a largely faithful adaptation of a Graham Greene novel published in 1936 about a deformed, sociopathic hit man named Philip Raven whose assassination of a socialist war minister leads his nation to the brink of conflict.[2] In addition to transposing the setting from England to California, softening Raven's character (both in terms of looks and of behavior) and simplifying the novel's political complexities, the wartime screen adaptation introduced a new, American wrinkle by turning the female lead, Ellen Graham (played by Veronica Lake), into a volunteer undercover operative charged with ferreting out a West Coast Axis sympathizer.[3] This traitor, likened to Benedict Arnold, is selling a secret chemical formula for poison gas to the highest bidders, who turn out to be Japanese. The screenwriters' decision to make the foreign enemy Japanese (whom we never see) was a bit unusual. Although 1942 marked the height of the spy thriller in Hollywood, with 60 percent of all war features devoted to espionage plots, nearly all of these focused on Nazis.[4] But making the agents Japanese would have resonated especially with California audiences, given that three months before the film was released, FDR had signed Executive Order 9066, leading to the emergency internment of thousands of Japanese Americans. In the film we eventually discover that the fifth columnist is the same decrepit captain of industry (derisively nicknamed "Old King Chloride") who in the beginning has hired Raven through an assistant to silence a threat (no longer the war minister as in the novel, but a blackmailer), so that this (un)common hit man unwittingly becomes mixed up in a case of international intrigue.

But unlike the prominent part played by the FBI in its obvious precursor *Confessions of a Nazi Spy*, the U.S. government appears only fleetingly in *This Gun for Hire*: a single, brief scene between Ellen and a Senator Burnett, who fearing being recorded by Dictaphones (no Walter Neff, he), has arranged a meeting in the backseat of a moving taxi. During their surreptitious ride he introduces himself as a member of a congressional "committee" dedicated to investigating "foreign agents" who seek to undermine the country from within. In 1942 audiences would have understood that "committee" to be HUAC, the very institution whose search for alien Trojan horses would lead five years later to Maltz's own blacklisting as a communist infiltrator. So in tweaking Greene's novel to turn the film into a patriotic meditation on the triumph of civic duty (the undercover

Ellen or the citizen writer, both involved in the fight against fascism) over self-interest (the alienated Raven's gun for hire or the rapacious capitalist), Maltz and Burnett in effect imaginatively opened up a space that would be filled after the war by HUAC's witch hunting.

Examining the discord between allegiance to country and self-interest, this chapter looks at a trio of noirs, starting with the wartime *This Gun for Hire*, directed by Frank Tuttle, moving to the postwar *Ride the Pink Horse*, directed by Robert Montgomery (1947), and ending with a more extensive analysis of Sam Fuller's cold war classic *Pickup on South Street* (1953), another tale of espionage. All three films feature what I will be calling "bad boys," psychologically damaged criminals out only for themselves who become enmeshed in matters of national security despite their best efforts to pursue nothing but their own selfish agendas of revenge and/or profit.[5] They are all laws sufficient unto themselves, or at least presume to be, until they become caught up in some sinister big business. These bad boys confront more obliquely the corporate sphere that consumes Neff in *Double Indemnity*. How and why they are damaged, how they are each reformed by women, and how they respond to the call of patriotism will be my focus. Unlike in the previous two chapters, here I invoke the concept of citizenship less to engage matters of geographical borders than a broader concern about a family member's responsibility toward his home, defined as the nation, however uncanny (to draw on Freud once again).

In all three movies, these marginalized tough guys explicitly reject "flag waving" as a spurious kind of commitment, and yet what serves as an alternative remains problematic. Certainly other midcentury film genres such as the western explored similar tensions between individualism and community, and of course the trope of the reluctant hero became something of a wartime staple—take *Casablanca* (1942) or *To Have and Have Not* (1944), for instance, both set outside U.S. territory. Yet in their willingness to entertain the possibility that their pathological misfits might be downright un-American, the three noirs I discuss push beyond the standard Humphrey Bogart vehicle to offer an unusually stark polarization between the estranged male loner, on the one hand, and the pressures of the state, on the other.

In their *A Panorama of American Film Noir, 1941–1953*, Raymond Borde and Etienne Chaumeton recognized *This Gun for Hire* as a crucial early contribution to the cycle by virtue of Alan Ladd's striking star debut as the icy but sensitive Raven. Their lyrical descriptions of the infirm industrialist Alvin Brewster (played by Tully Marshall) and his nemesis Raven remain unsurpassed. Here is the capitalist: "Ensconced in an imperial palace setting, funereal and grandiose, the spy master, a paralytic mummy hauled along in a wheelchair, transmits his murderous orders to his second-in-command, a gross and dangerous angst-stricken oaf. Their presence is not intended to lessen the feeling of malaise." And here is Raven: "Alan Ladd is a truly remarkable creation. His slight frame and his overly docile baby face, with its limpid eyes, its gentle, unobtrusive features, appear to come from some other planet, after all the huge and brutal killers who peopled prewar gangster films. Only his expressionless features in situations of great tension reveal a fearsome, inhuman frigidity in this fallen angel."[6]

Focusing on those expressionless features, Joel Dinerstein has recently made a case for the movie, as well as for several others made during the early 1940s, as "emergent noir" that represented "a delayed cinematic response to the traumatic experience of the Great Depression."[7] To work through that trauma, Dinerstein argues, hard-boiled protagonists like Raven and "Mad Dog" Earle (Bogart in *High Sierra*) assume a façade of indifference as they go about their brutal business as killers.[8] The result is a strange coolness that bespeaks a muffled despair at the heart of noir. While his historical contextualizing strikes me as overly general, given the political and cultural complexities of the United States in the 1930s, Dinerstein's emphasis on coolness as a kind of protohipsterism masking pain is promising, especially when applied to actors such as Bogart, Ladd, and Robert Mitchum—the coolest of the cool in *Out of the Past*, as I have previously remarked. But such an approach fails to account for another emotional strain prominently running throughout noir, from *Stranger* to *Touch of Evil*—overtly edgy feelings of paranoia, guilt, anxiety, disorientation, and menace that cannot be so easily contained and controlled by the men who excessively suffer this unrestrained confusion and dread. Consider, for instance, the tormented, frantic Michael in *Stranger*, the nervous, sweaty Neff in *Double Indemnity*, or the bitter, hapless Al Roberts in *Detour*, to name three central noir protagonists from the 1940s. These quintessential neurotics are anything but cool.

To complicate Dinerstein's reading, we need to trace a second important thread in the movie that supplements but also mitigates against this coolness, and that is domesticity, Raven's search for a home.[9] Throughout the narrative Raven is associated with two distinct sorts of props, his gun (a constant companion) and a series of objects or trappings that evoke the tenderness of the home: a kitten, a little girl in leg braces on a stairwell who asks Raven to fetch her toy ball, and a (fake) baby in a blanket that allows Raven to elude detection by covering up his telltale scar, significantly enough. Most notably toward the end, the mise-en-scène itself transforms into a dingy, dark, claustrophobic shack in which the couple spend the night holed up, surrounded by the police. This shadow-filled space serves as a temporary domicile that allows the fugitive killer to confess his abusive childhood to the surrogate wife-mother-spy Ellen.[10]

The gun, of course, is a prosthesis for masculinity, standing in metonymically for Raven himself, as the movie's title suggests (where *gun* is both the thing and the person). The weapon enforces Raven's code of self-sufficiency, his seemingly absolute refusal to accept any authority outside himself, as he concisely explains to Brewster's oafish assistant who has hired him: "I am my own police." The actual police in the movie are led by Ellen's obtuse fiancé, Detective Michael Crane (played by Robert Preston), who is a paragon of ineptitude, always arriving too late to be effectual. By contrast, Raven is supremely competent in his work as a professional assassin. That is one key aspect of his coolness. The only time he slips up, it is because of a moment of sentimental weakness, buying a dress with a marked bill for a washerwoman he had viciously slapped in the movie's memorable opening scene for mistreating his kitten. Later, to avoid being caught, he will smother to death another cat as Ellen watches, an omen to him that his "good luck" has finally run out.

Yet if sentimentality is a source of vulnerability for Raven, it is also what ultimately saves him in the nurturing figure of Ellen, to whom he divulges his innermost secrets during their long night trapped together: "Every night I dream. I read somewhere about a kind of doctor, a psych-something. You tell the dream, you don't have to dream it any more." Explaining the killer's derangement, James Naremore (and Dinerstein following him) interprets Raven as "a victim of Depression-era social injustice."[11] But this is not the whole picture, since the script's transparent Freudianism mixes sociological explanations with psychological ones: the hanging of his father, the early death of his mother, and then the trauma of being beaten and maimed by "a woman," a cruel aunt, whom he subsequently murders as a teenager to begin his long criminal career. The key here is that for Ellen to start to heal Raven's bottled-up hurt by way of a talking therapy, she must play the part of confidante as well as lover and caring surrogate mother. This role as therapist is closely linked to her covert identity as an undercover agent in the employ of the U.S. government, a duty even her detective boyfriend does not know about.[12]

In the dark shanty, during this scene of personal revelation, domesticity and national security begin to merge. Ellen understands that the only way to rouse Raven from his sullen solipsism (expressed in the opening scene as misogyny) is to appeal to a greater good, the safety of the homeland. At the same time she encourages him to confess while keeping her own secrets from him. For Ellen the issue is not whether or who you kill, but why you might do it. While most critics tend to dismiss the female's spy role as extrinsic wartime propaganda inserted into the movie merely for patriotic effect, it is actually crucial for grasping the underlying logic of the narrative, by which the criminal can be redeemed only insofar as he gives up his inner self for the sake of the state. As I have suggested throughout this study, political "propaganda" is not some sort of inessential overlay grafted onto the plot, but rather vital to the film's noirishness. While he emphatically turns down Ellen's appeal as mere "flag waving," Raven in the end conveniently need not choose between self and country: he indeed manages after all to serve as Ellen's proxy and to gain personal revenge by coercing a written admission of guilt at gunpoint out of the creepy capitalist Brewster. Before dying in a hail of police bullets, Raven closes the film with a question for Ellen: "Did I do all right for you?" The approval of the woman—mother, lover, government agent, therapist —restores moral order.

The slightly chaotic, rushed resolution of This Gun for Hire is profoundly conservative, containing and blunting the (sexy) strangeness of Raven, whose selfish rejection of state authority (recall "I am my own police") is potentially as threatening as the fifth-column treason of his double, the aging industrialist who sells weapons for profit to foreign foes (think "this poison gas for hire"). Hence the need for the gunman, along the lines of Poe's William Wilson, to murder his alter ego, and thereby destroy himself, although the movie oddly has Raven instead kill Brewster's buffonish assistant immediately after the aging industrialist suddenly keels over from a heart attack, with a glass of milk by his side. Perhaps the screenwriters' New Deal idealism dictated that greedy capitalism die a natural death, but in any case once Brewster and Raven are both out of the picture, Ellen and Michael can embrace, secure in the knowledge that analogous forms of domestic tranquility, their impending marriage and the nation, have been safely preserved from the enemy within.

It might be argued that such a conclusion was primarily a sop to Production Code Administration censors who always insisted on a happy ending. As Sherri Biesen points out, for example, the PCA during the wartime loosened restrictions against depicting graphic violence as long as that violence could be shown to aid the Allied march to victory.[13] In this view, filmmakers would give the PCA what it wanted in order to get what they wanted in return. But beyond the matter of regulation, the movie's ending efficiently serves to rid the state of transgressors like Raven while managing to make martyrs of them, in a kind of sacrificial purging that goes back to Stranger. If we push past the war to consider postwar bad boys, this pattern will become more apparent, even as these criminals no longer face literal banishment.

In Robert Montgomery's underappreciated Ride the Pink Horse (1947), released a few months before the much better-known Out of the Past, the loner Lucky Gagin is not a hit man disposing of a blackmailer but is himself the blackmailer. He comes to a small town in New Mexico seeking money and revenge for the death of his ex-soldier friend Shorty, killed by a crime boss for attempting the same act of blackmail. In shrewdly adapting the Dorothy Hughes novel of 1946 (with the same title) for the screen, the writers Ben Hecht and Charles Lederer made four key changes, all of a piece, that dramatically improved and complicated the Hughes narrative. First and foremost, they altered the setting from Santa Fe during the Zozobra Fiesta to a border town in which whites, Mexicans, and Indians mingle freely.[14] Second, they turned the main character—named Sailor in the novel, but only a common crook—into a severely traumatized, wayward veteran from the Second World War (played by Montgomery himself), more catatonic than cool, seeking to revenge the death of his comrade in arms. Third, they transformed the mobster, called the Sen in the novel (for Senator), from a conventional Chicago gangster, hardly recognizable as any sort of politician, into an ominous, nearly deaf war profiteer named Frank Hugo (Fred Clark) who has made millions by bribing government officials. Gagin has evidence of that corruption in the form of a canceled check he plans to sell back to Hugo, who resembles in this regard the corrupt fifth-columnist capitalist blackmailed in *This Gun for Hire*. Fourth, they changed a Chicago police detective hot on the trail of both the Sen and Sailor into a bespectacled, mild-mannered but relentless FBI agent, Bill Retz, played by an actor (Art Smith) who looks a lot like Harry S. Truman. As if to underscore this point, the suspicious Gagin begins calling the diminutive Retz "Uncle Sam" to his face.

Let us consider the implications of these changes, especially how they link up with one another to give the noir clear national and political dimensions. First, the locale: from the moment Gagin steps off the Greyhound bus in the opening scene, he is immersed in an alien environment, unrecognizable as part of the United States, filled with Indians wrapped in blankets, boisterous fiesta revelers, and Mexicans speaking Spanish. Wandering around the town looking unsuccessfully for a place to stay, it is as if he has been thrust back into an uneasy contact zone that recalls his recent war experience, as we shall see. This borderlands menace is most pronounced when he enters a bar and the music suddenly stops; a slow pan across the room shows everybody turning to stare at him. The stranger walks into a saloon: while this kind of scene is reiterated in dozens of westerns, the effect in this case is accentuated and given a noir twist by the absolutely disorienting foreignness of Gagin's surroundings. Even though we are still on U.S. soil, the patrons speak a mixture of broken English and Spanish and trade in pesos (neither of which Gagin fully understands; nor do we, presumably). Called by one local "the man with no place," Gagin keeps insisting that he is "nobody's friend," a stranger to himself along the lines of Raven in *This Gun for Hire*.

But what quickly breaks down this feeling of utter estrangement and homelessness is a matter of gender: the sameness of hard-drinking men across cultures and the nurturing of a woman (yet again). For the first time in the movie, the laconic, stiff Gagin (perfectly in keeping with Montgomery's wooden acting style) begins to loosen up in the bar as he is befriended by the curious Mexicans, one of whom (named Pancho, played by Thomas Gomez) gives him a place to sleep near his carousel (hence the film's title), taken by the generosity of the white man who buys drinks all around.[15] As we might expect, Mexicans like Pancho are more interested in friendship than money. If male bonding serves to smooth over national and ethnic differences in rather conventional ways in the film, so Gagin's interactions with women also offer an assuring stability. There are two main females in the narrative, foils for each other. One is the mobster Hugo's attractive moll, Marjorie (Andrea King), who pretends to help Gagin but turns out to be a treacherous back-stabber (literally). By 1947, thanks in part to roles like that of Phyllis Dietrichson in *Double Indemnity*, the Hollywood femme fatale had become such a familiar figure that the screenwriters spent little time or energy fleshing out this predictable character, whom even Gagin knows immediately to treat with suspicion and distrust. As she herself quickly realizes, "I'm afraid Mr. Gagin can't be seduced," while for his part the loner sums up the type nicely: she has "a dead fish where her heart ought to be."

Yet if one sort of stereotyped woman possesses no hold over the war vet, another one does—a young Indian waif named Pila (played by the Anglo actress Wanda Hendrix) who is just as much an outsider in the town as he is. Ignored by her female companions (older, Mexican, interested in picking up "muchachos"), the childlike Pila begins to follow Gagin around, offering guidance and spiritual protection, but also enabling Gagin to school her (more like a daughter than a lover), teaching her how to dress, wear modern clothes, and order food in a restaurant. Like the Seminole Indians in *Key Largo*, the indigenous Pila, inclined toward mysticism, signifies a natural innocence that vaguely points to an Americanism predating the founding of the nation-state. And so as in the case of the Mexican men in the film, the Indian girl (whom Gagin derisively nicknames "Sitting Bull") allows the stranger to find a place for himself in this border town as a kind of neocolonizer bringing civilization to the hinterlands.

However clichéd, Gagin's patronizing attitudes toward the natives (both male and female) are not quite as patently offensive as my description might imply. That is because we are constantly reminded of his own crippling trauma as a soldier who has served abroad. Reading postwar noir as the politics (and poetics) of maladjustment, Richard Maltby has made a strong, compelling, and detailed case for the centrality of the returning veteran in the cycle, who served to manifest the profound disillusionment felt by many American intellectuals after the Second World War.[16] In the wake of Maltby's influential arguments, the trope of the embittered war vet has become the ground of first resort for scholars (and students) who sometimes seek a quick way to historicize the cycle. *Ride the Pink Horse* is certainly not the first or last of a host of films noirs to focus on the war vet, more or less impotent. Think of the delusional Chuck Scott in *The Chase* or the heroic Frank McCloud in *Key Largo*.

But to my mind it is by far the most interesting portrayal for two reasons. First, the screenwriters work Gagin's trauma into the plot not simply by way of amnesia or psychosis, as these other movies tend to do, but by way of race; as he is teaching Pila in the restaurant how to look and act "human," her (red) face suddenly reminds him of his combat trauma: "For a minute I thought I was back in New Guinea again—only in New Guinea, they're [the native girls] darker." With this seemingly stray comment we are transported back to the field of battle for a second time; in an earlier scene negotiating a pay-off with Hugo, Gagin has similarly racialized his wartime experience, complaining that "while I was getting a tan in a place called New Guinea," Hugo was listening to "patriotic speeches" delivered by corrupt government officials. The Second World War has in effect blackened him, making him more likely to deal with crooks like Hugo than with civil servants like Retz. Having internalized the aliens he encountered in Pacific combat, Gagin is still haunted by this foreign enemy, now within, even after he returns home—a lurking menace he seeks to exorcise on the margins of his country in the figure of Hugo.

Second, and most important, *Ride the Pink Horse* is the only noir to directly link the battle experience of the disenchanted hero with the specific crimes of his antagonist. The brilliant stroke by screenwriters Hecht and Lederer is to turn Hughes's gangster Sen into a corrupt profiteer who stayed safely at home during the war making millions while soldiers like Gagin and Shorty sacrificed their lives. As Gagin sarcastically asks Retz, "Doesn't the government work for Hugo? It did all during the war." In a kind of residue of Popular Front ethics of the 1930s, the common man's loss unfairly becomes the rich man's gain. During and after the war, such widespread corporate profiteering was America's dirty little secret, akin to the white-collar crimes I discuss in chapter 2. That is why a detective is transformed into an FBI agent—there is here a federal offense that demands a federal cure. A dedicated public servant who continually reaches out to Gagin despite being rebuffed, "Uncle Sam" strives to counteract the war soldier's internalized, private foes by serving therapeutically as the veteran's friend in government. At the same time, the omnipresent agent relentlessly works to give Hugo "indigestion," as the war profiteer complains, boring into the world of the criminal who cannot easily consume or bribe him, so that he in effect becomes an enemy within for the corrupt gangster turned businessman.[17] We can now appreciate why Retz was strikingly cast to resemble Truman, who during the war, as Senator Truman, led a congressional committee (the flip side of HUAC, as it were) that conducted hundreds of hearings to investigate fraud and bribery in defense industries.[18]

Truman went so far as to deem such "legal profiteering" treasonous, a kind of economic fifth column. His vigilance against this lesser-acknowledged domestic threat was one reason FDR selected him as his running mate in the election of 1944. Earlier, when Retz "officially" requested the incriminating evidence to help arrest Hugo, Gagin replied in disdain, "Look copper, don't wave any flags at me." But after he is severely wounded, feverish, and so delirious that he thinks he is back in the jungle and that Pila is his dead war pal Shorty, Gagin becomes more receptive to Retz's way of thinking. Once push comes to shove near the end, when Gagin in an abject stupor listens to Hugo eloquently dismiss duty, honor, and responsibility as meaningless phrases in a last-ditch effort to buy him off with big money, the "small-fry" "haywire veteran" (as Hugo insults him) hands over the incriminating evidence to the FBI. Self-interest must necessarily take a backseat to his obligations as a U.S. citizen, renewed and restored by his loyal Mexican amigo Pancho and his female Indian charge Pila. At the close of the movie the gamin herself is integrated into the mixed-race community by virtue of her newly gained confidence as she recounts to her friends (in Spanish) her intimate association with the handsome (white) American. Poised between two kinds of conflict (hot and cold), *Ride the Pink Horse* retrospectively looks to the recent wartime past and geographically to the borders of the state to invent a revitalized patriotism for its sullen hero.

The crime of treason is also the central concern of Fuller's *Pickup on South Street*, a "nuclear noir" that poses the question most bluntly: what is the difference between a traitor and a pickpocket?[19] The film centers on the theft of a strip of microfilm containing government secrets vital to national security, along the lines of the canceled check in *Ride the Pink Horse* and the letter filled with chemical formulas in *This Gun for Hire*. But unlike these two paper documents, the purloined microfilm raises the stakes well beyond blackmail for money, or even war victory, since given the accelerating arms race of the early 1950s between the United States and the Soviet Union, such atomic secrets held in balance the ultimate fate of the planet. When in the opening scene a recently released petty convict named Skip McCoy (played by Richard Widmark) picks the purse of Candy, a prostitute (played by Jean Peters) who is unwittingly working as a courier for communist agents, he sets off a fierce contest between reds and feds vying for the information, with Skip and Candy caught in the middle. A microcosm of the Cold War, this skirmishing over the microfilm gives noir's distinctive set of concerns—transgression, disorientation, betrayal, sex, and moral ambiguity—the most explicitly political valence of all the narratives I have discussed in this study. In a close analysis of the movie, I aim to examine several related functions of the stolen microfilm: as self-reflexively calling attention to the materiality of the film medium and Fuller's role as a director; as dramatizing negotiations of scale and social space; as expanding the scope of crime from misdeeds against individuals to treason against the nation-state; and finally, as helping define the obligations of U.S. citizens during the Cold War, especially for outcasts like Skip and Candy.

Pickup was not Fuller's initial cinematic foray into cold war politics. Two years earlier he had scripted and directed *Steel Helmet* (1951), a low-budget production depicting a small band of GIs besieged in a Buddhist temple; this was the first American movie to be produced about the Korean War while the war was still inconclusively raging on. But unlike so many films made during the Second World War explicitly for propaganda purposes to boost U.S. morale, *Steel Helmet* refused to unequivocally endorse the country's latest military cause, focusing instead on a hard-nosed sergeant's more local struggle to survive alongside his men. In the absence of any clear historical retrospect to help make sense of the war, Fuller characteristically cast ideological issues into personal terms. For instance, when a captured North Korean officer affirms the superiority of communism and taunts a black medic and then a Japanese American soldier about racial segregation in the United States, explicitly referring to internment camps (a daring move on Fuller's part for 1951), the two soldiers are compelled to admit that they are second-class citizens, yet insisting still that they prefer to live in a land that values independence. As a result of such melodramatic scenes affirming Americanism as primarily an opportunity for individual autonomy, film scholars have generally not been kind to Fuller, concluding for the most part that his thinking about politics remains rather unsophisticated, if not downright crude, and praising his striking visual virtuosity at the expense of his ideas.[20]

Here I argue otherwise that Fuller's grasp of politics is anything but naïve, especially the way that *Pickup* treats the contested strip as precisely the (battle)ground between personal self-interest and the greater public good. Fuller's politics hinge on his representation of the miniaturized medium. The microfilm functions both as a token of personal gain and as an urgent but essentially empty compact signifier for the nation-state that generates a kernel of anxiety or tension in the story line. We understand that the film's suspense will not rest on the uncertain location of the secret information but rather on the curious fate of the small thing in which it is embedded. As in other noirs I have examined, here, too, the question of testing national boundaries remains central, but the crossing now refers to an object, not a person. At once tiny, nuclear, yet of national and global import, this microfilm requires a radical negotiating of perspective between the monumental and the infinitesimal. For Fuller that process of negotiation resolutely rests with individuals, not institutions such as the police or the FBI. The microfilm remains at the center of a series of complicated transactions among the film's socially peripheral characters, who during the narrative stake out various claims and urban terrains, personal as well as political, that tend to merge and comingle instead of staying self-contained. In the conspicuous absence of any clearly demarcated domestic sphere to regulate these roles, gender becomes entangled with national interests in particularly unstable ways.

As Susan Stewart has suggested, it is the human body that "serves as a 'still center,' or constant measure, of our articulation of the miniature and the gigantic," in other words, as that which enables us to comprehend and manage shifts in magnitude.[21] And even though microfilm, as a photograph of a text rather than a representation of the world, seems to be subject to infinite mechanical reproduction, it still retains a semblance of unique aura insofar as it remains intimately linked to the vicissitudes of the body, especially the female body.[22] Hence the paradox of microfilm for Fuller—the concealment and portability that makes it so effective as a personal medium for protecting and preserving information is also what makes it so vulnerable to theft and destruction, putting the nation's integrity at risk if these secrets were to be transported out of the country, with the violation of the border in effect leading to the loss of the state itself.

Given the seemingly formulaic role microfilm plays in many spy movies, with their invariably vague allusions to hidden government formulas and papers, cinema scholars have tended to ignore or slight (shall we say minimize?) its importance. It was Hitchcock, after all, who famously dismissed such things as mere "MacGuffins," insisting that "to steal plans or documents or discover a secret" makes no difference at all, since "the only thing that really matters is that in the picture the plans, documents, or secrets must seem to be of vital importance to the characters. To me, the narrator, they're of no importance whatever."[23] Seduced by the master's seeming indifference to matters of plotting, and perhaps not wanting to appear naïve, critics have followed Hitchcock's lead. But if microfilm is indeed a mere plot device, it is a MacGuffin of an exceptional sort, exerting a special kind of pressure in the narrative by virtue of its status as not just crucial information but a highly condensed object of volatile desire itself. This notion of microfilm as a charged signifier packing explosive potential takes on increasingly ominous significance in the course of *Pickup*'s plot. When a police captain named Dan Tiger (Murvyn Vye) early on warns the defiant pickpocket Skip about his victim Candy that "that girl was carrying TNT and it's going to blow up right in your face," we can appreciate how "blowing up" microfilmed atomic secrets might be more than a clever play on words.

At first glance the microfilm in *Pickup* would seem a perfect illustration of a MacGuffin. Offended by what they saw as the movie's anticommunist bias, the French retitled the film *Le port de la drogue* (*Port of Drugs*) and dubbed the dialogue accordingly to reflect the crime of drug trafficking instead of cold war surveillance.[24] Rather than cut out the scenes that so prominently foreground Skip peering at the strip, the French simply rewrote the dialogue to explain that the microfilm contained a secret new formula for the synthetic manufacture of drugs. From a narrative point of view this plausible if not seamless transition from spying to drugs underscores the blankness of the microfilm as a signifier and therefore would seem to confirm Hitchcock's MacGuffin theory. Yet the film's rather notorious history in France grows even more curious once we understand that Fuller initially based his screenplay on a story by Dwight

Taylor titled "Blaze of Glory" that originally made reference to narcotics.[25] Fuller changed the plot to highlight classified intelligence ostensibly to avoid Hollywood morals codes prohibiting movies about drug dealing. So sandwiched between two different drug tales, the source story and the subsequent French dubbed version, we have the film as it was released in the United States, clearly and deliberately a film about communist spies, the FBI, and microfilm. Even though Fuller himself in recounting his own "yarn" seemed a bit fuzzy about the presumed contents of that microfilm, falling back on the false explanation ("a new patent for a chemical formula," as if in direct echo of *This Gun for Hire*) that the duped courier Candy is at first given by her creepy ex-boyfriend, Joey (played by Richard Kiley), it is clear that this is no case of industrial espionage.[26]

In his terrific psychoanalytic exegesis of cold war movies, Michael Rogin shrewdly remarks: "The atomic spy trials of the late 1940s merged with the House Un-American Activities Committee investigation of Communist influence in Hollywood. Since HUAC exposed both Alger Hiss and the Hollywood Ten and since the accused spies, writers, and directors all went to jail, the distinction collapsed between microfilm and film. The celluloid medium of secret influence became the message."[27]

Rogin gives us a striking insight into the blurring of institutions that took place in the late 1940s and early 1950s in the name of national security. But he does not suggest how this celluloid collapse gets played out in some of the cold war movies themselves, especially ones like *Pickup* that invoke microfilm as a kind of self-reflexive shadow or parallel medium to the medium of film itself. Fuller may have prided himself on being one of the least self-conscious directors in Hollywood, but his screenplay for *Pickup* suggests otherwise.[28] Fuller's self-consciousness is especially on display in the context of the browbeating he claims to have faced while trying to have the movie released. As if to validate Rogin's point, Fuller relates how the film provoked Hoover to call the director and studio boss Darryl Zanuck in for a meeting. Hoover, Fuller says, was infuriated by Skip's "anti-American" stance and tried to dictate changes in the script. According to Fuller, Hoover was particularly offended by Skip's unpatriotic reply to the FBI agent in the movie who interrogates him about the missing microfilm. When the agent Zara (Willis Bouchey) cautions that "if you refuse to co-operate you'll be as guilty as the traitors who gave Stalin the A-bomb," the pickpocket responds, "Are you waving the flag at me?"

Although Zanuck convinced Hoover that Skip's surly line was in character and that it should stay (minus the adjective *damn*), we see how the FBI intimidation that Fuller claims happened outside the movie (about the film) mirrors the coercion dramatized inside (about the microfilm).[29] It is rather astonishing to imagine the head of the FBI taking such a personal interest in screenplay revision, micromanaging, so to speak, but it is true that Hoover often provided support for other cold war spy productions during the 1950s, even in one instance (*Walk East on Beacon*, another film featuring microfilm) taking credit for the movie's original story.[30] Just as Skip refuses to give up possession of the coveted microfilm to the feds, so Fuller refused to turn his film into a piece of cold war propaganda.

Fuller draws this analogy between the filmmaker and the microfilm thief in a number of ways. Beyond the familiar injunction "to co-operate" that helped spur the drama of the HUAC hearings, in Fuller's screenplay characters repeatedly refer to the microfilm simply as "film," such as when Tiger (anticipating Hoover) promises Skip "a nice fat bill of health for that strip of film." Although Skip is little more than a petty pickpocket or "cannon," Fuller also continually emphasizes his skill and professionalism; Skip for his part clearly takes pride in his work, bragging while caressing Candy (who admires his soft hands) that when he concentrates he never gets caught. Early on in the movie, when the professional stoolie Moe Williams (played by Thelma Ritter) is brought into police headquarters to help finger the thief, she dwells in loving detail on matters of criminal artistry, demonstrating with a folded newspaper how each cannon has "his own trademark" technique. Skip's artistry extends beyond his expert picking of Candy's purse to include his skill at picking an intricate hiding place for his stolen goods, including the envelope with the microfilm—a wooden box he dredges up from under the river, filled with cold beer bottles, with a false bottom containing a wrapped flat metal canister, precisely the sort used to store Hollywood 16mm or 35mm prints. Only with the film in the can, Fuller implies, will it be safe from the control of the meddling feds. And finally we note how near the end of the narrative Skip acts like a movie editor (or censor), cutting a key frame from the film strip to withhold important information from the communist agent Joey.[31]

To understand what the stolen microfilm variously signifies in *Pickup* thus helps us appreciate what Fuller's own film meant to him, including its wider political implications. The significance of Skip's opening criminal act (the "difference between a traitor and a pickpocket," as Zara draws the distinction) depends less on the microfilm contents per se than on how it is actively read. Fuller dramatizes this act of reading by showing Skip entering the New York Public Library newspaper room at one point to scan the pickpocketed film with a microfilm reader, a gesture resembling an editor reviewing a production's daily rushes. This curious scene foregrounds the process of "blowing up" information, but would seem to add little else to our knowledge. Clearly the scene is crucial for exposing the material means by which the cinema apparatus projects its images on the screen. Earlier we have learned that the strip is unique ("We can't get another copy of it," Joey tells Candy), since it records a single act of espionage that cannot easily be duplicated. As such it retains the vestige of its aura, the moment of its coming into being.[32]

Before he actually reads the microfilm, Skip as a cover has carefully requested a real newspaper to scan, a copy of the *New York Times* from January 5, 1947, seemingly a date picked at random, the front page of which he briefly glances at before replacing it with the strip of microfilm. The headline of this newspaper flashes on the screen for only a second or two. Yet thanks to the magic of DVD freeze frames, a sly inside joke by Fuller turns into a telling gloss on the politics of the entire film. The headline from the *New York Times*, actually dated December 31, 1946, reads "Truman Declares Hostilities Ended, Terminating Many Wartime Laws; Republican Chiefs Commend Action," and it continues by indicating in smaller font that "51 Statutes to Die," even though, in still smaller headline font, "States of Emergency and War Continue." The article itself goes on to discuss how Truman's surprise end-of-year declaration technically rescinds laws related to the "state of hostilities" but not the "state of war" itself, nor FDR's "state of emergency [1939] that consists of limited and unlimited emergency and special emergency." Analyzing Truman's motives, the reporter Bertram D. Hulen explains: "The President's action was generally regarded here as chiefly important from the psychological standpoint. It was viewed as a move to demonstrate that he wants to be a constitutional President and not to hold on to excessive powers granted to the Chief Executive through emergency proclamations and a state of war."

Because Skip does not take the time to read the article, which for him serves as a mere pretense, neither can we. Yet this bit of text momentarily caught and imaged in the microfilm projector and then analogously projected onto the big screen actually offers an accurate historical context (literally a subtext) that underlies *Pickup*'s complex representations of cold war dynamics. In fact, even though the news story does not directly mention the Soviet Union, it is hard to imagine any more revealing moment to pinpoint and encapsulate the start of the war. What Fuller brilliantly suggests by deliberately, covertly inserting this headline (which must have escaped even Hoover's keen eye) is that from the vantage point of 1953, FDR's states of emergency and war are still firmly in place, despite a shift in enemies, but with little else changed. Lying dormant for more than fifty years, *Pickup*'s ironic jest is to mock the finality of Truman's proclamation of December 31, 1946: poised precisely at the transition between the official end of one war and the beginning of another that was shortly to emerge unofficially the following year. "Hostilities" are declared over, yet only to have another sort of hostility commence. Both in terms of the domestic front, those internal security measures centering on the fear of infiltration and espionage, and of conflict abroad, in Korea, where fighting was continuing unabated when *Pickup* was released in the summer of 1953, the United States had never stopped being at war. The rhetoric of war (hot and cold) in fact infuses the images and words of the film, from the blood-drive posters casually plastered on New York subway stations ("For Defense: Blood Means Life"; see figure 18) to the fleeting headline Skip glimpses, to the curious metaphors that various characters invoke to describe their reactions to foreign agents operating in their midst. At the core of this rhetoric resides the microfilm itself.

It may be reasonably objected that however telling a comment pinpointing the moment of the Cold War's emergence, "Truman Declares Hostilities Ended" cannot properly be worked into an interpretation of *Pickup* because it is too transitory to register for any audience seeing the movie. That is true, if we limit ourselves to the phenomenological experience of viewing moving images as they temporally unfold before our eyes to tell a story. But if we take a broader approach to the ontology of the cinematic medium, surely this image of text embedded in the narrative merits analysis once the new technology of the DVD pause button makes it readily available to us, just as it makes available for inspection those blood-drive Korean War posters that otherwise simply recede into the mise-en-scène of Fuller's subway station mockup, cobbled together in a few weeks on a Twentieth Century-Fox studio back lot. More interested in money

18 Korean War poster, from *Pickup on South Street*

than global events, the indifferent pickpocket ignores the newspaper he has requested. Yet for us to discover the headline "Truman Declares Hostilities Ended" secreted in the film is like stumbling across and opening a hidden PDF file attached to a document we thought we already knew inside and out. Crafty journalist that he was before he became a director, Fuller relies on this concealed news to uncannily make his political point. And while it may be objected that even in freeze frame only the headline is visible and not the specifics of the article itself, I would argue that, as with any allusion or reference "outside" the text, we are encouraged to supplement the image of the headline with the full substance of the news story beneath.

It might also be objected that I am indulging in sheer speculation by attributing the insertion of the headline to the director himself, when in fact a whole range of people could have been responsible, from the production designer, an art designer, a set decorator, or even a prop assistant. Because filmmaking is such a collective industrial process, is it not risky (if not downright foolish) to give agency to a single person? Here my granting Fuller a subtle political agenda (one he later would explicitly disavow) by way of this fleeting headline raises a troublesome French term perhaps even more feared these days among some cinema scholars than *noir*: *auteur*.[33] There has lately been something of an academic backlash against high French film theory, which initially developed in part from and in response to *Cahiers du cinéma* celebrations of idiosyncratic mavericks like

Fuller in the 1950s. Given this aversion to theory, auteur as well as apparatus, especially to its cruder popularized versions, attention has gradually
shifted away from the stylistic analysis of individual Hollywood directors
and films to concentrate on the institutional and historical complexities of
studio production. But this tendency strikes me as ill advised in the case of
Fuller, for this film at least, since he exercised enormous power over it by
virtue of being also its sole screenwriter—a combination of roles unusual
in the early 1950s, especially for a major studio director, that enabled him
through the movie's plotting to explore these very questions of control.[34]
As my reading of *Pickup*'s autobiographic dimension has emphasized, to
the extent that Skip is pressured by contending cold war ideologies, so was
Fuller. His hands are all over the movie (as shifty as Skip's), even if we
cannot definitely prove that it was his idea to stick in that particular
newspaper headline.

In this regard, although the projected *New York Times* headline is
directly analogous to the stolen microfilm, it also stands in stark contrast
to a pair of images we see earlier on when the pickpocket first inspects the
object of his theft. The movie's initial close-up of the microfilm's contents
simply reveals a negative of six sprocketed frames, each with rows of
numbers and equations that could mean anything. Unlike the *New York
Times* text, they specify little here beyond vaguely signifying some sort of
scientific formula. Filling the entire screen, this fleeting close-up is followed immediately by a midrange shot of Skip holding up the strip verti-
cally against a glassless window in his riverside shack that frames the
distant Brooklyn skyline (see figure 19). In this emblematic shot, Fuller
contrasts the smallness of the microfilm with the bigness of the contained
city, with the outline of the strip formally mimicking the silhouettes of the
various skyscrapers. As Edward Dimendberg has suggested, *Pickup* opens
with similar sorts of dramatic negotiations of scale. An exterior of a lighted
subway train racing through a dark tunnel, like a whirring reel of celluloid
(see figure 20), cuts to an interior of a crowded subway car, where Skip
lifts the wallet of the oblivious Candy, lips sensuously pursed, eyes half
closed, in front of two FBI agents trailing her. The car's jostled, utterly
silent passengers are at once in intimate contact and utterly anonymous
to one another. Immediately after this scene of tight close-ups of tired,
vacant faces, the camera moves to a crane shot, an overhead long view
that follows Candy exiting the station from the vantage point of a high-

19 Negotiating
matters of scale,
from *Pickup on
South Street*

20 Rushing subway
as reeling celluloid,
from *Pickup on
South Street*

rise building across the street, reducing the individuals walking below to little figures.[35]

The way in which *Pickup*'s promiscuous urban camera eye enlarges and shrinks people not only corresponds to the volatile shifts in mood between Candy and Skip, from tenderness to aggression, but also matches the logic of the microfilm itself as an object of longing that characters variously interpret, value, and use. For Skip, the information he has inadvertently stolen is simply a way to cash in, even as he cynically distrusts everyone he deals with. As a measure of the intense desire of others, the strip for him means money, pure and simple, apparently with no other content or ideo-logical baggage attached, as he remarks to Candy: "I'll do business with a red, but I don't have to believe one." Skip does not seem to believe in anything besides himself, so that this comment is less an attack on communism than simply an assertion of his complete independence from all institutions. Although he is contemptuous of authority, he does participate in a loose code of honor among his fellow petty criminals, refusing to get angry at the mother figure Moe when he discovers that she has turned him in, for example. Appreciating that "she's gotta eat" too, Skip implicitly acknowledges how the lower classes must struggle to get by under capitalism.

But beyond these occasional bouts of sympathy, the bad boy remains alienated, solitary, insolent, and self-sufficient, regarding the microfilm only as a means to personal gain. The film represents nothing more than what he himself stands to get from it, a hard-boiled attitude that Fuller tended to adopt when he discussed his own filmmaking. Yet immediately after the pickpocket flaunts his defiance to the FBI, Zara asks, "Do you know what treason means?" His crucial question translates the microfilm from the personal to the national, drastically enlarging the scope of its significance. Theft becomes treason only when the security of the entire nation-state is at risk, a proposition Skip quickly rejects as bogus patriotism. Although Zara, needing by definition to keep cold war secrets secret, remains vague about the "military information" on the film, his subsequent reference to the A-bomb strongly suggests that nothing less than nuclear holocaust may be at stake.[36]

It is instructive to compare Skip's attitude with Raven's in *This Gun for Hire*.[37] As I have suggested, Fuller closely follows the earlier movie's plot by replacing fifth-column spies with communists, who are also foiled by a disgruntled, alienated outcast in the end. But Fuller's updating suggests several crucial differences. Although both Raven and Skip are not above slapping a woman (decking one cold, in Skip's case), Skip seems to enjoy himself more than the melancholic Raven. Skip's defiance is gleeful, Raven's morose. (Just consider their names in this regard.) And it is not simply that Fuller's misfit Skip survives while the tormented Raven does not, or that even though he is less lethal than Raven, the sneering, smirking Skip (who insists "I never used a gun in my life") seems to embrace his sadism. The key difference is that Raven's twisted menace is sympathetically given psychological motivation, whereas the sources of Skip's instability and discontent remain something of a mystery. In *This Gun for Hire*, the film's psychology and wartime politics are clearly intertwined;

suffering from a misshapen childhood and an abusive aunt, Raven leans on Freudian trauma for support. While it might be argued that he acts heroically in the end only for Ellen's sake, not for the war cause, insofar as Ellen the undercover spy also stands for the good mother he never had, his sacrifice is ultimately redemptive. In Fuller's cold war version, by contrast, Skip never abandons his self-interest, even for a good woman, let alone to fight communism; when Candy, trying to get closer, innocently asks, "How'd you get to be a pickpocket?," Skip suddenly explodes in anger, sarcastically repeating her question as he brutally pushes her aside, shouting, "How'd you get to be what you are? Things happen, that's all." This is a direct mockery of the kind of diagnosis *This Gun for Hire* attempts to perform.

In its rejection of 1940s (pop) psychology as well as 1930s (pop) sociology, which claimed that bad environments produced delinquents, *Pickup* would seem to disavow any explanation for the underclass of small-time losers who figure so prominently in the narrative. Yet Skip's repeated references to the costs of doing "business," shared by every other character in the film, patriotic, un-American, or simply "a regular kind of crook" (as Moe at one point calls Skip), does suggest how the logic of commerce drives Fuller's plot. Echoing Skip's realization "she's gotta eat," Moe is constantly talking about the rising cost of food as a way to justify her "crummy business" as a professional stool pigeon. Personal (economic) security and national security remain closely linked. The movie's crossing over from common crime into state treason by way of the stolen microfilm does not leave financial considerations behind, but simply reinforces them, as government and spies go about their business precisely as a business. Trying to downplay the melodrama of espionage for a radio audience in 1945, Hoover emphasized the professionalism of his office by insisting that "spying is just like any other business"—an oddly reassuring sentiment *Pickup* would seem to have taken literally.[38]

In this sense the FBI and the reds in the movie double one another, as Rogin and Frank McConnell have pointed out, with the state security apparatus twinned by the equally bureaucratic communist spy bosses. Showing a meeting between the agitated Candy and the nervous Joey with his two handlers, Fuller depicts the calmly smoking pair of agents as bland, well-dressed, corporate types, not nefarious villains speaking with thick accents.[39] Even the way in which Fuller composes this scene suggests the

Manichaean mirroring of the Cold War, moving back and forth from tight close-ups of individual faces to a midshot illuminated by two starkly lit lamps symmetrically framing the quartet. As a paid agent for the communists, Joey falls into a slightly different category from his two bosses. He is less concerned with ideology than in trying to make a buck even as he seems in sympathy with the communists who hire him to deliver the microfilm. Constantly rendered in low-angle close-ups that highlight his profuse perspiring, Joey is a parody of sleazy, un-American cowardice, the objective correlative, it would seem, to Arthur Schlesinger's description in *The Vital Center* (1949) of communist totalitarianism as "pervert[ing] politics into something secret, sweaty and furtive."[40] But like everyone else in the film, he means business. Hence the irony of his initially duping Candy into thinking the celluloid in her purse holds urgent trade secrets, a "cutthroat" matter of "big business," he tells her. Similarly, the corporate and the personal become conflated in Moe's insistence that "everyone of them [pickpockets] has got his own trademark" with "his own way of doing things," at once a celebration of individual technique and a tacit admission that such individuality inevitably belongs to a larger proprietary economy marked by exclusive patents and trademarks.

Candy's position in that economy represents perhaps the most interesting case. Throughout the film she exhibits rather complex responses to the microfilm. After all, she (and we) initially experience the intimate theft of her wallet as an act of personal violation, a kind of rape that, judging by the expression on her face, Fuller would have us believe she unconsciously enjoys. Thinking it strictly a mercenary matter, as Joey has insisted, Candy therefore has no trouble trying to seduce or pay Skip into giving the microfilm back. No problem for a girl who has "been around," in Joey's phrase, a hooker on her way to becoming an ex-prostitute by the movie's end. When Skip disingenuously asks what is on the film, she invents an obvious lie about her "old lady" wanting pictures of her brother, a "war hero in Korea." The cold war comedy here is to mix up personal family values with national ones, the local with the global, as both Candy and Skip understand in their tense, erotically charged banter, with Skip responding, "How much is your brother worth?" Similarly, when Moe asks Candy what Skip took from her, she merely says "something personal," while Moe in a salacious but perhaps maternal turn then asks, "How personal?" Over and over again Fuller as a matter of fact links the stolen microfilm with sex, Candy at one point provocatively asking Skip, "How many times have you been caught with your hand where it doesn't belong?" Yet despite this somewhat crass association, the instant she hears from Skip that she has been dealing with communists, not businessmen, she suddenly and strangely gets insulted and slaps Skip in the face—the only moment in the entire movie that she matches in full frontal assault his own flagrant physical aggressions toward her. However jaded, Candy treats Skip's revelation as a kind of accusation; betraying her country, not her body, thus represents the true stain against her virtue.

So despite other characters' confusions between corporate, national, and personal motives, for Candy business (including sex) is clearly one thing, communism quite another. Her powerful reaction to the microfilm as containing state secrets distinguishes her from Skip, a man only out for himself, and aligns her closely with the values of the film's other woman, Moe, suggesting how gender is central for grasping *Pickup*'s cold war politics. Seeing how Skip is caught between two equally unsavory alternatives, feds and reds (one and the same, really), critics have struggled to articulate Fuller's vision of a third option. Focusing on the torrid passion that develops between Skip and Candy, McConnell in the 1970s found a kind of radical utopian solution in the couple's liberating sexuality, whose subversive energies, pace Norman O. Brown and Herbert Marcuse, serve to "abrogate the twin economies of Communism and capitalism both."[41] Surely McConnell's optimistic proposition that love is all you need is seriously undermined by the film's rather traditional ending, in which Candy suggests that she will make an honest man of Skip, the sort of normative heterosexual closure we find in almost every Hollywood romance of the period.[42] Rogin in his analysis offers a far darker assessment, admitting how *Pickup* was the only film during the Cold War that was complex enough to give the lie to Hollywood's patriotic pandering, but arguing how Fuller simply displaced such pieties onto a reactionary posture harkening back to nineteenth-century "predatory individualism," and nothing more.[43]

Here Rogin seems to have equated Fuller with his sadistic alter ego Skip, an easy-enough thing to do considering the self-conscious conflation between film and microfilm, director and professional thief, that I have been elaborating. Yet as a source of vital data in the movie, the microfilm Skip seizes is rivaled by another medium, Moe's little black book, in which she meticulously records her transactions with the police, as well as the names and addresses of all the lowlife criminals she interacts with. As she puts it, "I peddle information," unlike Skip, who steals it. And whereas Skip refuses to acknowledge any difference between his role as a pickpocket and the label traitor that Zara tries to pin on him, Moe for her part indignantly insists that earning a living as a stoolie is not the same as being an "informer." While a year later in his HUAC parable *On the Waterfront* (1954), Elia Kazan would try to make a virtue of naming names, for Moe selling out Skip to the FBI (but not to Joey) is less a virtue than an economic necessity. In a cold war climate in which "the *principle* of betrayal" was "a norm of good citizenship," as Mary McCarthy described life in the 1950s, Moe is attempting to survive and chart some course of integrity, although of course Fuller conveniently positions her heroic silence against the communists, not the FBI.[44]

As in *Key Largo*, an older woman of dubious social standing activates and actualizes the movie's morality.[45] It is the motherly, nurturing Moe, not Skip, who remains at the center of *Pickup*'s network of knowledge and secrecy, speeding up the detectives' old-fashioned and tedious review of thousands of criminal mug shots, earning a buck by bargaining hard with the police without giving them too much to go on, while still commemorating the "trademark" professionalism of criminals. From Moe's first appearance in the police station, Fuller's camera signals that she will be the film's focus of attention. The scene mainly consists of two mobile long takes. Kneeling to put down her battered briefcase (filled with ties she constantly tries to sell), Moe is initially given a close-up, followed quickly to a medium shot of her and Tiger. While Moe discusses the one issue that exposes her vulnerability, her wish for a fancy funeral, the camera moves in closely, capturing Moe's expressive face again and edging Tiger to the right margin of the frame. Her extended celebration of the art of picking pockets ("It's the technique") is matched by virtuoso camera movement, zooming in and out on Moe, sometimes with a tight close-up, sometimes framed between Tiger and Zara, but always with her in the center. In a subsequent long shot, with Moe still dominating the composition and Fuller still preferring a fluid, rotating camera to more conventional shot–reverse shot editing, her animated demonstration culminates in a declaration of truth ("I know") as she walks toward the back of the room, followed by the camera as if drawn by her thought process. Both men are rendered peripheral bystanders who can only witness and admire Moe's dramatic performance, and once Zara is ushered out by Tiger (in the same continuous take), Moe assumes prominence again in the foreground while writing down the names of possible suspects: it's the technique, indeed.

The scene of Moe's weary but defiant encounter with Joey (who is seeking to pay her for Skip's address) similarly works by establishing an intense identification between the tired old woman and the camera, which stays fixed on her at the center of the composition while Joey nervously paces to the left and right of her almost motionless figure propped up in bed, surrounded by ties hanging from the bed frame. Joey's sweaty pacing and darting eyes make us nervous, but the exhausted Moe stays still except for her pathetically quivering lips. At the close of their confrontation, there is a slow pan to the left onto a spinning phonograph record as it reaches the end of a sad French love lyric, right before we hear, but do not see, Moe get shot, as if the camera could not bear the sight of her death.

Before finally (and fatally) refusing to play ball with the communists, Moe has also encouraged Candy's growing love for Skip. As in her interactions with the law, here, too, she plays the role of a kind of information go-between or matchmaker driven by a curious mixture of intuition and calculation. Candy cannot say why she hates the reds, and Moe would seem to do only a bit better, remarking to Joey just before he kills her: "What do I know about Commies? Nothing. I know one thing—I just don't like them." Abandoning rationality for personal animus, here Moe would seem to be echoing (parodying?) American liberalism's notorious lack of ideological substance, such as Gary Cooper's famous HUAC testimony about Soviet influence in Hollywood: "From what I hear, I don't like it because it isn't on the level."[46]

Taking place in Moe's bedroom, a rare invocation of intimate domestic space in the movie, Moe's poignant resistance is *Pickup*'s most telling moment. Yet however visually compelling, this scene looks like a case of Fuller trying to have his cake and eat it too, rejecting communism while still refusing, like his antihero Skip, to commit to any countercollective formation such as "the American way." At her death Moe thus makes good on her earlier vow to Skip that "you've got to draw the line somewheres." Here again Moe's colorful rhetoric closely follows familiar cold war discourse: the battle lines still being drawn between North and South Korea, and Schlesinger's more philosophical question about internal security: "Is there not some point in advance of 'clear and present danger' where free society must draw the line if it is to preserve its own inner moral strength?"[47] But on what basis is that line being drawn? It is one thing for Moe to despise the cowardly "crumb" Joey, whom the camera continually marks as clammy and shifty-eyed. Yet to graft such individual dislike onto an entire group, while flaunting your ignorance of these persons, seems a rather dubious kind of politics, as if communism or capitalism were simply a matter of personal taste devoid of ideas. But unlike Skip's own brand of brutal individualism, Moe's works outward from private desire to take an interest in the wishes and ultimate well-being of others.

We can best gauge her distance from Skip by tracing the social geography of the film's various misfits. In her cover job selling ties, she takes pleasure in trying to match particular individuals with specific ties, which she calls "personality neckware," a business that acknowledges personal difference as inevitably part of a larger economic structure or system (a dollar is a dollar, or "the rising cost of pork and beans," as she says). Skip lives a liminal life in a shack on the outskirts of the city, and Candy is a kept woman living in an apartment apparently subsidized by Joey (and his communist paymasters). But Moe lives independently in the heart of New York City (above a tattoo parlor, no less). In this sense she may be more of a "solid citizen," as she half jokes to Candy, than she realizes in her struggle to adhere to a kind of cold war politics of personality apart but not entirely removed from the corporatist nation-state. She recognizes what Skip does not, that you have to live somewhere, dwell inside something bigger than yourself, if only to resist the pressures of the state. In the shadow of the Brooklyn Bridge, as Fuller visually reminds us, Skip's rundown waterside bait shack may have no electric lines to connect it to an urban power grid, but it does have an address ("66 South Street"). Although Moe, no "informer" she, is murdered for not divulging this particular fact, it is a secret, like all others, subject to public knowledge, specifically a slip of paper (another tiny text) that Joey eventually finds in Candy's purse, the original hiding place of the microfilm, we recall.

Moe's lone bourgeois indulgence (reflecting the screenplay's own sentimental indulgence) is to save up to buy a "private" cemetery plot on Long Island, so that she can finally become "exclusive," her own self-sufficient person, achieving a kind of dignity denied her in life. Such privacy bespeaks her desire for social approval. But to be private, for Moe, we understand, is to be dead. Fuller in effect grants her this dream of privacy, for she is not only Joey's sacrificial victim but the director's sad scapegoat as well, allowing us to emotionally savor Skip retrieving and rescuing her body from an anonymous grave in Potter's Field. Moe is the one character in the movie least concerned with the microfilm, having too many of her own secrets to keep, and yet it is she who must die for it. In the end the communists are thwarted and beaten to a pulp, and so the nation is saved (although the FBI is conspicuously absent), while Candy and Skip walk off together hand in hand, presumably to start a new life, in front of the policeman Tiger, more upset than satisfied, personally frustrated by his failure to put Skip back in jail where he belongs. But laid to rest, Moe remains *Pickup*'s most compelling alternative to both feds and reds, indeed an alternative to the miniaturized microfilm itself—a source of human intelligence whose scale we can easily comprehend.

Insofar as *Pickup on South Street* locates its politics of personality in the vulnerable body of Moe, it offers us a way out of the cold war standoff between the global ideologies of communism and capitalism that Fuller so openly despised and the selfish individualism of the pickpocket he professed to applaud. She is a citizen, neither patriot nor un-American. Her own boss and yet concerned about the well-being of others, the mother figure Moe is more intimate than the impersonal bureaucratic formations of reds and feds, but also more magnanimous than Skip, who thinks of himself as a purely private, pleasure-seeking monad accountable to nobody and nothing outside of himself. The information Moe picks up and dispenses also helps us put the microfilm in perspective. As a medium of desire, the microfilm, like the film *Pickup* itself, retains value only in relation to those who can assimilate its volatile abstractions into some kind of shared experience. To protect the film is to preserve that community— outcasts perhaps, but solid citizens no less.

Darkness Visible

"Ah, you folks American citizens?"—opening line of *Touch of Evil*, 1958

Pickup on South Street (1953) represents a fitting end for this book, explicitly returning us to those fears about domestic espionage that resonated so profoundly in *Confessions of a Nazi Spy* and *Stranger on the Third Floor*. Locating the crime thriller specifically in the context of cold war anticommunism, Sam Fuller's film foregrounds the continuity in uncanny political affect that I have been discussing throughout my study, from devious interlopers perceived to threaten national security to another sort of treacherous enemy boring from within following the end of the Second World War. But this similarity between prewar strangers lurking in the house and *Pickup*'s rendition of a state of emergency is also marked by difference, not only in regard to Fuller's skepticism about the efficacy of the government to combat subversion but also in terms of his inspired gendered recasting of the informer. Instead of a menacing, censoring father figure (e.g., Meng in *Stranger*), Fuller gives us a weary, nurturing, matronly soul (Moe) who insists that her sociable peddling of intelligence keeps her a loyal American, not a betrayer of either her country or her criminal cohorts.

By so removing conventional traces of Oedipal drama from his narrative, Fuller exposes and undermines a foundational feature common to many earlier noirs such as *Stranger* and *Double Indemnity*. Without these intimate Freudian dynamics, authoritarian structures like the FBI and the CPUSA seem more blandly bureaucratic than overtly sinister. Even though the Soviets already possessed the atomic bomb by 1949, as Agent Zara remarks to the pickpocket Skip, safeguarding weapons technology was clearly still a security concern in 1953. But the loss of military secrets in *Pickup* seems less pressing a threat than the loss of personality and personal freedom that the daily policing of subversives would entail. Moe's benign good nature, a perfect mixture of pathos and humor brilliantly played by Thelma Ritter, along with bad boy Skip's gleeful, cackling insolence (in Richard Widmark's manic performance), suggest a new sort of tongue-in-cheekiness for the noir thriller. *Pickup* thus points to a change in the tone and direction that the cycle would take in the 1950s, or at least a certain strain of it, as I will suggest by looking briefly here at a key trio of films spanning the decade: *Gun Crazy* (1950), *Kiss Me Deadly* (1955) and *Touch of Evil* (1958), the latter a dizzying blur of border crossings. At the same time that these transformations were largely intrinsic to noir as it grew prone to self-reflexive parody, they also closely corresponded to changes in cold war culture more broadly during the early years of the Eisenhower administration. The perceived danger of sedition began to recede, to be overshadowed by a more diffuse array of preoccupations and perturbations: juvenile delinquency, homosexuality, mass culture and conformity, race relations, civil defense, and so on.

Three political episodes that converged the year following the release of *Pickup* help us appreciate this shift in domestic security priorities. The year 1954 marks the passage of the Loss of Citizenship Act, which for the first time established the legal grounds for native-born members of the CPUSA to have their citizenship revoked—a punishment formerly reserved under the Constitution only for those convicted of treason. It appears that Informant T-10 (Ronald Reagan) finally got his wish. But the great irony, of course, is that by 1954 there were hardly any card-carrying members left in the CPUSA other than those on the FBI payroll, the party having been well-nigh destroyed by the ceaseless intimidation of McCarthy and HUAC.

This criminalization therefore largely proved an empty gesture. Thanks to McCarthy's sensational allegations, HUAC's investigative hearings of 1947 and 1951, and the Smith Act prosecutions of communist party leaders (1948), the damage was already done. By 1954, fear of widespread fifth-column infiltration at home, as opposed to fear of an atomic bomb dropped from above, would test even the most fanciful imagination. In the mid-1950s anticommunist feelings powerfully lingered, no doubt, but it was becoming more and more implausible to believe that a handful of homegrown "Reds" were taking their orders directly from Moscow. Only by continually insisting, increasingly against common sense, that these subversives were not "free agents" but merely Soviet lackeys, could they still be construed as grave dangers to the stability of the state.[1]

J. Edgar Hoover, in fact, consistently opposed such overt penalizing of native-born communists, arguing that turning them into criminals would simply drive the members underground, therefore making them more difficult for the FBI to track via its elaborate system of files. On this strategic matter, among many others, he began to break ranks with HUAC and McCarthy, leaving Senator Joe to twist in the wind, as they say, even though the FBI had been supplying him with information redacted from its files for years. When Congress during the army hearings of April 1954 began investigating McCarthy for his reckless accusations purporting to uncover communist infiltration in defense plants and the CIA, Hoover sided with Eisenhower and refused to support his former ally's claims.[2] In the wake of this riveting, televised spectacle, watched by a "jury" of millions, as McCarthy called the live audience, the Senate by the end of the year had officially censured the junior senator from Wisconsin, effectively ruining his career as a witch hunter. The result was double-edged. On the one hand, public hysteria about domestic communism, no longer so openly fueled by demagogic politicians, died down. But on the other hand, cold war liberals and moderates relieved by McCarthy's abrupt exit tended to give their unqualified trust to professional bureaucrats like Hoover on matters of national security; as a result, intelligence gathering (i.e., spying) on Americans grew unimpeded, with "subversive activity" now a convenient excuse for the bureau to monitor, with no congressional oversight, the private affairs of thousands of U.S. citizens. So while the CPUSA did not go underground, the FBI did.

Yet another important governmental action in May 1954 helped redirect domestic attention away from an internal red menace: the Supreme Court decision *Brown v. Board of Education* ruling against segregated schools. From the 1930s onward there was a convergence of interests and energies between the CPUSA and African Americans, with many black activists and union leaders assuming key roles in the party. What happened between the mid-1930s and the mid-1950s is a multifaceted story too complex to trace here, particularly the wartime and postwar disenchantment of some black intellectuals like Ralph Ellison.[3] But suffice it to say that by 1954 the burgeoning church-based civil rights movement was no longer so closely aligned with communism, even though the FBI continued to investigate (and fabricate) connections well into the 1960s. For most mainstream whites and blacks during the Eisenhower years, race was perceived as an autonomous issue, with its own contours and quandaries that ostensibly had little to do with anxieties over homeland security. For those who thought seriously about social problems, by the mid-1950s race relations had become a more pressing domestic concern than communism. Blacks were not enemy aliens who warranted expulsion but U.S. citizens, albeit second-class ones, and it was precisely their status as socially unequal that drove the decade's activism, as well as political resistance to change. Briefly discussed in my introduction, the Harlem jazz scene in *When Strangers Marry* (1944) suggests an early affinity between the blackness of noir and less figurative matters of race. But a decade later, noir's oblique pessimism would have little to do with the restlessness of Americans who were demanding to be more fully integrated into the national community.

As I have already indicated in the case of *Pickup*, this waning urgency over communist traitors would be registered by the profound irreverence in tone of certain important crime thrillers. Emerging from a culture in transition, these curious movies began refiguring precursor films of the previous decade, in effect offering a kind of self-conscious commentary on the form and content of noir itself. As early as 1950, with *Gun Crazy*, a complex self-mockery beyond mere farce starts to work its way into the cycle.[4] Originally released under the lurid title *Deadly Is the Female*, *Gun Crazy* is a remarkable movie, one of the greatest of films noirs, but also one of the funniest (a fact mostly lost on French intellectuals who adored its romanticism). "Goofy" and "noir" would not normally go together in the same sentence, but there is no better way to describe the film's male protagonist, Bart Tare (played by John Dall), from the little boy who freaks out at shooting a baby chick, to a teenage rebel with a fondness for guns, to an adult (well, sort of) falling hard for a pistol-packing seductress who introduces this disaffected vet to a criminal life on the run. Part of his goofiness may be attributed to Dall's silly habit of inappropriately flashing a toothy grin in the midst of his supposed angst. But the movie's entire logic—from the acting to the mise-en-scène (partially set in a traveling sideshow) to its hyperkinetic narrative to its daring visual style—is shot through with an exaggerated, exuberant sense of the carnivalesque. Bart's childhood gun fetish is clearly a pop psychology burlesque of Freud and the phallus, while the courtroom scene in which the teenager is somberly sentenced to reform school mocks the juvenile delinquent panic that had begun to spread soon after the end of the war.[5]

Commenting on the movie's baby chick killing, jokingly presented as a sort of primal scene that purports to explain and disclose all there is to know about Bart's anguished psyche, James Naremore remarks that the dead bird "looks like something that had been lying around the property department for weeks."[6] But this seems to me precisely the point: the film does not try to disguise its low-budget artifice, instead continually calling attention to it. Otherwise why gratuitously insert an extreme close-up of something that looks so fake? To assume that the laughter provoked by *Gun Crazy* today is "unintended" or "unwanted," as Naremore asserts more than once, is to underestimate the deliberate shrewdness of the director Joseph H. Lewis and of the uncredited coscreenwriter Dalton Trumbo, who shortly after completing the script was blacklisted and imprisoned, and who after his release in 1951 left for Mexico with his family in self-imposed exile.[7] Certainly earlier noirs sometimes had a staged look about them, especially those by European-trained directors like Robert Siodmak and Edgar Ulmer, accustomed to filming in highly controlled studio settings. The initial diner sequence of Siodmak's *The Killers* (1946), for example, is noteworthy for its shadowy theatricality, akin to an Edward Hopper painting.

But *The Killers* feels positively like cinema vérité in comparison to the first scene in *Gun Crazy*, featuring a dark street, rainy and empty, illuminated by a sign predictably flashing "HOTEL." This opening riffs on the visual dynamism of prior noirs such as *Detour* (1945), *The Killers*, and *Out of the Past* (1947), which each open with road scenes shot through the windshield of the interiors of speeding cars (so that the window functions as a sort of screen for the audience), a technique perfected to stunning effect later in *Gun Crazy*. But Lewis chooses to begin his film more statically by having the camera placed on the inside of a store window looking out at the iconic combination of wet pavement and neon. Starting with the opening credits, this inert composition makes us aware that we are watching a kind of show filled with props, whose fourth wall will suddenly, surprisingly be shattered when the teenager Bart breaks the window with a rock (an assault aimed directly at us) to steal his fetishized gun, only then to run away and fall (literally) at the feet of the law (yet another familiar noir trope), but this time figured less ominously as a concerned neighborhood cop. Set in a grassy, fog-filled marsh, the ending of the film appears even more unnatural, as if the smoke machine Ulmer used in *Detour* to cheaply conjure up New York City's Riverside Drive had been transplanted to some unspecified wilds and left on high for five years. Beginning with a studio-set noir city street, and fatally closing, like *The Asphalt Jungle* (1950), with an ostensible return to nature or innocence, a weird bog built for two that looks like something out of a cheesy Japanese science fiction or horror movie, *Gun Crazy* from start to finish invites us to enjoy the contrivance of its stylized design (see figures 21–22).

The parodic tendencies of the film are most pronounced in relation to matters of identity. From *Double Indemnity* (1944), where Walter Neff pretends on the train to be his lover's disabled husband, to *Detour*, where the hapless Al Roberts steals a dead man's clothes, papers, car, and father, to *Border Incident* (1949), where a government agent goes undercover to pose as a criminal, film noir, as many have noted, obsessively probes the unstable foundations of American selfhood. *Gun Crazy* self-consciously transforms this serious preoccupation into children's role play or make-believe. The female lead, Annie Laurie Star (Peggy Cummins), is an amalgamation of two legendary American women, the Buffalo Bill sharp-shooter Annie Oakley and the gangster Bonnie Parker, with a British background thrown in for good measure. During their wild robbing and shooting spree across the country, she leads Bart in a game of dress up, as he masquerades as a cowboy, a soldier, and, most improbable of all, a respectable office worker employed by a meat-packing plant. (After robbing the plant the couple runs through rows of hanging carcasses.) When Bart confesses at one point that he fears he is living a terrible "nightmare,"

21–22 Stylized artifice from start to finish, from *Gun Crazy*

invoking noir's obligatory dark feeling, here made all too painfully explicit, Annie reminds him that when he wakes up with her sexy body beside him every morning, she is "real" and belongs to him. While on the bad trip that is America, Annie realizes, you might as well have some fun along the way. A dreamscape that emerges from flimsy studio sets, endless highways, and a couple of alienated outcasts wearing grown-up costumes, noir has been converted into sheer mannerism or attitude emptied of affect, with the possible exception of the emotion seemingly least likely to be found in these movies, true love.

As the film's original title suggests, reinforced by the couple's over-the-top role play, it is the performance of gender that drives *Gun Crazy*'s extravagant display of style for style's sake. Annie exhibits all the well-worn character traits of the stereotypical femme fatale—she is alluring, greedy, treacherous, venal, toxic. But she embraces these clichés with such joyful abandon that her turn as a castrating bitch becomes a lark, while Bart for his part plays the emasculated, manipulated noir sap or sucker more as an endearing schlub than as an embittered masochist. The odd result is that when the two profess their adoration in that fog-shrouded swamp at the end of the movie, before he shoots her and is in turn gunned down by police, something touching lingers that goes against everything we have conventionally been taught to think about film noir. Declaring that "I wouldn't have it any other way," Bart's final affirmation certainly has lethal consequences, but it lacks the grim fatality that marks a precursor like *Out of the Past*. Equally surprising, Annie's earlier decision to stick with her man over the money (a love scene played out between two departing convertibles) dramatically swerves from the underlying logic of betrayal so exquisitely plotted in *Double Indemnity* and other crime movies of the 1940s that followed in its wake.

Drastically undermining audience expectations, giving us a loyal relationship rather than a mutually treacherous one, *Gun Crazy* in effect sets us up by sending up the noir cycle itself. Against the objection that noir was a critical construct after the fact that should not be accorded the status of a cinematic genre, we have the evidence of a film like *Gun Crazy*, whose thrills depended on viewers at once recognizing its formulaic visual and thematic elements (dark rainy streets, titled camera angles, aimless war veteran, aggressive siren, pat Freudianism, and so on), while being shocked by its high-spirited exaggeration or deviation from these conventions. Audiences and reviewers at the time may have found the movie more baffling than comic, but from the retrospect of half a century, *Gun Crazy*'s postmodern tone of pastiche is unmistakable.[8]

In *Kiss Me Deadly*, the director Robert Aldrich and the screenwriter I. A. Bezzerides push this sort of playful pastiche to the verge of absurdity. The genius of the movie is that it consistently refuses to take itself seriously at the same time that it succeeds in whipping up its viewers into an ever-escalating state of anxiety and confusion. Instead of the Brechtian estrangement effects that mark pivotal moments in *Gun Crazy*, *Kiss Me Deadly*'s politics depends less on carnivalesque excitement than on dread: a pervasive fear all the more unnerving for being detached from any clear-cut source of menace. There is a fascinating photograph of Aldrich taken in 1956 on the set of his war movie *Attack!*, in which he holds a copy of Raymond Borde and Etienne Chaumeton's pioneering book, *Panorama du film noir américain*, published in 1955, the same year that *Kiss Me Deadly* was released.[9] While not exactly a smoking gun because of that one year differential, the photo clearly belies the common misconception that noir was a concept unknown to Hollywood practitioners until Paul Schrader introduced it in his seminal essay of 1972.

I am less interested here in claiming direct influence between critics and the filmmaker than in appreciating how ten years after French intellectuals coined the term in response to a cluster of U.S. motion pictures screened right after the war, the first study of these movies quickly found its way back across the Atlantic in the grasp of an American director, who may not have understood a word of French but certainly could judge a book by its cover, especially one that announced itself with the bold word NOIR, in capital letters (see figure 23). Looking more carefully at the photograph, we note that the dust jacket features a close-up of an intense, staring Widmark lighting a cigarette, a still from his stunning turn as a beleaguered, petty con man in *Night and the City* (1950). By design the adjective *américain* even manages to inch its way across the actor's forehead. And so in a kind of *mise en abyme*, we have a film of 1950 about an American abroad (in London) covered by two French authors, whose book, tilted at a crazy noir angle, is held in the hands of a Hollywood director captured posing (head also tilted) alongside a movie camera. And would it be too much to detect a slight, enigmatic smile on Aldrich's lips? Corresponding to this transnational circulation (chronologically 1950, 1955, 1956), we also have a succession of widening frames: picture (Widmark), text (*Panorama du film noir américain*), and picture (Aldrich, who is self-consciously identified as a maker of moving images).

As in the case of the post-Occupation French recognition and naming of film noir in 1946, here, too, a decade later we see on display in this photograph a perfect instance of what Jacques Rancière calls a regime of visibility—a particular distribution of the sensible by which intelligibility emerges (in both senses of the word *sense*) via an ongoing exchange between words and images.[10] Rather than assume critical discourse as secondary to the autonomous work of art, it helps constitute the picture itself. That is what I mean by calling attention to the profoundly parodic

23 A regime of visibility: Robert Aldrich grasps French Hollywood cinephilia

inclinations of certain movies of the 1950s, which explicitly come to apprehend and redefine film noir as a kind of metacommentary about noir. A passage in Borde and Chaumeton spells out how this metacommentary specifically works for *Kiss Me Deadly*. Had Aldrich been able to read the French book in his hands, at the end of a chapter titled "Toward a Definition of Film Noir," he would have encountered this summary: "It is easy to come to a conclusion: the moral ambivalence, criminal violence, and contradictory complexity of the situations and motives all combine to give the public a shared feeling of anguish or insecurity, which is the identifying sign of film noir at this time. All the works in this series exhibit a consistency of an emotional sort; *namely, the state of tension created in the spectators by the disappearance of their psychological bearings.* The vocation of film noir has been to create a *specific sense of malaise.*"[11]

Shortly I will examine that specific malaise, but for now I simply want to point our how this account of noir's "vocation" precisely describes Aldrich's film. The French book, in fact, reads (in slightly reversed chronology) like a programmatic blueprint for the making of the movie. Stripping the narrative of coherence beyond a very loose quest romance plot that finally does not add up and draining characters of psychological complexity or points of identification, so that they mostly simply pop in and out of the movie as recognizable but slightly warped Hollywood caricatures (assorted tough guys, wanton women, a grizzled boxing manager, etc.), the filmmakers leave us with as series of visually arresting,

largely self-contained vignettes crafted to maximize feelings of disorientation. An early scene is exemplary. Suspecting that some hostile intruder
is lying in wait for him, the private detective Mike Hammer (played
by Ralph Meeker) nervously tiptoes from room to room in his own apartment, while on the soundtrack high-pitched flute trills heighten our tension. As he cautiously turns one corner after another, he finally encounters . . . nobody. Yet beyond the anticlimax of an empty home, filled now
with nothing but dread, the movie camera's fluid tracking of Hammer as
he traverses domestic space reveals something interesting in the mise-en-
scène: a large television console in the corner of the living room, modern
art hanging in the bedroom, and (in a nod to *Double Indemnity*'s Dictaphone) a tape machine on the wall set up to record phone messages. How
cool, my students invariably exclaim, a reaction that presumably would
have been even stronger for 1950s audiences unaccustomed to such technology. At the same time that the film constantly stirs us into a stew of
anxiety, then, it also calls attention to its glamorous surfaces and objects,
things associated most often with the protagonist Hammer; it is this
strange, seemingly impossible mixture of coolness and mounting panic
that drives the movie and makes it so striking a gloss on noir itself.

In the "Postface" to their book Borde and Chaumeton call *Kiss Me
Deadly* "a fascinating and somber" conclusion to the "social critique of the
United States" that they have defined as the cycle's primary impetus.[12] By
virtue of a similarity of plots (the search for a mysterious treasure), they
remark how the movie resembles its precursor *The Maltese Falcon* (1941),
but I think *Out of the Past* offers a perhaps more interesting point of
comparison. In both films we get a detective with a hard, impassive exterior, at once bewildered, framed, and vulnerable to the wiles of duplicitous
women and yet apparently in perfect self-control, at ease in a wide range
of social settings, from opulent gangster mansions to African American
nightclubs. *Kiss Me Deadly* even echoes *Out of the Past*'s Harlem scene by
showing us, a bit gratuitously, how Hammer seeks solace in a black club in
Los Angeles—another curious blending of raw emotion, this time agitation and grief at the death of his Greek friend Nick, combined with a too-
insistent hipness, as the black bartender gives us three choice pieces of
slang ("beat," "lean," "wasted") when one would do. While such coolness
here and elsewhere is clearly associated with race, it is more consistently
linked throughout the movie to commodities and consumerism. In *Out of*

the Past, Jeff Bailey (Robert Mitchum) is admired for what he does and says, not for what he wears (a rumpled trench coat), drives (an old station wagon), or the décor of his home (which we never even see). But Hammer's smooth attitude depends on and is measured by dress, "va-va-voom" sports cars, and fashionable furnishings, a self-absorbed showiness that the waif Christina Bailey (note the last name, played by Cloris Leachman) chides him for early on in the film. Calling him a narcissist who loves only himself, she quotes for good measure the feminist philosopher Simone de Beauvoir's *The Second Sex* (first published in English in 1953): this is yet another way that French intellectualism insinuates itself into what otherwise seems to be a very American panorama.[13]

There is a shorthand explanation for this change from iterations of hard-boiled masculinity in 1947 (think Bogart as well as Mitchum) to a more exhibitionist brand in the mid-1950s: *Playboy*, a magazine founded in 1953, that pioneered male consumerism. At once shaped by changing gender roles and more actively shaping those very roles and values, *Playboy* in the 1950s encouraged American men, especially bachelors, to escape the oppressive workplace (recall *Double Indemnity*) in order to assume some dominion over domestic space, a traditionally feminine realm defined mainly by the acquisition of commodities. A model and guide for an emergent new taste, *Playboy* helps us understand why and how an obvious philistine like Hammer would have such classy abstract paintings in his apartment, which is laid out along the lines of an enticing magazine photo spread educating its readers/lookers about how to furnish and arrange themselves.[14]

So linking 1950s masculinity with a rampant materialism, *Kiss Me Deadly* ups the stakes by signaling modern art's complicity in all this. As if to anticipate, wryly, Naremore's influential thesis arguing for film noir as combining high modernism with a tough criminal sensibility, *Kiss Me Deadly* turns the detective into a literary exegete trying to interpret a Christina Rossetti poem; features classical music (self-consciously identified as such) played on radios, which also broadcast Nat King Cole blues, horse races, and boxing matches; introduces an opera singer who alludes to the atomic riddle at the heart of the mystery (what is both big and small?); and includes a collector of modern art, one Mr. Mist, whose gallery figures prominently near the end of the movie.[15] These latter two figures, the singer and the collector, are treated rather badly by the sadist Hammer, who grows increasingly cruel and thuggish in his single-minded quest for the treasure, snapping the singer's cherished recording of the maestro Caruso and slapping Mist senseless—except that he is already senseless, having frantically downed a sleeping potion in anticipation of Hammer's beating.

As this last example underscores, brutal inquisition methods on all sides of the quest repeatedly fail in *Kiss Me Deadly* to divulge any useful information. To make matters even stranger, Mist's potion was prescribed by the movie's supposed master villain, the nefarious Dr. Soberin (with a name like that, how can we take him seriously?). Soberin (Albert Dekker) has a pretentious habit of spouting mythological and biblical allusions, even after he has been shot by his femme fatale associate, Gabrielle (Gaby Rodgers), a "Pandora," as Soberin dubs her, who simply wants to know "what's in the box." Getting one in the belly at close range, Soberin continues to pontificate about Cerberus guarding the gates of hell, but no longer with a straight face. Up to this scene, our view of the story's nemesis has been confined to his shoes, so any look at his face is most welcome, even if while dying. Soberin's twisted demeanor only reflects a mildly unpleasant surprise, as if he had just eaten a bit of spoiled food, like the key that Christina, tortured by this evil man, earlier swallowed to preserve her secret. And in a few minutes, with the head of Medusa exposed for all to see, so Soberin says, the world will be blown to smithereens.

This entire lineup of modernist tropes (existentialism, poetry, music, painting, mythological quest romance, apocalypse) constitutes the narrative and thematic backbone of *Kiss Me Deadly*. But these tropes are red herrings, false clues that ultimately reveal little about the case of the glowing radioactive Whatzit that so captivates Hammer. The whole movie functions as a kind of undoing of detection; in contrast to Moe's intelligence in the companion nuclear noir *Pickup*, we are constantly reminded of Hammer's lack thereof. Given the crucial role that art seems to play in *Kiss Me Deadly* as the ostensible grounds of intelligence, the implication is that modernism itself has become commodified into a series of hollow gestures—mere affectation drained of any affect beyond fear. To put it another way, the film generates more sensation than sense. While Naremore sees noir as fusing high and low culture, and while Rancière generally has described the relation between high and low in "political art" as a kind of "border crossing," *Kiss Me Deadly* more radically pulps modernism into a hash, leaving little meaningful but a residue of disturbing uncertainty.[16] In a similar vein, we note how the threat of atomic annihilation is overtly presented to Hammer by his cop friend Pat (Wesley Addy) as a hodge-podge of signifiers, words like *Trinity* and *Manhattan Project* that are nothing but a "bunch of letters scrambled together," the lieutenant admits. So, too, when Sorberin drugs Hammer with the truth serum sodium pentothal, a communist brainwashing technique that soon after the Korean War gained press attention in the United States. Expecting intimate access to Hammer's "subconscious," Freudian or otherwise, Soberin instead only gets some nonsensical mumblings.

The detective's gibberish under interrogation is perhaps the film's most cunning comment on itself. And yet *Kiss Me Deadly* is more than an elaborate joke at the expense of modernism insofar as it manages to keep its viewers on edge, plunged into the movie's chaos, rather than put off by it. Here I would recall Borde's and Chaumeton's notion of film noir depending on a *"specific sense of malaise,"* but one that the Frenchmen seem too arch to pinpoint. That noir malaise, I have been contending throughout this study, centers in many cases on matters of citizenship, the question of who belongs in the United States and who does not. These cold war films are fueled by anxiety attached to detecting and casting out enemy subversives, whose un-American crimes might lurk at the level of thought, as antisedition measures such as the Smith Act proposed. But what happens when such dark feelings can no longer be linked to any recognizable object of malignancy at all? While a noir from the 1950s like *Pickup* evacuates communism of all ideological content in favor of a politics of preference ("I just don't like them"), at least we have some cowardly, sweaty figures on screen held up in tongue-in-cheek derision. *Kiss Me Deadly*, on the other hand, gives us almost nothing: Soberin remains only a stentorian voice for most of the narrative, a mere shadow (a pair of shoes, more accurately) whose allegiances are unclear—no Soviet agent, he. All we learn in the end is that he plans to take the radioactive treasure out of the country to sell it to the highest bidder, destination unknown, although we can note a tourist poster of Mexico hanging on the wall during his final confrontation with Gabrielle. And while this duplicitous femme fatale is the one who actually opens the deadly box to loose destruction on the world, her gesture is portrayed as more haphazard than demonic, in keeping with the movie's refusal to solve the mystery by assigning culpability to anyone besides a paranoiac "they."

If Americans could no longer take seriously the danger posed by domestic communists in their midst, the primary thing left to fear was the bomb itself, which *Kiss Me Deadly* progressively equates with the spreading terror about it. In other words, radioactive contagion and social panic turn out to be one and the same in the movie's representation. This is the film's specific noir malaise: civil defense. By the middle of the decade, the main security problem facing the country was not espionage but how to control citizens' responses to the threat of nuclear assault, a public hysteria that was potentially as damaging as an attack. Assuming Americans to be "frivolous, superficial, and selfish" (think Hammer), dedicated to materialist pleasure in the aftermath of the Second World War, defense strategists sought to counteract these irresponsible tendencies by building a kind of national consensus or resolve that required the banishment of feelings of dread. To give in to such terror would lead to the breakdown of the social order and to the dissolution of all moral restraint, these specialists theorized in hypothetical scenario after scenario. Addressing "the problem of panic," as it was called, meant convincing Americans that a nuclear attack could be survived with the proper preparation and practice, as well as with the appropriate mental attitude—what cold war cultural historians Guy Oakes and Andrew Grossman have dubbed "public emotion management," a system or "strategy for the mobilization, administration, discipline, and control of emotional life." Cutting panic down to size entailed a process of "internalization—transposing the nuclear threat from the domain of politics to that of psychology, from the sphere of public policy to that of private therapy."[17]

This was something new. In preparation for the U.S. entrance into the First World War, President Wilson had established the Creel Committee on Public Information to disseminate official pro-war propaganda, and in response to this enormously effective state educational apparatus, writers like Walter Lippmann and Edward Bernays during the 1920s began to examine how the government, news media, and private enterprise decisively shaped public opinion, for better or worse.[18] But in the wake of the Second World War, government propaganda aimed less at manufacturing consent about the enemy (agreement was clear enough during the Cold

War) than at managing more intimate feelings of vulnerability. *Kiss Me Deadly* makes a mockery of this psychologized civil defense, drawing on the counteraffect of noir insecurity to amplify and expand wild emotions of panic instead of trying to control them. Unhinged from any clear objects or causes, these ugly feelings of dread in the movie continually grow more pervasive and overwhelming, until, in the end, the very terror of annihilation effectively triggers that annihilation.

Whereas *Kiss Me Deadly* ends with an explosion, *Touch of Evil* famously begins with one. What is left of film noir after Welles's bomb goes off is an open question. In their "Postface" added in 1979 (twenty-five years after their book was initially published), Borde and Chaumeton call Aldrich's film of 1956 "in every respect" for the noir cycle "a point of no return."[19] Presumably the Frenchmen were not interested in retrospectively thinking about *Touch of Evil*, and who could blame them? A failure at the U.S. box office when released (but well regarded in Paris at the time), the film has subsequently garnered much academic attention. Extending well beyond cinema studies, this scholarship has focused on Welles's complex rendering of a state of emergency or exception marked by the uncertain borderline between the United States and Mexico, which becomes the site of an apparent contestation between justice and law, with the bloated, dissolute cop Hank Quinlan (played by Welles), on the one side, and the stalwart government official Mike or Miguel Vargas (played by Charlton Heston), on the other. As his dual first names suggest, Vargas's transnational status has occasioned considerable perplexity, compounded by Heston's perfect English, poor Spanish, and racialized brown face. My aim here is not to reiterate or revisit this impressive array of critics, which includes the likes of Homi Bhabha, Michael Denning, and Donald Pease, but rather to briefly examine the film's peculiar affect, a question central to my understanding of noir in general.[20]

For a variety of reasons, the tone of *Touch of Evil* is much more difficult to decipher than that of other noirs from the 1950s such as *Gun Crazy*, *Pickup*, and *Kiss Me Deadly*. In these other crime films we can detect a strong current of parody that not only mocks certain cinematic conventions and expectations but particular and dominant American mores as well. To the degree that *Touch of Evil* obsessively scrambles geopolitical and cultural boundaries, my concern throughout this study, it serves as a highly self-conscious culmination of the entire cycle of films from *Stranger on the Third Floor* on—in effect becoming noir's epitaph, as it has some-times been described. Yet if Welles aimed to put a nail into noir's coffin, what sort of nail was it?

Unlike Lewis, Fuller, or Aldrich, Welles seems to take himself and his film quite seriously in a number of ways. Buying into the plot of detection, he is careful to include clues such as Quinlan's missing cane, an incriminat-ing piece of evidence that Welles takes the trouble to visually foreshadow by giving us a sign (literally) as Quinlan leaves the crime scene without it, so that the childlike Pete Menzies (more son than partner, played impec-cably by Joseph Calleia) must eventually acknowledge that his beloved hero is guilty of Joe Grandi's (Akim Tamiroff) strangulation. Welles even works in a psychologically compelling, traumatic back story (the stran-gling of Quinlan's wife by an unpunished "half-breed") to explain Quin-lan's deep racism and corruption. At that thematic level, Welles deploys his Freud with a similar gravity, opening the narrative with the violent death of the father that triggers all events to follow. The movie's dialogue, between its main characters at least, seems equally freighted with import. While *Gun Crazy* gives us lines such as Bart's to Annie, "We go together, like guns and ammunition," Vargas incisively shares with Quinlan the insight that being a policeman enforcing the law is a tough business, "only easy in a police state."

The film can also profitably be read allegorically as a kind of autobio-graphical last stand, with Welles the auteur intent on casting the film to contemplate his botched career in relation to cinema history more generally.[21] His poignant ruin is self-embodied by the obese, debauched Quinlan: "You're a mess, honey"; and, "your future is all used up." At the same time his nostalgia for the medium is figured in the enigmatic gypsy, Tana, played by Marlene Dietrich in a soft-focus homage to her early femme fatale turn in *Blue Angel* (1930), who breaks this bad news and has the last word in the movie. Most pointedly, Welles expresses his disdain for the Hollywood studio system by wonderfully miscasting Vargas, played straight by a clueless, self-righteous Heston, still fresh from his triumphant performance as Moses in another cold war epic, *The Ten Commandments* (1956). And certainly the movie's visual style is in perfect keeping with what we have come to expect from noir: dark, oppressive, claustrophobic, and confusing, a disorientation that matches our inability to track which side of the border we are on at any given moment in the film.

All this bespeaks a certain ambition or pretension (to be a bit less generous) that would appear to demand our most sophisticated herme- neutic skills just to keep up. And yet . . . there is something funny going on here, as Uncle Joe Grandi might say. It is not just that Grandi (an "Ameri- can citizen," he insists) is one of a number of strange, clownish figures whose presence in the narrative tends to undermine its solemnity.[22] Nor is it that Quinlan's suspicion about the guilt of the bomber Sanchez (Victor Millan), despite his framing by the police, turns out to be correct. An echo of the little man inside that inspires Keyes in *Double Indemnity*, Quinlan's intuitive hunch in the end wins out over the ostensibly more rational detective methods employed by his foil Vargas. Nor it is that Vargas himself is exposed as something of a fraud, neglecting his (white Ameri- can) bride, Susan (Janet Leigh), and resorting to the same sort of sur- veillance tactics to catch Quinlan that he had previously associated with a police state. Nor even that his mixed-up transnational markings (accent, dress, attitude, moral certitude, brown face) make little sense. All of these seeming baffling anomalies can and have been explained (most persua- sively by Pease) in terms of the movie's headlong plunge into a state of emergency that puts law outside the law. Extravagantly crisscrossing na- tional boundaries to test the limits of citizenship under this state of excep- tion, Welles caps two decades of American film noir.

But unlike *Stranger*, or Welles's own *Citizen Kane* (1941), for that matter, the noir nightmare of *Touch of Evil* appears at once too private, directed by and for Welles himself, and too Grandi-ose. I assume that pun is not mine but Welles's, and that is part of the issue: the film's possibilities of inter- pretation seem endless, and yet Welles appears to have self-consciously preempted every single one of them by working them all into the narrative itself, barraging us with sign after sign in quick succession. As the twitchy country hick/hotel night man (Dennis Weaver) keeps moronically repeat- ing, "they got another thing coming," reducing powerful feelings of resent- ment and paranoia to mere imbecility. To take everything in the movie seriously, scholars risk ending up looking a little like Heston, whose recti- tude renders him oblivious to the absurdity taking place around him, Mexican lesbian druggie hoodlums in drag included (in a memorable cameo by Mercedes McCambridge). Welles may be heavily invested in the meaning of his production, but we match him at our peril.

Certainly prior parodic noirs like *Kiss Me Deadly* offered mixed messages (Hammer is cool; Hammer is a malicious jerk), not to mention violent mood swings, from farcical to frightening. But these movies nonetheless manage to sustain a consistent core of the political uncanny (intruders in the house), despite or because of abandoning coherent plotting. But the suffocating self-consciousness of *Touch of Evil* tends to turn feelings of dispossession into a more flamboyant creepiness. When Susan, abed in the sleazy Hotel Ritz, for instance, slowly rouses from her drug-addled delirium (induced by sodium pentothal, as in *Kiss Me Deadly*) to meet the strangled Grandi's bug-eyed look (see figure 24), upside down, tongue protruding, the sensation is less terrifying or alienating than grotesque, a masklike effect accompanied by garish Afro-Cuban jazz (too loud for the diegesis) and blinking neon lights, heightened by the dead man's extreme eye makeup and missing toupee—his "rug," as one his nephews has previously referred to it in typically incongruous slang. This image may be quoting un-American Peter Lorre near the end of *Stranger*, but what a difference. By so monumentalizing noir, trying to capture and encompass all of its history, themes, and visual tropes in a single movie, Welles manages to blow up its predominant sensibility. Making its darkness all too visible (to indulge in a literary pretension of my own), straining always to keep another exaggerated thing coming, *Touch of Evil* can assure only that film noir will go out with a bang.

24 Turning noir on its head, from *Touch of Evil*

Notes

Introduction

1 Quoted in Whitfield, *The Culture of the Cold War*, 142.

2 Reagan's complete HUAC testimony is reprinted in Bentley, *Thirty Years of Treason*, 143–47; the quotation here occurs on 146–47. For every unfriendly witness who was asked if he or she had ever been a member of the Communist Party, a friendly witness was asked if such membership should be outlawed.

3 See especially Navasky, *Naming Names*; and Ceplair and Englund, *The Inquisition in Hollywood*. For an excellent overview of the year 1947 in film that emphasizes the anxieties both embodied and engendered by HUAC, see Williams, "1947."

4 J. Edgar Hoover, HUAC testimony, March 26, 1947, quoted in Schrecker, *The Age of McCarthyism*, 127–33.

5 The term *fifth column* was introduced in a Spanish radio address in 1936 by Emilo Mola, a rebel (pro-Franco) general who called for a fifth column of support in Madrid to aid his four military columns laying siege to the city from without. The fifth-column betrayal of Spanish loyalists by a high-ranking rebel infiltrator plays a central part in the first Hollywood narrative made about the Spanish Civil War, *Blockade* (1938), with a rather muddled screenplay by John Howard Lawson.

6 For attempting to fuse politics with affect, two pioneering cultural studies of the period deserve special mention, although my emphasis on the uncanny aspects of citizenship differs from theirs: Polan, *Power and Paranoia*; and Graebner, *The Age of Doubt*. Both studies are noteworthy

for treating the 1940s as a single, unbroken decade, rather than one divided by the Second World War, as is customary.

7 Dimock, "Aesthetics at the Limits of the Nation," 538. Dimock does not explain why she finds the word so striking, which in my reading is remarkable precisely because of its evocation of the uncanny. Lest the term seem a strictly exceptional American coinage, I should point out that in an unread statement presented to HUAC by Bertolt Brecht during his testimony in 1947, the playwright described how in the Weimar Germany of the late 1920s certain "humanist, socialist, even Christian ideas were called 'undeutsch' (un-German), a word which I hardly can think of without Hitler's wolfish intonation." See Bentley, *Thirty Years of Treason*, 221.

8 For an interesting linguistic analysis of prefixes such as *un-* that frequently modify a positively valued adjective, but not a negatively valued one, see Zimmer, *Affixal Negation in English and Other Languages*.

9 Truman, quoted in Whitfield, *The Culture of the Cold War*, 124. During one of the most intellectually substantial exchanges in the entire course of the HUAC hearings, the American Civil Liberties Union (ACLU) lawyer Arthur Garfield Hays in 1948 vigorously attacked plans to outlaw the CPUSA, sarcastically proposing a bill to "appropriate $10,000,000,000 to set up a commission to invent a mental reading machine which when applied will say 'Communist' when the individual is not a loyal citizen." Hays also, when mentioning HUAC itself, dropped the key word *activities* to mockingly refer to HUC, "the un-American Committee." Quoted in Bentley, *Thirty Years of Treason*, 252.

10 Quoted in Goodman, *The Committee*, 14.

11 See Theoharis, *Spying on Americans*. For more about these emergency measures and about how they engage the earliest film noir, see chapter 1. These presidential directives, FBI memos, and dozens of other documents are usefully collected and reprinted in Theoharis, *The Truman Presidency*. The term *thought control* is contemporaneous, used both by anticommunists like Hoover to describe communist methods and by liberals to describe anticommunist tactics. For a remarkable collection of essays, the proceedings of a conference held in Los Angeles in July 1947 organized by progressives such as John Howard Lawson and Adrian Scott (both subsequently part of the Hollywood Ten) in anticipation of HUAC's October hearings into communist infiltration, see Salemson, *Thought Control in the U.S.A.*.

12 For a discussion of Freud's essay on the uncanny in relation to U.S. citizenship, see Wald, *Constituting Americans*, 5–7; and, more generally, Arnold, *Homelessness, Citizenship, and Identity*.

13 Freud, "The Uncanny," 17:226.

14 Ibid., 17:222, 226.

15 The best book on wartime "enemy aliens" is MacDonnell, *Insidious Foes*. As MacDonnell points out, fears of domestic communist subversion surface earlier

during the Red Scare Palmer Raids of 1919 and harken back to nineteenth-century nativist hostility toward foreigners. See, for instance, Higham, *Strangers in the Land*; and Bennett, *The Party of Fear*.

16 The phrase *constitutional birthright* comes from Earl Warren's dissent in *Perez v. Brown* (1958), where he drew on the Fourteenth Amendment to conclude: "United States citizenship is thus the constitutional birthright of every person born in this country." From the beginnings of the United States, the native born were automatically citizens, and most foreigners immigrating from abroad gained citizenship through a process of naturalization, although of course immigrants could be excluded (such as the Chinese in the 1880s) and unwanted or illegal aliens deported. Once gaining U.S. citizenship, persons rarely lost that status, unless they voluntarily renounced their nationality or it was subsequently discovered that their citizenship had been procured by fraud.

17 Aleinikoff, "Theories of Loss of Citizenship," 1477. Examining the Immigration and Nationality Act (also known as the McCarran-Walter Act) of 1952, passed by Congress over President Truman's veto, Siobhan B. Somerville points to the Cold War's refiguring of U.S. citizenship, arguing that "when the explicit language of race disappeared, the underlying fantasy of national purification—an unadulterated Americanness—was articulated instead through the discourse of sexuality," although she misses an opportunity to discuss at length the emergent discourse of "un-Americanness" more generally driving cold war immigration reform. See Siobhan B. Somerville, "Queer Loving," 355. Defending the 1952 act against its critics (including the CPUSA and President Truman), its coauthor Senator McCarran insisted that "we have in the United States today hard-core, indigestible blocs which have not become integrated into the American way of life but which, on the contrary, are our deadly enemies." Quoted in Bennett, "The Immigration and Nationality (McCarran-Walter) Act of 1952, as Amended to 1965," 133. For another pertinent discussion, see Bosniak, "Citizenship Denationalized," 447. See also Schuck and Smith, *Citizenship without Consent*. Schuck and Smith argue that children of illegal aliens who are born in the United States should not automatically be considered U.S. citizens. Given my emphasis on feelings of uncanniness that collapse boundaries, I have not always distinguished sharply between nation and state in the present study, or between citizenship as a legal concept and a psychological one more akin to belonging or affiliation.

18 Aleinikoff, "Theories of Loss of Citizenship," 1487 (emphasis original), 1499, 1500. Of course as the histories of Asian Americans and other immigrants in the country make painfully clear (not to mention the second-class status of African Americans, women, and homosexuals), under the Constitution not everyone has been treated equally. First-generation Japanese immigrants (Issei) were never allowed to become naturalized U.S. citizens, for example, making them more vulnerable to detention or deportation than other ethnic/racial groups, while Mexican braceros starting in 1942 (the same year as Japanese American intern-

ment) were brought into the country as raw labor power under an emergency work program without any pretense to grant them full rights, as I discuss in chapter 4.

19 Agamben, *State of Exception*, 1, 24, 33; emphasis original. See also Agamben, *Homo Sacer*.

20 Agamben, *State of Exception*, 35; emphasis original.

21 Ibid., 31. For the phrase *zone of anomie*, see 23, 36, 50, 59.

22 For the most comprehensive critique, see Neale, *Genre and Hollywood*, 151–78. For another interesting discussion of noir's place in film studies, see Young, "(Not) the Last Noir Essay." Rather than imply that there is an engaged debate about noir, it might be more accurate to say that many recent studies are still so heavily invested in traditional notions of noir that in willful ignorance they continue to perpetuate the same stereotypes, subgenres, and taxonomies. On this matter, issuing a call for new insights, see Dana Polan's review of Lee Horsley's *The Noir Thriller* in *Intensities*. One excellent recent study that fits Polan's call, published after my own book was completed, is Fay and Nieland, *Film Noir*. The authors show how film noir is and always has been international, emerging from the effects of globalization and linked to anxieties about the contours of national culture. Theirs is a fresh, wide-ranging analysis that complements my own emphasis on U.S. citizenship.

23 Vernet, "*Film Noir* on the Edge of Doom," 1, 25.

24 Neale, *Genre and Hollywood*, 154.

25 Altman, *Film/Genre*, 206; see also 86–87. Altman is particularly good at sketching out how the concept of noir became essentialized from an adjective to a noun (60–61). References to borders as conceptually delimiting genres can be found on pages 6, 11, 16, 18, 50, 69, 132, 205, and 207.

26 See, for instance, Koppes and Black, *Hollywood Goes to War*.

27 Vernet, "*Film Noir* on the Edge of Doom," 5, 4, 11.

28 Neale, *Genre and Hollywood*, 2–3. For one excellent example of this recent trend, see Lewis and Smoodin, *Looking Past the Screen*.

29 Rancière, *The Future of the Image*, 82, 75–76. For his essays devoted to cinema, see Rancière, *Film Fables*. See also Conley, "Cinema and Its Discontents." As he does in his own theorizing on film, Conley locates the intersection between word and image for Rancière in the figure of the hieroglyph.

30 Chartier, "The Americans are Making Dark Films Too," 27. For a discussion of how the adjective was used negatively in France during the 1930s, see Charles O'Brien, "Film Noir in France." See also Vincendeau, "Noir Is Also a French Word."

31 See Auerbach, *Body Shots*.

32 Neale, *Genre and Hollywood*, 168.

33 Vernet, "*Film Noir* on the Edge of Doom," 21.

34 The photograph is reproduced in Silver and Ursini, introduction to *Film Noir Reader*, 10; and in Silver and Ursini, *What Ever Happened to Robert Aldrich?*, 170;

as well as in other coauthored books by Silver and Ursini. This photograph is also briefly mentioned by Naremore, *More Than Night*, 4. I discuss this intriguing image at some length in my postscript.

35 Borde and Chaumeton, *A Panorama of American Film Noir, 1941–1953*, 13; emphasis original. The passage in the original *Panorama du film noir américain, 1941–1953* (Paris: Éditions de Minuit, 1955) reads as follows: "Il est facile de conclure: l'ambivalence morale, la violence criminelle et la complexité contradictoire des situations et des mobiles concourent à donner au public un même sentiment d'angoisse ou d'insécurité, qui est la marque propre du film noir à notre époque. Toutes les œuvres de cette série presentent bien une unité d'ordre affectif: *c'est l'état de tension né, chez le spectateur, de la disparition de ses repères psychologiques*. La vocation du film noir était de créer *un malaise spécifique*" (15).

36 Ngai, *Ugly Feelings*.

37 For an interesting if sometimes quirky analysis of the producer Val Lewton's horror movies in relation to the Second World War that is somewhat akin to my own efforts to contextualize film noir, see Nemerov, *Icons of Grief*. Nemerov identifies grief as the predominant feeling pervading these movies, but he only intermittently links this emotion to Americans' wartime experience, preferring instead to make intricate and rather fascinating associations among films, paintings, and literary texts chiefly by way of the career roles of actors in these movies.

38 For the "age of anxiety," see Henriksen, *Dr. Strangelove's America*. See also Graebener, *The Age of Doubt*.

39 Maltby, "The Politics of the Maladjusted Text." In one aspect of his argument, Maltby anticipates Neale's subsequent critique by suggesting that in terms of sheer output and popularity, film noir was a relatively minor category of movies during the 1940s and 1950s. But this kind of empirical approach to assessing canonicity strikes me as ill conceived. As canon-formation theorists are quick to point out, whether in relation to literature, music, or painting, sheer numbers tell us little about how certain works become culturally privileged over other, more popular ones. Or as the she-devil Vera from Edgar Ulmer's *Detour* (1945) might energetically respond, "So what?"

40 Naremore, *More Than Night*, 6, 2 (for "mythology"). Along with Vernet, Naremore offers one of the most nuanced intellectual histories of the French postwar reception of noir. Other studies that thoughtfully discuss the significance of that reception include Krutnik, *In a Lonely Street*; and Palmer, *Hollywood's Dark Cinema*.

41 Just as cinematic noir is not uniquely uncanny, it is also not uniquely a cold war film genre. As many cinema scholars have noted in some detail, in the 1950s one science fiction movie after the other expressed deep-seated terror about nuclear holocaust and/or an invasion by aliens or mutants threatening "our way of life." A bit more unusually, the western has similarly been treated as an important cold war genre, with cowboys in hugely popular movies of the 1940s and 1950s acting as cold warriors. Because the western predominantly deals with moral issues set

on the frontier, these films mostly engage debates about U.S. foreign policy, military expansionism, imperialism, and the acceptable use of force for deterrence, not so much how the consequences of internal security raised specific concerns over national belonging. For science fiction, see Biskind, *Seeing Is Believing*, 101–59; and Rogin, *"Ronald Reagan," the Movie, and Other Episodes of Political Demonology*, 236–71, among many such treatments; for the politics of the western, see Corkin, *Cowboys as Cold Warriors*.

42 Clearly in its generic instability (or richness) film noir has a rather complex genealogy. To cite one very intelligent recent overview, Andrew Spicer notes nearly a dozen cultural influences: hard-boiled crime fiction of the 1930s, the gangster film, gothic romance, German expressionism, the Weimar *Strassenfilm* (street film), émigrés coming to Hollywood, French poetic realism, Universal Studios horror movies, and Orson Welles. There are also a variety of historical contexts: postwar adjustment, McCarthyism, existentialism, and the popular impact of psychoanalysis. If individually these influences and contexts remain insufficient to define noir in a satisfying way, taken together they certainly help do so. See Spicer, *Film Noir*, 1–26.

43 Dimendberg, *Film Noir and the Spaces of Modernity*, 66–76. Dimendberg's account of space is striking in its deft merging of history and theory, but it remains curiously inattentive to questions of tone in noir.

44 Sobchack, "Lounge Time."

45 In this introduction I have not dwelled on the defining visual style of the films that I briefly discuss. But in subsequent chapters I do try to attend to the formal features of noir in my more detailed analyses of individual movies. Having previously concentrated on questions of representation in early cinema, short movies often without character or plot (what I like to think of as paying my film studies dues), I would hope to do similar justice to matters of visuality in noir, even if at the same time I carefully track narrative and affective structures embedded in particular lines of dialogue (being trained in literary criticism as I have). It seems to me that in their emphasis on the visual, some cinema scholars tend to inadequately appreciate the density of language displayed by these films; in this regard, when I measure Wilder's *Double Indemnity* against Shakespeare, I mean for the comparison to be taken seriously.

46 For one account of film noir strongly inflected by feminist psychoanalytic theory, see Oliver and Trigo, *Noir Anxiety*. For a study that emphasizes another concept closely associated with anxiety, see Pratt, *Projecting Paranoia*, 48–86. In his analysis of postwar political paranoia, Pratt gives a useful historical background, but he does not closely integrate this material with a detailed analysis of specific films. For a recent study more focused on summarizing films than examining cultural context, see Dixon, *Film Noir and the Cinema of Paranoia*.

47 See, for instance, Kemp, "From the Nightmare Factory"; Neve, *Film and Politics in America*, 145–70; and May, *The Big Tomorrow*, 215–56. See also Naremore, "From Dark Films to Black Lists: Censorship and Politics," in his *More Than*

Night, 96–135. For an important collection of essays on this period, mostly production histories, see Krutnik et al., *"Un-American" Hollywood*. This collection reprints (with a new afterword) the influential essay by Thom Andersen, "Red Hollywood" (225–75) of 1985, which introduces the notion of *films gris*, movies made between 1947 and 1951 that were leftist and sociologically inclined in criticizing American capitalism. Andersen's argument helped pave the way for a recent more extensive account of noir in relation to social class: Broe, *Film Noir, American Workers, and Postwar Hollywood*. In an appendix that reflects his taxonomic methodology throughout, Broe includes a valuable if somewhat arbitrary catalog of crime films under a series of categories such as "Depression-Era Drifter," "Middle-Class Fugitive," and so on. Broe's attempt to link midcentury American labor strife with certain noir character types is admirable, if unconvincing at times, dependent on overly rigid narrative and periodization schemes. For example, the emphasis on surveillance Broe sees taking hold in McCarthyite police procedural crime films after 1950 is clearly on display in the prewar spy films I discuss in chapter 1. For a more supple treatment of noir subgenres and cycles emphasizing the psychology of masculinity, see Frank Krutnik's excellent *In a Lonely Street*.

48 For the concept of "structure of feeling," see Williams, *Marxism and Literature*, 128–35.

49 Buhle and Warner, *Radical Hollywood*, 321–68; the quote is taken from 323. Even if Buhle and Warner are more nuanced and thorough in their efforts than some other film scholars, it is somewhat ironic that their quest to uncover radicals in Hollywood basically mirrors the positivistic approach of HUAC members, who were similarly convinced that subversive content could be covertly yet unambiguously smuggled into movies.

50 Jerome Christiansen, from a chapter in his *America's Corporate Art*. Christiansen's argument is indebted to the seminal analysis of postwar disillusionment by Maltby, "The Politics of the Maladjusted Text." For cold war liberalism's aversion to ideology, see especially Daniel J. Boorstin, "How Belief in the Existence of an American Theory Has Made a Theory Superfluous," in his *The Genius of American Politics*, 8–35; and Bell, *The End of Ideology*.

51 Borde and Chaumeton, *A Panorama of American Film Noir, 1941–1953*, 10.

52 In addition to writing the story for *Song of Russia* (1944), the *Tomorrow* co-screenwriter Guy Endore also fronted for his friend, the blacklisted Dalton Trumbo, in *He Ran All the Way* (1951), so that Bill's walking out of jail to confront the harsh realities of cold war America can plausibly be read as akin to how blacklisted writers might have felt trying to reintegrate into society after serving their prison sentences for contempt of Congress.

53 I am playing with the titles of three important noir films: *Raw Deal* (1948), *Detour* (1945), and *Where the Sidewalk Ends* (1950), all favorites of mine, *Raw Deal* directed by Anthony Mann, the latter two directed by émigrés from Europe, Edgar Ulmer and Otto Preminger. That Borde and Chaumeton in their book

make no mention of either *Detour* or *Stranger on the Third Floor* (my focus in the following chapter), both crucial films that closely fit their definition of noir, leads me to conclude that they were not familiar with these low-budget, limited-distribution movies.

54 On race in noir, see Lott, "The Whiteness of Film Noir"; and Murphet, "Film Noir and the Racial Unconscious." For a very interesting analysis of jazz scenes in noir, one that does not, however, mention the wartime *When Strangers Marry*, see Sean McCann, "Dark Passages: Jazz and Civil Liberty in the Postwar Crime Film," in Krutnik et al., *"Un-American" Hollywood*, 113–29.

55 With this passing reference to Carol Reed, let me clarify that the scope of my analysis in this study will be limited to American films and questions of U.S. citizenship, although of course British noir is an important subject in its own right that demands a careful consideration of similar issues of national belonging, as Reed's suspenseful narrative about an IRA operative on the run suggests. And of course Reed's *The Third Man* (1949), set in the shadows of postwar Vienna, would also be crucial here as well. The complex relation between British and U.S. noir especially warrants its own study. To give just one example, Sam Fuller's visualizing of Moe's murder in *Pickup on South Street* (see chapter 5) closely echoes a similar cut from the body to a revolving phonograph record in Brian Desmond Hurst's striking and bleak *On the Night of the Fire* (1939).

56 Statistics quoted in Theoharis, *The FBI and American Democracy*, 3.

57 See, for one instance, Gilbert, *A Cycle of Outrage*. On the FBI more generally, see Kessler, *The Bureau*; and Powers, *Broken*.

58 It is telling that in his excellent, wide-ranging study of film noir as an outgrowth of modernism, James Naremore only mentions the FBI director Hoover once in passing; see his *More Than Night*, 101. On Hoover, see Powers, *Secrecy and Power*; Theoharis and Cox, *The Boss*; and Gentry, *J. Edgar Hoover*. For more specialized studies, see O'Reilly, *Hoover and the Un-Americans*, on Hoover's relationship with HUAC; Stephan, *"Communazis"*; Batvinis, *The Origins of FBI Counterintelligence*, on various spy cases; and Charles, *J. Edgar Hoover and the Anti-interventionists*, on Hoover's surveillance of FDR's political enemies.

59 See Schlesinger, *The Vital Center*; and Chase, *Security and Liberty*, 80. For an excellent analysis of these liberals' acquiescence to the authority of Hoover, see Keller, *The Liberals and J. Edgar Hoover*. One exception was Truman's advisor Max Lowenthal, who in 1950 published a very harsh historical assessment of the FBI, including criticism of deportation raids, labor surveillance, and the bureau's filing system. See Lowenthal, *The Federal Bureau of Investigation*.

60 See Theoharis, *The FBI and American Democracy*, 53. The asymmetry of Hoover's catalog is revealing—two concrete ethnic/national designations, followed by the more problematic classification "Communist." The official FBI Web site (foia.fbi.gov), under the Freedom of Information Privacy Act, lists 34,207 pages of information and names pertaining to the Custodial Detention Program, which

under pressure from the attorney general was seemingly disbanded, but actually continued under a new title, Security Index, apparently without notification to either the Justice Department or the attorney general Francis Biddle.

61   Hoover, "Letter to Sidney Souers, July 7, 1950."

62   Gary, *The Nervous Liberals*, 243–44.

Chapter One: *Gestapo in America*

1   There are a few earlier major studio films like *Black Legion* (1937) that address the threat posed by homegrown fascism, but these movies do not mention Hitler as a possible inspiration for racial hatred. Joseph Breen of the Production Code Administration frequently warned studios during the 1930s against stirring up any controversy abroad that might cut into foreign market revenues. See Mac-Donnell, *Insidious Foes*, 31, 46. As listed in Internet Movie Database, the only American nondocumentary predating *Confessions* that deals with Nazis is *I Was a Captive of Nazi Germany* (1936), an obscure, low-budget dramatization of the memoirs of a woman (Isobel Steele) arrested for espionage. See Nugent, "Review of *I Was a Captive of Nazi Germany*."

2   See, for instance, *The Long Night* (1947) and *Sorry, Wrong Number* (1948).

3   Discussing the relation between the two films in terms pivotal for the argument of this chapter, Krims admitted, "I always knew Fascism was an enemy. I once believed Communism was a friend. It is a trying process to discern friends as well as enemies." Quoted in Giovacchini, *Hollywood Modernism*, 212. Fears of enemy aliens lurking in the United States clearly predate the Second World War, as indicated by *The Hun Within* (1918), directed by D. W. Griffith's assistant Chester Withey, starring Dorothy Gish, and featuring Erich von Stroheim as a nefarious German spy.

4   On Jews and noir, see Brook, *Driven to Darkness*. Because Ingster did not directly flee Hitler, he is given only a passing mention by Brook, whose valuable historical study is sometimes marred by dubious interpretations that strain to discover Jewish themes or concerns in these films, such as Vera's consumption in Ulmer's *Detour* (1945), although there is little indication that this character is Jewish. Like many other film noir scholars, Brook also strikes me as overly preoccupied with taxonomy.

5   The entry for the movie in Silver and Ward, *Film Noir*, puts the case most succinctly: "*Stranger on the Third Floor* is the first true film noir: and it represents a distinct break in style and substance with the preceding mystery, crime, detection, and horror films of the 1930s" (269). Despite the consensus among cinema scholars that *Stranger* marks the start of film noir, there is remarkably little critical analysis of the movie, and none that argues for any kind of political dimension to the film. For a beautiful poem claiming the Highlands chase scenes in Hitchcock's *The Thirty Nine Steps* (1935) as "the first film noir landscapes," see Stanley

Plumly, "Against Narrative," in *Old Heart*, 54. Perhaps more appropriate for poetry than for scholarship, bold assertions about "firsts" are notoriously risky to make about film history, especially for a category as problematic as noir.

6 For a great demonstration of how Hollywood narratives often manage effortlessly to mix escapist entertainment with more serious political engagement, see an exemplary reading of *Casablanca* in Polan,"The Limitless Potentials and the Potential Limits of Classical Hollywood Cinema." And yet despite this formal ease, Polan goes on to show, the end results are often ambiguous narratives that may carry confused and contradictory ideological implications.

7 The actor Paul Lukas played the part of a nefarious German agent in a number of previous spy thrillers, including Hitchcock's *The Lady Vanishes* (1938), where his character is also a physician. The British spy thriller dealt with Nazism well before Hollywood and is an important precedent for *Confessions*.

8 For details of the Rumich spy case, see MacDonnell, *Insidious Foes*, 49–62.

9 Giovacchini, *Hollywood Modernism*, 94–98; and MacDonnell, *Insidious Foes*, 62–72. See also Koppes and Black, *Hollywood Goes to War*, 27–30; and Ross, "*Confessions of a Nazi Spy*," especially 52–57. See also the excellent essays by Leo Braudy (26–37) and Dana Polan (39–47) in Blakley and Kaplan, *Warner's War*.

10 On the German-American Bund, Kuhn, and the Madison Square rally, see Bell, *In Hitler's Shadow*; Diamond, "The Bund Movement in the United States"; and McKale, *The Swastika Outside Germany*, 91–92. For a breathless firsthand account of the rally, see John Carlson, *Under Cover*, 26–28, a bestseller.

11 MacDonnell, *Insidious Foes*, 66. Kuhn also spoke in Los Angeles on April 30, 1939, in a rally covered by the local press. See Bahr, *Weimar on the Pacific*, 5.

12 Kuhn, "Address." Of course what GAB leaders professed in public and published in pamphlets such as this one presumably differed markedly from their less guarded, more private speeches. The phrase *Jew Deal*, for example, does not appear in the pamphlet, although it was widely invoked by GAB speakers in the late 1930s.

13 For an interesting contrast between Soviet and Nazi spying, see Weyl, *The Battle against Disloyalty*: "Instead of recruiting agents among nuclear physicists and other pure scientists [like the Soviets], they [the Nazis] gathered up skilled mechanics, technicians, and production engineers" (154).

14 Beyond this scene, maps play an important role throughout the movie, from the map of the United States that hangs prominently in Renard's FBI office to the gigantic world map that the Goebbels figure (unidentified as such) in Germany gestures toward while instructing Kassel about his propaganda mission. For Litvak the map is a convenient image of the spatial reach of Nazism, indicating its menace as well as its potential containment.

15 On the history of HUAC, see Goodman, *The Committee*. For a highly detailed account of its early years, see Ogden, *The Dies Committee*. Unable to look ahead to the Cold War, Ogden's study of 1945 concludes by dismissively pronouncing the committee a "failure" with no foreseeable future.

16 Quoted in MacDonnell, *Insidious Foes*, 43.

17 Ibid., 76. As MacDonnell points out (3), the term *fifth column* was another journalistic phrase that originated in 1936 during the Spanish Civil War. See also Maddux, "Red Fascism, Brown Bolshevism"; and Adler and Paterson, "Red Fascism." Crediting the term *Commu-Nazi* to a story published by Frederick Hazlitt Brennan in February 1940, Adler and Paterson remark: "Once Russia was designated the 'enemy' by American leaders, Americans transferred their hatred for Hitler's Germany to Stalin's Russia with considerable ease and persuasion" (1046).

18 Quoted in Goodman, *The Committee*, 14.

19 Quoted in Ogden, *The Dies Committee*, 51, 43.

20 See Diamond, "The Bund Movement in the United States," 192–93.

21 For a discussion of how Americans typically viewed and represented the FBI and Hoover, see Powers, *G-Men*. On the adulation of Hoover by liberals otherwise suspicious of political witch hunts aimed at subversives, see Keller, *The Liberals and J. Edgar Hoover*, 3–71. Keller makes a persuasive case that in the aftermath of war, trusting liberals like Schlesinger Jr. enabled the establishment and growth of the U.S. state security apparatus by putting their faith in the professionalism of the FBI to conduct intelligence operations with no oversight. In terms of *Confessions*, it is interesting to note that Hoover and the FBI objected to the film's depiction of their efforts as overheated "Americanism" designed primarily to gain audiences. The FBI might have had this reaction because the bureau was angry that one of its own agents had sold his story to newspapers to cash in on the case, but Hoover also feared the movie would create "a good deal of public hysteria about spies which is a bad thing because the spy situation is not one-tenth as bad as the yellow journals present" (quoted in MacDonnell, *Insidious Foes*, 67). This, of course, was written in a personal note to his assistant Clyde Tolson; in public Hoover took a much harder line against subversion, and MacDonnell offers a nuanced assessment of Hoover's balancing between reassuring and alarming Americans about the enemy within during the war (157–83).

22 For a discussion of this secret directive of 1936 that led under Hoover to the supplementing of criminal investigations with a variety of intelligence operations aimed against "subversion," see Theoharis, "The FBI's Stretching of Presidential Directives, 1936–1953"; and Charles, *J. Edgar Hoover and the Anti-interventionists*, 30–34.

23 On these emergency measures, see Theoharis, *Spying on Americans*, 65–86. See also O'Reilly, *Hoover and the Un-Americans*, 21–22.

24 See Bacevich, *The Long War*. Remarking in his introduction (vii) that "when World War II ended, history has (apparently) begun new, thereby endowing the Cold War with an aura of remarkable singularity," Bacevich (and other historians) assumes that the emergence of a national security apparatus bred of an intensified sense of American exceptionalism began only after the Second World War, but I would argue the Cold War started in the late 1930s, with these security measures aimed against foreign subversives at home.

25 Quoted in Theoharis, *The FBI and American Democracy*, 46.

26 In one of the more interesting cold war propaganda productions, *I Was a Communist for the FBI* (1951), also from Warner's studio, during a brainstorming session among American communists, one party member actually evokes the name of Fritz Kuhn and the Bund as a model for subversive agitation worthy of emulation.

27 The Smith Act of 1940, 54. Stat. 670, 671, title I, §§ 2–3 (June 28, 1940), current version at 18 U. S. C. § 2385, sec. 2.

28 For two conflicting views of this trial, see the prosecutor's account, Rogge, *The Official German Report* and the defendants' version, St.-George and Dennis, *Trial on Trial*. On Rogge and the Special Defense Unit (SDU), see Gary, *The Nervous Liberals*, 229–36. Gary quotes Rogge as claiming to defend free speech to avoid prosecuting what he called "sincere Americans" (302n70).

29 Both the majority opinion and the Douglas dissent are discussed in Steinberg, *The Great "Red Menace,"* 224. See also a review of this book by Alan Filreis, "Words with 'All the Effects of Force.' " For a wider ranging discussion of the relation between national security advocates and free speech defenders within the Justice Department between 1939 and 1954, see Gary, *The Nervous Liberals*, 175–251.

30 See Charles, *J. Edgar Hoover and the Anti-interventionists*. Douglas is one of the few historians who locates in the prewar actions of Hoover and FDR the emergence of a national security apparatus putting the United States on a perpetual emergency wartime footing. See also MacDonnell, *Insidious Foes*, 137–56.

31 For a recent overview of the history of deportation that stresses the legal incoherence of U.S. policies and practices, see Kanstroom, *Deportation Nation*. He notes "how the deportation system is better understood when it is functionally decoupled from the formal citizenship-alienage line and viewed as a system of extraordinary majoritarian power operating outside of well-accepted legal norms" (206–7).

32 Powers, *Secrecy and Power*, 36–55.

33 However generally revered, the FBI on occasion was not above direct comparison with the Nazis. Responding to FBI raids and arrests of U.S. veterans who fought in the Spanish Civil War in early 1940, the *Milwaukee Journal* accused the bureau of acting like "a Gestapo that can haul citizens off to prison . . . without accountability." Quoted in MacDonnell, *Insidious Foes*, 171–72. After the war, President Truman frequently in private referred to Hoover and the FBI as the "Gestapo." See Powers, *Broken*, 202.

34 Dies, *The Trojan Horse in America*.

35 Debate about whether native fascism could grow on U.S. soil was spurred by the publication in 1935 of the Sinclair Lewis novel *It Can't Happen Here*, loosely based on the career of the populist demagogue Huey Long. Plans to turn the best-selling novel into a movie were halted by MGM after Joseph Breen of the

Production Code Administration (PCA) warned Louis B. Mayer about the "inflammatory" potential of the film overseas. See MacDonnell, *Insidious Foes*, 31.

36 For the most complete account of the film's production history, marketing, and reception, see Biesen, *Blackout*, 22–32. After the war, Partos and Litvak teamed up again to make the award-winning *The Snake Pit* (1948).

37 Pertinent here is the discussion of Kafka and the Law in Agamben, *State of Exception*, 63.

38 As Biesen points out in *Blackout* (24), PCA censors were less concerned about the film's vivid descriptions of violence (the gory throat slashing) than about Michael's self-address as a symptom of mental illness. It is difficult for me to come up with a prior film, either American, British, French, or German, in which such pervasive voice-over musing fills the soundtrack, although Sergei Eisenstein (one of Ingster's mentors) as early as 1930 planned to film Theodore Dreiser's *American Tragedy* for Paramount using the protagonist's "interior monologue" for extended sequences. See Schatz, *The Genius of the System*, 77. Fredric Jameson briefly makes some suggestive general remarks about the relation between film noir and "radio culture as it resonates out into other genres and media," but he does not try to explain why it took a full decade for sound film to incorporate this type of radio narration, nor its various rhetorical functions in the original medium. See Jameson, "The Synoptic Chandler," 36. Surprisingly, in his fine study of voice-over narration in noir, J. P. Telotte does not even mention *Stranger*. See Telotte, *Voices in the Dark*.

39 Biesen in *Blackout* (26) also calls attention to this line, which she reads as a comment on the film's low budget. In general Biesen's excellent production history of film noir is marred by her overinsistence on financial constraints as fundamentally shaping the style and themes of these movies. This sort of economic determinism risks underestimating the astonishing aesthetic potential of cheaply made films like *Stranger*.

40 Polan, *Power and Paranoia*, 208. Vivian Sobchack elaborates on Polan's insight about this negative existentialism and its particular implications for noir in her essay "Lounge Time," 138.

41 The soundtrack is one of the most experimental and innovative features of the film, which anticipates *Detour* (1945) in tending to break down the distinction between diegetic and nondiegetic sounds, so that we are uncertain at times whether characters in the movie hear what we do on the soundtrack from outside the story. On the importance of nondiegetic sound as a "bath of affect" and a source of empowerment for the cinema audience, see Gorbman, *Unheard Melodies*, 5–23.

42 The character actor playing Meng, Charles Halton, shows up in a minor role as an American newspaper man aiding the fight against fascism in *Foreign Correspondent*, a Hitchcock spy movie released the same day as *Stranger*, August 16, 1940. George Sanders (a high-ranking Nazi officer in *Confessions*) plays a patri-

otic British correspondent in the Hitchcock movie. Audiences following individual actors rather than fictional characters in these wartime films would often have their allegiances sorely tested.

43 On the luminosity of objects and bodies in German expressionism that seem to both reflect and radiate light, such as the Stranger's hand, see Elsaesser, *Weimar Cinema and After*, 251. I should note in passing that at the end of this book (420–44), Elsaesser mounts a formidable frontal assault on the conventional scholarly linkage between German expressionist cinema and American film noir, a linkage he finds overly simplistic and reductive. But I trust my pairing of *Stranger* (so obviously indebted to German expressionism) with *Confessions* would at least suggest an alternative genealogy to the connections evoked automatically by many film critics.

44 In one of the few critical discussions of the film, Frank Krutnik interprets Meng's look at the two women as a lascivious leer, which supports his compelling reading of the Meng-Michael relationship as a kind of Oedipal doubling and rivalry. But I would argue that Meng is less a sexual rival than a sexual censor and informer—what makes him Gestapo—seeking to suppress the reporter's expression and desire. See Krutnik, *In a Lonely Street*, 48. For another nonpolitical reading, see McCarthy and Flynn, *King of the Bs*, 155–60.

45 The phrase *mind laundering* and its variations produced no hits on the JSTOR database, and the first instance of *brainwashing* that came up was dated 1952. I like to think that Nathanael West was responsible for this contribution to the script, but of course there is no way to tell.

46 It is also worth noting that directly after they exit the apartment, it is Jane, not Michael, who proposes they move in together and get married. She is the more sexually aggressive of the two.

47 Bentham, *The Rationale of Reward*. Bentham is specifically defending the paid informer, but his analysis is enlightening more generally, particularly in its complete neglect of the social psychology of informing, which we can appreciate in the sadistic pleasure that Meng takes in exposing the transgressions of others, as well as in Michael's extreme fear and hatred of his neighbor. As Bentham's discussion suggests, the term *informer* was frequently used in the early modern period to refer to persons who denounced violations against religious doctrine.

48 One equally subversive and disturbing representation of American justice that might have actually served as an inspiration for the film is an edgy, noirish Disney cartoon called *Pluto's Judgement Day* (1935), which depicts the rascally dog scolded by Mickey for chasing a kitten, falling asleep by the fire, and then having a nightmare that finds him in a surreal, shadow-filled courtroom composed of a jury of cats, who declare his guilt in a minstrel-show chorus, then rushing over to lynch and burn him before Pluto wakes up (his tail burnt by a fire ember) and makes friends with the kitten at Mickey's urging. Slavoj Žižek reads this remarkable cartoon of 1935 in relation to Moscow show trials, but it seems more compelling to view the film in the context of race, both Hitler's Nuremberg race

laws (1935) and the oppression of African Americans during the 1930s. To be black in a white-dominated society is like being a Jew among Nazis, or a dog in a world run by cats. See Žižek, *The Universal Exception*, 135.

49 In a final tag scene that parodies PCA requirements for happy endings, we find Michael and Jane reunited at the luncheon counter for the last time, now able to afford to move in together. Michael ominously teases Jane about the need to return to the courthouse, but this time only to procure a marriage license, and the two are whisked off to get hitched by none other than the falsely accused Joe Briggs, now a gainfully employed taxi driver who with a big smile offers them a free ride—no hard feelings, naturally.

50 Simmel, "The Stranger." I note in passing that Simmel's essay was originally published the same year that the America Bureau of Investigation (later renamed the FBI) was founded.

51 On Lorre, see Youngkin, *The Lost One*.

52 The twinning of Mike and the Stranger, who only briefly encounter each other twice during the entire movie, is reminiscent of another film made in 1940 explicitly about Hitler, Charlie Chaplin's *The Great Dictator*, in which the dictator's violent and growling speech is offset by the stoic muteness of his shopkeeper double. *Stranger* inverts the relation between speech and silence by making the protagonist Michael the incessant talker (if mainly to himself), while the sinister Stranger keeps quiet (presumably preferring to direct action from behind the scenes). Appealing perhaps to Ingster's Russian roots, the crime story of *Stranger* also more classically resembles Dostoyevsky's *The Brothers Karamazov*, where the guilt for the murder of an abusive father (Meng) is shared by three brothers (Briggs, Michael, and the Stranger).

53 Working on the metaphor of Hollywood as a dream factory—a comparison that would become a commonplace in the 1940s and 1950s—the nightmare can be read as a self-reflexive parable about moviemaking, complete with a mindless, docile audience vulnerable to mass suggestion, namely, the sleeping jurors in the courtroom. Like the news reporter, but less self-consciously tormented, they are subject to an analogous sort of mind control, governed by the massive moving images and shadows playing on the walls/screens around them. I am indebted to Michael Tratner for suggesting this line of inquiry. For an important analysis of how Hollywood has responded to fears about cinema's capacity to collectively sway audiences, see Tratner, *Crowd Scenes*.

54 The Stranger's motive for initially murdering Nick remains something of a mystery, but we might surmise that he resents the successful assimilation of the Greek immigrant into U.S. society.

55 Among the film's many prescient concerns, perhaps the most striking is its anticipation of the problem of statelessness facing displaced persons in the wake of the war. See, for example, Arendt, "The Stateless People"; and Arendt, *The Origins of Totalitarianism*, 275–89.

1   See Sobchack, "Lounge Time." As Jeff Bailey (Robert Mitchum) jokes to the gangster Whit Sterling (Kirk Douglas) in *Out of the Past* (1947) about his humble job owning a gas station, "we call it earning a living. You may have heard of it somewhere." For an alternative view of work in noir, making an unusual claim particularly for the significance of office space, see Christopher, *Somewhere in the Night*, where he calls the modern skyscraper a "compressed, complex, tautly wired microcosm of the city at large" (115). His analysis of John Farrow's *The Big Clock* (1948) along these lines is especially insightful. But I would argue that this postwar film also carries strong traces of prewar ideology, particularly in its rendering of the villain, a malevolent publishing magnate who harkens back to New Deal depictions of rapacious, tyrannical capitalist bosses. Similarly, the movie's fixation with the building's "big clock" itself as exerting inexorable pressure on the narrative, whose innocent protagonist must frantically race against time to avoid getting caught, strikes me as somewhat akin to Charlie Chaplin's Depression-era representation of the relentless blue-collar factory line in *Modern Times* (1936). Other postwar film noir excursions into the corporate world include *Pitfall* (1947), *They Won't Believe Me* (1947), *Shakedown* (1950), and *Steel Trap* (1952), but in these cases the motives for crime centers on professional ambition, boredom, greed, or womanizing, combined with simple opportunity, tending toward a single impetus rather than a more complicated clustering of feelings. Compared to these other films, *Double Indemnity* remains a richer psychological exploration of the dark side of business in the United States at midcentury. For my purposes perhaps the most interesting of these later white-collar noirs is *Steel Trap*, whose assistant bank manager (played by Joseph Cotton, with an extensive voice-over narration) embezzles nearly 1 million dollars, less for the sake of the money itself than to fulfill his "strange fascination" with breaking the conformity of his bourgeois life by fleeing the United States with his unsuspecting wife for Brazil. As one minor character puts it, "you must want to get out of the country awfully bad." But quickly his story bogs down in procedural details, having more to do with the stress of travel than anything else.

2   In this regard *Double Indemnity* can be viewed as the first of what I would call Wilder's corporate trilogy, the other two movies (both cold war comedies) being *The Apartment* (1960, also starring MacMurray), and *One, Two, Three* (1961). Wilder's interest in corporate culture pervades his oeuvre, beginning as early as his coauthored screenplay for *Hold Back the Dawn* (1941), a film about a European refugee stuck in Mexico who is desperately trying to immigrate to the United States, as I discuss in chapter 4 of this study. When this gigolo briefly and illegally crosses the border, he immediately drives to Hollywood to try and sell his story. Other movies directed by Wilder that feature business and businessmen include *Sabrina* (1954), *The Seven Year Itch* (1955), *Avanti !* (1972), and *The Fortune Cookie* (1966), which is about insurance fraud.

3 On the role of voice-over narration in the movie, see Telotte, *Voices in the Dark*, 40–56. See also more generally Kozloff, *Invisible Storytellers*; and Chion, *The Voice in Cinema*.

4 While waiting for Phyllis to get dressed, her maid cautions Neff that the liquor cabinet is locked, to which he jokes in reply that "I carry my own keys," one of two such puns on keys/Keyes suggesting how he has from the start internalized the disapproving claims manager. The second pun occurs near the end, when Neff phones Phyllis to meet her for the last time at her house, remarking "Don't worry about Keyes. Just leave the front door unlocked and put the lights out." The dropped definitive article and upper case spelling (as printed in the screenplay) here give priority of meaning to the name of the claims investigator.

5 Wilder and Chandler, *Double Indemnity*, 20.

6 Although the poster's phrase "surrender rates" reinforces the ferocity of Keyes's attack against the immigrant, the term is fairly benign, referring to the number of policy holders who cash in their insurance.

7 Lott, "The Whiteness of Film Noir," 546.

8 I use the term *bourgeois* for Neff pointedly, since in casting MacMurray, who usually played light comedy, Wilder claimed that he "wanted a decent, bourgeois man," not a stereotypical criminal. See Schickel, *Double Indemnity*, 59.

9 For an excellent analysis of the film's music, as well as for one of the best discussions of the movie in general, see Brown, *Overtones and Undertones*, 120–33.

10 In the screenplay, right before he begins talking about his "little man," Keyes quizzes Gorlopis about his family (a wife and two kids) and his eating habits (meatloaf with garlic)—personal details that Wilder presumably cut from the film because he wanted the culprit to remain foreign yet otherwise anonymous, which is how Keyes unsympathetically sees him. Since many speeches in the movie reveal minor variations between the screenplay and the final version as filmed and released, I have quoted directly from the film, not the shooting script, unless otherwise noted.

11 Cain, *The Postman Always Rings Twice, Double Indemnity, Mildred Pierce, and Selected Stories*, 129. Subsequent references to Cain's *Double Indemnity* are cited parenthetically in the running text from this edition. In the film, Neff says, "All you need is a plant out in front, a shill to put down the bet."

12 Quoted in Sikov, *On Sunset Boulevard*, 200.

13 Irwin, *Unless the Threat of Death Is behind Them*, 71–92.

14 At the risk of rehashing stale biographical anecdotes, it is tempting to read the Neff-Keyes relationship in the movie as a reflection (doubling?) of the Wilder-Chandler studio collaboration: an odd-couple pairing featuring a rumpled older man (in his mid-fifties, whom Wilder recalled looking like an accountant), well-versed in the ways of detection (that genre of fiction, at least), contentiously interacting with a younger, sociable man (in his mid-thirties) noted for his drinking and womanizing, as well as his talent for selling himself to Hollywood.

While it is impossible to attribute individual lines to either author, I would surmise that the romantic spin on Keyes as a caring father figure looking out for Neff owes much to Chandler, whereas the more cynical view of Keyes as an interfering bully owes much to Wilder. So where does Phyllis fit in? Intriguing here to complete the triangle is Wilder's comment that in hooking up with Chandler, he had "cheated" or committed adultery on his steady writing partner Charles Brackett (Sikov, *On Sunset Boulevard*, 197). If we prefer to read the movie's plot in relation to Paramount studio politics, then Keyes's disdain for Norton's meddling in the case resembles Wilder's own notorious disrespect for front-office authority. For biographical information on Wilder, see Sivok, *On Sunset Boulevard*; Horton, *Billy Wilder*; and Crowe, *Conversations with Wilder*. For Chandler, see MacShane, *The Life of Raymond Chandler*; and Hiney, *Raymond Chandler*. Because much of this material is familiar, repetitive, and circular, with the film glossing stories about the writers' collaboration, as much as vice versa, I have largely refrained from discussing the production history of the movie. For one concise overview of production and reception, see Biesen, *Blackout*, 96–111.

15 Manon, "Some Like It Cold." Manon's close reading is impressively detailed, including a moment in the film in which Neff distractedly kicks back a folded corner of his rug, indicating the very spot of their adultery. Of course PCA censorship meant that sex could never be explicitly depicted, but Manon's point is that its deferral and displacement suggests something about Neff's desire for loss.

16 Wilder and Chandler, *Double Indemnity*, 107.

17 Tyler, *Magic and Myth of the Movies*, 175–89. Overly fond of wordplay, Tyler shifts his brilliant opening analysis of their company roles to Keyes's function as Neff's sexual claims adjuster, thereby spawning a slew of queer readings of their relation that I find utterly unpersuasive, for reasons that will become apparent as my argument develops. For the most extensive queer reading, see Gallagher. " 'I Love You Too.' "

18 For an interesting discussion of the gas chamber scene in relation to tabloid journalism, see Pelizzon and West, "Multiple Indemnity."

19 The only similar character I can think of is the gun-toting insurance investigator Jim Reardon (played by Edmund O'Brien) in Robert Siodmak's *The Killers* (1946), although his close association with the police lieutenant Sam Lubinsky (Sam Levene) puts him more closely in league with state law enforcement than Keyes, who acts alone and only for his company in *Double Indemnity*.

20 Sikov, *On Sunset Boulevard*, 23.

21 Sutherland, "White-Collar Criminality," 44. See also Sutherland, *White Collar Crime*.

22 Smigel and Ross, *Crimes against Bureaucracy*. Given Sutherland's emphasis on such crimes as learned, imitative behavior, it is precisely the relation between how bosses act and how employees do that demands clearer analysis.

23 As an oil company white-collar employee, Chandler became intimately familiar with a number of frauds and scandals roiling the industry during the 1920s, including the arrest of his own company's chief accountant for embezzlement, a corporate crime Chandler himself helped expose and which led to the doubling of his salary when he was promoted as the chief accountant's replacement. See Hiney, *Raymond Chandler*, 50–59.

24 Quoted in Pells, *The Liberal Mind in a Conservative Age*, 193. Pells offers an excellent overview of these cold war intellectuals (183–261).

25 Kracauer, *The Salaried Masses*, 88, 99. In the latter passage Kracauer uses the word *entrepreneur* (*der Unterrnehmer* in the original German) to slightly finesse the classic Marxist distinction between the proletariat and the owners of capital, and in fact Keyes may be so hostile to Mr. Norton's incompetent stewardship of the company because he has somehow (falsely) convinced himself that he has some financial stake in the business. Other aspects of Kracauer's analysis of *die Angestellten* that apply to the movie include his discussion of the emphasis by salaried workers on superficial appearances, the "morally pink complexion" (38) that Neff projects (and here consider Eric Lott's racial reading), as well as some of his thumbnail ethnographic sketches of employees themselves, including a dashing young cigarette salesman whose glib personality closely resembles Neff's (68–69). For a reading of Kracauer's study in relation to Wilder's movie *The Apartment*, see Gemünden, *A Foreign Affair*, 125–35.

26 See Szalay, *New Deal Modernism*, 222–25; and McCann, *Gumshoe America*, 73–75.

27 Miller, *Taylored Citizenship*. See also Graebner, *The Engineering of Consent*.

28 Cain, *The Postman Always Rings Twice*, 3. Subsequent citations from this edition will be given parenthetically in the running text.

29 Agamben, *State of Exception*, 23.

30 Sollors, *Interracialism*, 5.

31 On the function of blacks in the movie as alibis for white subjectivity, see Lott, "The Whiteness of Film Noir." Mexico plays a small but equally crucial role in the film, as suggested by references to the intoxicating perfume Phyllis has purchased from Ensenada and to Neff's desire to escape "across the border" at the end of the film. In Cain's novel the couple commits suicide while sailing off the coast of Baja.

32 Copjec, "The Phenomenal Nonphenomenal." For a Foucauldian reading that emphasizes (overly so, in my view) how Neff's resistance is incorporated into the disciplinarity he seeks to transgress, see Shumway, "Disciplinary Identities."

33 Hacking, "Biopower and the Avalanche of Printed Numbers," 279.

34 Boorstin, *The Americans*, 165.

35 Defert, "'Popular Life' and Insurance Technology," 212, 232. See also Ewald, "Insurance and Risk." Keyes appears even more sinister from yet another perspective, that of the Frankfurt School critique of enlightenment rationality, utility, and calculability. Theodor W. Adorno's and Max Horkheimer's *Dialectic of Enlightenment* was completed in Los Angeles the same year that *Double Indemnity* was released (1944).

36   Robert D. Putnam's influential essay of 1995 was expanded into a book, *Bowling Alone*.

37   Copjec, "The Phenomenal Nonphenomenal," 180.

38   Ibid., 193.

39   See, for instance, two other wartime movies, *Stranger on the Third Floor* (1940) and *Detour* (1945), as well as *Out of the Past* (1947) and *I Walk Alone* (1948), where the gangster (played by Kirk Douglas) responds by insisting that the woman enjoys the pain.

40   Bronfen, "Femme Fatale." For another critique of how the femme fatale is conventionally represented in film studies, see Grossman, "Film Noir's 'Femme Fatales' Hard-Boiled Women."

41   Ngai, *Ugly Feelings*, 12–16.

42   Naremore, *More Than Night*, 90.

43   Gunning, *The Films of Fritz Lang*.

44   Schickel, *Double Indemnity*, 50.

45   Naremore, *More Than Night*, 92. My reading of the film resembles Naremore's, with three key differences: he locates Wilder's sensibility primarily in Weimar modernity, whereas I try to give it a more precise American historical context through white-collar crime; his focus on rationalization falls on the film's visual and verbal metaphors ("straight down the line" trolley cars, bowling lanes, and so on), whereas I emphasize the corporate rivalry between Keyes and Neff; and finally, he tends to buy into the love between the two men, thereby mitigating the most disquieting aspects of the claims manager's surveillance, whereas I do not. Right before his "closer than that, Walter" line, Keyes gives another reason for his failure to detect Neff—"You can't figure them all"—that is more in keeping with his actuarial mentality throughout. For another attempt at historical contextualizing of the film that argues for the importance of Wilder's status as a German émigré, see Gemünden, *A Foreign Affair*, 30–53. Both Naremore and Gemünden briefly mention Wilder's close ties to Frankfurt School intellectuals living in Los Angeles (292n62 and 49–50, respectively). For an uncommonly harsh, albeit brief, critical assessment of Keyes, see Selby, *Dark City*, 12–16. Spencer asserts that "Keyes' absolutism forces him to deny the humanity of his victims. He refuses to try to understand them because such understanding would undercut his simplistic characterization of evil" (16). I would say that given his statistical outlook, Keyes does not actually have any concept of evil, which is more disturbing than having a simplistic one.

Notes to Chapter Three: *Cuba, Gangsters, and Vets*

1   See especially Maltby, "The Politics of the Maladjusted Text."

2   Pérez, *Cuba and the United States*, 109. As he remarks elsewhere in this volume, "North Americans considered Cuba essential to the political-military security of the United States; Cubans looked upon the United States as vital to the socio-

economic well-being of the island" (xvi). See also his *On Becoming Cuban* and his *Cuba in the American Imagination*, where he claims that "the destiny of the nation [the United States] seemed inextricably bound to the fate of the island" (1). Pérez suggests that "it is not likely that North Americans were more familiar to any other people in Latin America than Cubans, and vice versa" (*Cuba and the United States*, xviii), and yet given his single-minded focus on the United States–Cuba dyad in these three books, there is hardly a mention of Mexico, even though this Spanish-speaking country was also less than two hundred miles from Cuba.

Clearly United States–Cuba–Mexico relations cry out for a complex cultural and political analysis that triangulates these three nations. What that analysis might entail is suggested by one fleeting reference to Mexico by Pèrez, who describes the U.S. ambassador Sumner Welles's attempts in 1933 to remove Gerardo Machado from power, followed by the ambassador's endeavors to destabilize the reformist, nationalist government that soon after replaced Machado. When this government announced an agreement with Mexico to train Cuban military officers, training formerly done only by the United States, Welles protested that such a move was a "deliberate effort by the present Government to show its intention of minimizing any form of American influence in Cuba" (Pérez, *Cuba and the United States*, 196).

3 Polan, "Stylistic Regularities (and Peculiarities) of the Hollywood World War II Propaganda Film," 41. For another brief but interesting discussion of Ripley's film that argues for it partaking in "the myth of the tyrannized island," see Dick, *The Star-Spangled Screen*, 235–36. Calling *Prisoner of Japan* a "strange picture," the scriptwriter Edgar Ulmer took credit for taking over the film's direction from Ripley. See the interview reprinted in McCarthy and Flynn, *King of the Bs*, 397–98. It is fitting that in the movie, until his ultimate patriotic sacrifice, David is the (failed) son of a great astronomer famous for his treatise on "island universes."

4 Borde and Chaumeton, *A Panorama of American Film Noir, 1941–1953*. The screenwriter for *The Chase*, Phillip Yordan, was a master of evocative, dreamy noir, in addition authoring or coauthoring *When Strangers Marry* (1944), the surreal *Suspense* (1946), and the violently sexual *The Big Combo* (1955), which some regard as the greatest film noir.

5 Rovner, *The Cuba Connection*, 31–56.

6 For naval base activity during the Second World War, see Murphy, *The History of Guantanamo Bay*, chap. 12. "U.S. Ship in Caribbean Is Sunk by Torpedo," *New York Times*, April 20, 1943. For a fascinating account locating the base in a broader social context that includes Cuban workers at midcentury, see Lipman, *Guantánamo*, especially 29–60.

7 On Martí's influence and activities in Key West, see Ronning, *José Martí and the Emigré Colony in Key West*, 4.

8 Hemingway letter quoted in Ogle, *Key West*, 151. For a fascinating discussion of

Hemingway's multiple national affiliations (American, Cuban, and Key West, or "Conch") within various cultural histories, see Miyamoto, "Papa and Fidel."

9 In his autobiography, Huston amusingly describes Robinson in the bathtub as looking "like a crustacean with its shell off." See Huston, *An Open Book*, 151.

10 See Ogle, *Key West*, 176–81.

11 Ibid., 181.

12 Here I would mention a fourth Robinson performance from the 1940s in a film I do not discuss, *The Stranger* (1946), in which he plays a War Crimes Commission investigator hunting down an ex-Nazi living in Connecticut. Closely linked to his prewar role as the FBI agent Renard prosecuting spies, the part of a postwar investigator functions as a kind of bookend to the job of destroying fascism, although the movie is less uncanny than unconvincing, since an isolated, solitary stranger in our midst, after the defeat of Germany, does not carry the same noir feelings of dread and menace as it did at the war's onset. That is why certain films shifted postwar to targeting communists as the enemy within, something the director Orson Welles resolutely refused to do. Huston worked on *The Stranger* as an uncredited writer alongside Welles.

13 Arguably Robinson's vilest role was that of the cowardly informer Dathan in *The Ten Commandments* (1956), frequently read as a key cold war text.

14 Grieveson, Sonnet, and Stanfield, *Mob Culture*, 1–10. Stanfield discusses Robinson on 252.

15 Cavell, *The World Viewed*, 75–76.

16 Sarris, *The American Cinema*. Sarris's assessment of Huston is notoriously harsh in this book.

17 It may be objected that I am confusing two related but distinct terms, *canon* and *genre*, the latter being a far more capacious concept, I concede. Yet insofar as commercial studios seek to duplicate their successes, as defined both by box-office receipts and reviewers and critics, it seems to me the process of academic canon formation cannot be isolated from Hollywood's own constructions of genre. But recovering and analyzing previously neglected movies remains a crucial task.

18 For Freud in relation to film noir, see Krutnik, *In a Lonely Street*, 75–85. For one discussion of the impact of psychoanalysis on U.S. culture more broadly, see Lunbeck, *The Psychiatric Persuasion*.

19 Studlar, "A Gunsel Is Being Beaten." For one such influential pop analysis infamously positing the new pathology of "momism," see Wylie, *A Generation of Vipers*.

20 Studlar, "A Gunsel Is Being Beaten," 138.

21 This convergence between soldier and gangster genres might be traced to *The Roaring Twenties* (1939), which begins with the demobilization of buddies from the First World War, a scene that in 1939 would have reminded audiences of the impending conflict in Europe.

22 For the sake of brevity, all subsequent references to the movie's script will credit

its director and coauthor Huston alone, although Brooks also played an important part in shaping the film's implied politics.

23 Borde and Chaumeton, *A Panorama of American Film Noir, 1941–1953*, 78.

24 Anderson, *Key Largo*, 111.

25 Huston explicitly addresses the political intentions of his film in his autobiography, where he remarks, "The high hopes and idealism of the Roosevelt years were slipping away, and the underworld . . . was again on the move, taking advantage of social apathy. We made this the theme of the movie" (Huston, *An Open Book*, 151).

26 On these films, see Desser "The Wartime Films of John Huston"; and Edgerton, "Revisiting the Recordings of Wars Past." In his effort to see *Key Largo* as a film noir emerging directly from Huston's trilogy of war documentaries, Desser in my view drastically overestimates the dark qualities of the film, especially in regard to Frank, who may be mildly cynical but is hardly the typical dysfunctional and traumatized veteran we find in so many far bleaker noirs of the period (which Desser does not discuss). It makes sense to view *Let There Be Light* as a kind of noir in its own right, but to link noir itself to the documentary's therapeutic sensibility seems highly problematic to me, since in Hollywood's fictionalized versions, such "therapy" often means undergoing additional criminal violence.

27 Given the amount of analysis devoted to Bogart's stardom, I will say relatively little here, but for an excellent discussion of the actor's projections of masculinity, see Cohan, *Masked Men*, 79–121. The best book on masculinity and film noir in general remains Krutnik, *In a Lonely Street*.

28 Edna Buchanan, "Lucky Luciano," *Time*, December 7, 1998, 130–32.

29 *Key Largo* is not the first Hollywood movie to be based on Luciano's life. In 1937 Warner released *Marked Woman* (1937), loosely patterned after Luciano's prostitution trial and coauthored by Robert Rossen, which starred Bette Davis and Bogart as the Thomas Dewey district attorney figure. For an interesting albeit brief discussion of the movie that argues for its linking of gangsterism and fascism, see Dick, *The Star-Spangled Screen*, 45. For Luciano's own take on Hollywood gangster movies, including *Little Caesar*, see Gosch and Hammer, *The Last Testament of Lucky Luciano*, 300.

30 For one explanation for Hoover's well-known dismissal of the existence of the Mafia as "baloney," see Powers, *Secrecy and Power*, 333. My own surmise for his denial is that he simply could not imagine a national nemesis as organized and rationalized as his beloved bureau. On Anslinger and the FBN in relation to Luciano, see Rovner, *The Cuba Connection*, 65–73. On Luciano and the mob in Cuba, see English, *Havana Nocturne*, 3–29.

31 Quoted in Rovner, *The Cuba Connection*, 69, 70.

32 On Operation Underworld, see Costanzo, *The Mafia and the Allies*. For a briefer discussion that focuses on Luciano's drug trafficking in the United States and Italy, see McCoy, *The Politics of Heroin*, 24–45.

33 For one interesting postwar fictional treatment set in Italy, see Robert Siodmak's

Deported (1950). As early as *Scarface* (1932), immigrant hoodlums in films were threatened with expulsion, as one reformer remarks while urging that "teeth" be put in the Deportation Act: "These gangsters don't belong in this country. Half of them aren't even citizens."

34 Quoted in Blum, *Killing Hope*, 27. But to a greater degree than during the Red Scare of 1919, many cold war "subversives" living in the United States were immune from deportation because they were native born.

35 See Blum, *Killing Hope*, 27–34. Quotation from *Time* magazine on 29.

36 See Grobel, *The Hustons*, 312. The same year that *Key Largo* was released, Claire Trevor played a similar role in Anthony Mann's brilliant *Raw Deal* (1948). But in this case the older woman's neglect is mitigated by her first-person voice-over, no less than eleven times during the film. This very rare instance of female narration in noir (*Kiss of Death* [1947] is another, briefer example) suggests how not the male protagonist's feelings but her own predominate in the story: adoration, anxious waiting, jealousy, all accompanied by the haunting sounds of a theremin.

37 To add a few quick remarks on *Key Largo*'s other, younger woman, Nora, who intermittently acts defiantly in response to Rocco's lustful advances but otherwise plays a pretty tepid role in the movie: This was the fourth and final pairing onscreen between Hollywood's ideal couple Bogart and Bacall, but without generating the sexual sparks of earlier ones like *To Have and Have Not* (1944), for two reasons, I think. First, they had already been married for three years, so the newness of the romance might have been wearing off for audiences; and second, since she is playing the part of the grieving widow of Frank's war buddy, it would not make sense or be in good taste for the pair to show affection too quickly or strongly.

38 Her theft of his weapon undermines a claim the gangster made earlier in the narrative: "There's a lot of guns out there, but there's only one Johnny Rocco."

39 On Huston's view of the Viertel salon, see Huston, *An Open Book*, 136, 165. See also Giovacchini, *Hollywood Modernism*, for the role of this Los Angeles émigré community in helping shape Hollywood filmmakers and films in the 1930s.

40 On the making and reception of the film, see Sklar, "Havana Episode." Sklar does not connect the movie to *Key Largo*. For Hemingway and Huston, see Huston, *An Open Book*, 165–70, as well as Viertel, *Dangerous Friends*. Describing how Hemingway educated him about the Machado assassination attempt and Cuban politics more generally, Viertel drops the tantalizing tidbit that "Papa went on to say that the most recent plots against the government had involved some of the football stars at the University of Havana and that the Irish-American coach of the team was at the center of much of this activity" (34), but it is unclear how and if this is related to Fidel Castro's alleged shooting of the sports director Manolo Castro (no relation) outside a Havana cinema in February 1948.

41 See Quirk, *Fidel Castro*; and Skierka, *Fidel Castro*. The detail about *Das Kapital* can be found on 28 of Skierka.

Chapter Four: *North from Mexico*

1 For James M. Cain's *Postman*, see chapter 2. Beyond his noir phase, Cain continued to be interested in Mexico throughout the 1930s. See, for instance, his novel *Serenade* (1937), about an opera singer who hooks up with a Mexican Indian woman in Mexico City before moving back with her to the United States. Two other notable films noirs of 1946 take place in Latin American locales: *Notorious*, set in Brazil, directed by Hitchcock and scripted by Ben Hecht, and *Gilda*, set in Argentina and directed by Charles Vidor, both involving sinister Germans (former Nazis). The role of Latin America in noir is briefly discussed in Naremore, *More Than Night*, 230.

2 It is suggestive that Welles would set his elegy for film noir on the Mexican–U.S. border, but *Touch of Evil* has already generated so much critical commentary that I will refrain from examining it extensively in this chapter and only remark on it briefly in my postscript. For a provocative set of reflections on the movie to which I am indebted, see Pease, "Borderline Justice / States of Emergency." Pease does an excellent job of analyzing the important scholarship on the film. In his interesting discussion of Welles's Popular Front politics, Michael Denning notes in passing how "Mexico had long been Hollywood's other." See Denning, *The Cultural Front*, 401. For a reading of antebellum historical romance that shows how Mexico "stands in as the U.S.'s uncanny imperial other" in the nineteenth century, see Alemán, "The Other Country," 409. For an earlier sympathetic account of Mexican laborers exploited (indeed, enslaved) by an Anglo boss, see the Hopalong Cassidy B western *Border Patrol* (1943), scripted by Michael Wilson. As this example makes clear, Mexico is certainly not the exclusive domain of film noir: from the silent era onward, the Mexican-U.S. border has been the site for dozens of westerns depicting the transgressive activity of outlaws, thieves, and smugglers. For an important collection of essays broadly germane to my analysis, see Dudziak and Volpp, "Legal Borderlands."

3 One other film is worth noting here, *Jeopardy* (1951), about an American wife and mother (played by Barbara Stanwyck) vacationing in Mexico who is terrorized by a ruthless escaped American convict (played by Ralph Meeker). Only in *Border Incident* do Mexicans play significant roles in these noirs set south of the border.

4 I take my title for this chapter from the classic study by Carey McWilliams, *North from Mexico* originally published in 1949.

5 The political fates of the cast and crew soon after making the movie are worth mentioning. Both the assistant director Howard Koch and Da Silva were blacklisted during the 1950s for their leftist leanings, while Murphy in 1964 went on to become a Republican senator representing California. In his autobiography, Murphy credited his sophisticated political grasp of the intricacies of the bracero program as stemming from his acting experience in *Border Incident*. While running for the Senate, he expressed his support for continuing the guest-worker

program by infamously declaring, "You have to remember that Americans can't do that kind of work. It's too hard. Mexicans are really good at that. They are built low to the ground, you see, so it's easier for them to stoop." See "Who is the Good Guy?" *Time*, October 16, 1964, 36. See also Murphy with Lasky, *Say . . . Didn't You Used to Be George Murphy?*, 2–3; and Koch, *As Time Goes By.*

6 Wicking and Pattison, "Interviews with Anthony Mann," 37. Mann specifically remarks "John and I had thought of doing *Border Incident*, because the guys there were also involved with the federal agents and T Men. Through the research we made with *T Men* we found the fantastic story of the *Border Incident* boys." See also his remark that "one must be very careful of words. A word can destroy an image . . . it is vital that what you see is real, rather than what you hear." Quoted in Koszarski, *Hollywood Directors, 1941–76*, 337. I am precisely interested in the relation between word and image in *Border Incident*, particularly in how images can destroy words (the reverse of Mann's concern).

7 For the film's original title and the details of its purchase by MGM, see American Film Institute, *American Film Institute Catalog of Motion Pictures Produced in the US*, 280. On MGM and Schary, particularly his disputes with Louis B. Mayer, see Schary, *Heyday*, 157–82; Crowther, *The Lion's Share*, 287–303; Carey, *All the Stars in Heaven*, 282–300; and Biesen, *Blackout*, 209.

8 For a blistering, brilliant contemporary critique of these social problem films, see Tyler, "Hollywood as a Universal Church." Specifically evincing *Border Incident* to ponder the vexed relation between social realism and film noir, Raymond Borde and Etienne Chaumeton in 1955 posed a key question: "Can one speak of noir violence in a work that treats of an objective economic phenomenon and that is inspired, even atrociously so, by authentic news stories?" See Borde and Chaumeton, *A Panorama of American Film Noir, 1941–1953*, 113. My response will be to show precisely how this assumed distinction between the "oneiric" (as Borde and Chaumeton frequently characterize noir) and the "objective" tends to collapse in the wake of the braceros' nightmarish border crossings.

9 For a discussion of the resonant phrase *bootlegged alien* that locates the term in the smuggling of persons as well as liquor during the Prohibition, see Ngai, *Impossible Subjects*, 62.

10 On the bracero program, see Anderson, *The Bracero Program in California*; Galarza, *Merchants of Labor*; Ngai, *Impossible Subjects*, 139–47; and Camacho, *Migrant Imaginaries*, 67, 62–111. For a fascinating account of Mexican Americans' mixed reactions to the program, see Gutiérrez, *Walls and Mirrors*, 133–51. I have deliberately used the term *manpower* because, at its inception, the program only contracted Mexican men as workers.

11 For an excellent, detailed, and eye-opening account of Roosevelt's aggressive implementation of the mass evacuation, see Robinson, *By Order of the President*. Robinson stresses how FDR tended to consider Japanese American citizens as aliens loyal to Japan who could not be assimilated. Hoover's opposition to mass evacuation is discussed in Powers, *Secrecy and Power*, 249–50. For an interesting

analysis of key court cases triggered by the internment, see Irons, *Justice at War*. That Japanese Americans living in Hawaii (under martial law) were not evacuated and that there were no mass internments of Americans of German or Italian descent during the war all suggest the inconsistency of FDR's policies. Interestingly, there are relatively few spy movies made during the war that address the West Coast internment, presumably too close for comfort to Hollywood, but see *Little Tokyo, USA* (1942), and *Betrayal from the East* (1945), both fifth-column plots along the lines of *Confessions of a Nazi Spy*. *Little Tokyo, USA*, even makes reference to an "oriental bund" and concludes with newsreel footage of a mass evacuation that the movie has worked to justify. For a discussion of the Office of War Information's (OWI) negative reaction to *Little Tokyo, USA*, whose plot confirmed FDR's own sense of Japanese Americans' loyalty to Japan, see Koppes and Black, *Hollywood Goes to War*, 72–77. For a glowing portrait of Japanese American soldiers who fought in the famed 442 Regimental Combat Team, see *Go For Broke!* (1951), which refers to the internment only in passing.

12 See Chan, *Asian Americans*, 130.

13 I should point out, however, that the Japanese Americans were primarily owners of small farms, whereas the braceros were brought in to work large tracts run by big corporate agribusinesses. Another sort of connection, by way of space, between the internment and the migrant labor program is made in Camacho, *Migrant Imaginaries*, when the author points out that former Japanese internment camps were used to house Mexican nationals, suggesting "the ideological continuity linking the formation of a subordinated caste of foreign workers and the denial of citizenship to people of Asian and Latin American origins" (90).

14 Goodman, *The Committee*, 154. Lippmann quoted in MacDonnell, *Insidious Foes*, 87. For an intriguing account of the mixed reaction of German exiles living in Los Angeles to Executive Order 9066, see Bahr, *Weimar on the Pacific*, 90–94. The words *alien* and *enemy* were so closely associated during the 1940s (both during and directly after the war) as to be interchangeable, with each being used as either an adjective or a noun in conjunction with the other ("enemy alien" or "alien enemy").

15 Rossiter, *Constitutional Dictatorship*, 8, 314.

16 "North of the Border," *Time*, November 1, 1948. See also Gutiérrez, *Walls and Mirrors*, 157, who calls the incident a "near riot"; and Ngai, *Impossible Subjects*, 153.

17 Quoted in Galarza, *Spiders in the House and Workers in the Field*, 31. Galarza's entire book is devoted to this banned film (currently available from the Holt Labor Library, San Francisco) and its twenty-year ordeal in the courts. Although midcentury documentaries shared a certain generic similarity, *Poverty in the Valley of Plenty* begins in a nearly identical fashion to *Border Incident*, with sweeping panoramic shots of agricultural fields accompanied by a narrator intoning, "This is the San Joaquin Valley." Insisting that the striking farmworkers "are not migrants," the documentary unsympathetically emphasizes how Mexican

"wetbacks" acted as scabs for the farm industry; in the only clearly fictionalized scene in the film, these "illegal entrants" are shown climbing from a car into the back of a waiting truck as their smugglers are surreptitiously paid off.

18 The same year as this documentary, a Mexican fictional comedy was released, *Pito Pérez se va de bracero*, *Pito Pérez Becomes a Bracero*, (1948), that portrayed its villainous coyotes as Italian, which is interesting in relation to my subsequent discussion of the figure of the German Ulrich in Mann's movie. For an account of this early film, as well as other representations of braceros in Mexican cinema and literature, see Fox, *The Fence and the River*, 97–118. See also Herrera-Sobek, *The Bracero Experience*.

19 See, for example, "DiGiorgio Sues for $2,000,000," *Los Angeles Times*, November 8, 1949.

20 On police procedurals at midcentury, see Wilson, *Cop Knowledge*, 57–93.

21 Bosley Crowther, "'Border Incident,' Adventure Film about US Immigration Service, Opens at Globe," *New York Times*, November 21, 1949.

22 It might be argued that the term *all* signifies inclusion rather than exclusion, meaning that the canal is open to both sides, but in fact the aqueduct acquired its distinctly patriotic name when built in the 1930s to replace the Alamo Canal, which was located primarily in Mexico, underscoring how transnational sharing remains an illusion throughout the movie. The Overseas Highway connecting the Florida Keys that I discuss in the previous chapter underwent a similar nationalizing of nomenclature (to "U.S. 1") when completed in the 1940s. The CBS show *Sixty Minutes* reported on May 2, 2010, that more than 550 Mexicans have drowned in the All-American Canal trying to enter the United States illegally.

23 As Dana Polan points out in his DVD commentary, Alton's camerawork amounts to a textbook of visual techniques subsequently to be identified as film noir: deep-focus compositions that triangulate characters in the foreground and background to emphasize a sense of menace and entrapment; figures cast in inky black shadows whose faces are frequently illuminated by strong lighting (most explicitly by flashlights); and awkward off-angle long shots and close-ups. Alton in the movie even manages to give plowed lettuce fields the stark chiaroscuro effects reminiscent of Venetian blinds in so many urban thrillers of the 1940s. Contemporaneous westerns with noir-inflected narratives filled with matter-of-fact treachery, brutality, and obsession, frequently identified as "psychological" at the time, include *Ramrod* (1947), *Pursued* (1947), and *Blood on the Moon* (1948).

24 Agamben, *Homo Sacer*, 129.

25 In passing I should mention a second sort of visual allegory running through the film that Polan also notes, a Dantean descent into hell, but I am less interested in this mythological pattern than in the film's political allegorizing.

26 In an otherwise suggestive article on "border noirs" that appeared after my own chapter was completed, Dominque Bregent-Heald mistakenly locates the quicksand on the U.S. side in her brief discussion of *Border Incident*. See Bregent-

Heald, "Dark Limbo: Film Noir and the North American Borders," 128. Bregent-Heald's concerns are similar to my own, although she does not engage questions of citizenship in her emphasis on Americans who cross into Mexico in these border narratives. Eric Lott has also noted in passing that "film noir is a cinematic mode defined by its border crossings," but he reads these crossings more in terms of race than nationality. See Lott, "The Whiteness of Film Noir," 548.

27 For a classic American studies account of the imposition of technology on the landscape, see Marx, *The Machine in the Garden*.

28 One other cultural difference between the two nations merits mention: Mexicans stab while Americans shoot, in keeping with their tendency to occupy a more distant, detached perspective in the film.

29 The three other women are a Mexican shopkeeper who allows Jack to use her phone, a Mexican housekeeper who curtly ushers in Cuchillo and his comrade as they enter Parkson's home, and the farm foreman Amboy's wife, Bella, who near the end briefly holds Pablo at gunpoint when he tries to call the immigration authorities for help. Given the almost complete absence of women in *Border Incident*, it is interesting to note that a day after the film was released on November 20, 1949, *Life* magazine ran a cover story on Ricardo Montalban featuring his upcoming MGM war picture, *Battleground* (also with George Murphy), that called Montalban "a new kind of romantic movie hero: honest, serious, brave" (94). That a male lead could be deemed "romantic" in two successive films without any women in them is worth further consideration.

30 For a different reading of this scene that stresses how we are inclined to "sympathize with the tortured villain," see Basinger, *Anthony Mann*, 73.

31 Ngai, *Impossible Subjects*, 5, 4.

32 For a similar argument focusing on how Asians since the nineteenth century have been admitted into the United States because of "emergency" economic imperatives at the same time that the state has acted to exclude them from citizenship, see Lowe, *Immigrant Acts*.

33 Coutin, "Illegality, Borderlands, and the Space of Nonexistence," 174–75. See also Momen, "Are You a Citizen?"

34 Consider *Blue Dahlia* (1946), *Somewhere in the Night* (1946), and *The Crooked Way* (1949), to name just three amnesia plots featuring veterans of the Second World War, a trope I discuss briefly in chapters 3 and 5. For a discussion of films from the 1940s in relation to paranoia, see Polan, *Power and Paranoia*.

35 Agamben, *Homer Sacer*, 49–58.

36 Comments about Operation Wetback from the commissioner general of the INS, Joseph M. Swing, quoted in Ngai, *Impossible Subjects*, 155. See also 56–95 on U.S. deportation policies.

37 Basinger, *Anthony Mann*, 72. Basinger's assessment in 1979 of the film's brutality might seem a bit quaint by today's standards.

38 See, for example, Krutnik, *In a Lonely Street*, 15–17; Naremore, *More Than Night*, 9–39; and Neale, *Genre and Hollywood*, 151–77.

39 For the term *meta-genre* as applied to film noir, I am indebted to Yoichiro Miyamoto. Arguing against film noir's exceptionalism (contra the assumptions of Pease and others), Jonathan Munby, in his invaluable study of gangster films from the 1930s, including how they mutated after the war, similarly calls film noir "a non-genre-specific 'second order' textual category." Munby, *Public Enemies, Public Heroes*, 142. See also Naremore, *More Than Night*, 220–33 for a discussion of noir's liminality; and, conversely, Hantke, "Boundary Crossing and the Construction of Cinematic Genre," which argues that the claustrophobic "diegetic totality of the noir universe" is always encapsulated, rendering escape to any outside impossible.

40 Pease, "Borderline Justice/States of Emergency," 87. As Pease's emphasis on naming and narrative suggests, his Lacanian treatment of noir as a kind of submerged language tends to slight the nonverbal aspects of film, certainly a drawback or limitation for an essentially visual medium like cinema, as my focus on the subversive potential of Alton's camerawork has suggested.

41 These lines are reprinted in Sikov, *On Sunset Boulevard*, 101. As Sikov points out (105), the slowness of the United States to fill its quotas has been interpreted as a deliberate tactic to keep unwanted refugees out. The cockroach scene is also discussed by Gemünden, *A Foreign Affair*, 1.

42 On female gothic, see Doane, *The Desire to Desire*; and Waldman, "'At Last I Can Tell It to Someone.'" Beyond discussing how voice-over operates in this film (150–51), Doane perceptively notes how Mark's theory of felicitous space perversely reverses the logic of German expressionism, since in this case a room determines rather than reflects events within (134–35). On female voice more generally, see Silverman, *The Acoustic Mirror*. On voice-over in cinema, what Michel Chion calls "acousmêtre," see Chion, *The Voice in Cinema*, 24; and Kozloff, *Invisible Storytellers*.

43 A second example might be the drug-induced voice-over of Louise Howell (Joan Crawford) in *Possessed* (1947), although I would argue that this narration is a more outer-directed recounting of plot events rather than of personal feelings.

44 Gunning, *The Films of Fritz Lang*, 340–67; and Bronfen, *Home in Hollywood*, 157–95. See also Oliver and Trigo, *Noir Anxiety*, 73–96; and Cowie, "Film Noir and Women." Gunning is especially strong in his comparisons between Lang and Hitchcock. Because Bronfen (like Cowie before her) is intent on treating the movie as a film noir, she emphasizes two passing references in the narrative about Mark's wartime experience, thereby associating him with the familiar trope of the maladjusted war veteran, a figure I discuss elsewhere in this study. I should point out in passing that Mexico is nowhere to be found in the film's source novel of 1945, *Museum Piece No. 13*, by Rufus King.

45 Maltby, "The Politics of the Maladjusted Text," 39. Maltby's analogy is more than clever, since it draws on a deep-seated link between communists and gangsters that many Americans felt after the war, a connection based on the prior wartime association between Nazis and gangsters. Later in this same essay (46) Maltby

speculates that the narrative may also function as a metaphor for the traumatized war veteran trying to readjust to American normalcy, but there is no indication that Jeff has been a soldier, and little indication, given Mitchum's cool performance, that he is suffering from "guilt" and "obsessive neuroses" beyond a fleeting reference he makes in the film to having "been afraid of half the things I ever did." For more on the trope of the war veteran and noir, see chapters 3 and 5.

46 For an excellent discussion of the film's lighting effects created by Nicholas Musuraca, the same cinematographer that shot *Stranger on the Third Floor*, see Naremore, *More Than Night*, 178–86. Given its familiarity, I have not bothered to give a full summary of *Out of the Past*'s story line, especially the second half of the film's San Francisco segment, whose derivative plot is as confusing and convoluted as *The Big Sleep* (1946), but with fewer clever lines.

47 As do *Border Incident* and *Key Largo*, the film begins its Mexican segment with an aerial shot from a plane landing in Mexico City, but instead of an authoritative police procedural narrator, we have the detective Jeff's voice narrating his tracking down Kathie. Although the domestic Mexican movie industry was quite robust in the 1940s, the tourist town of Acapulco would most likely be showing American films, although this is not made explicit one way or another in the narrative. For a reading of the movie similar to mine that emphasizes the timeless, fantasyland aspects of Mexico and that also speculates on the sort of movies that might have been shown at the Cine Pico, see Fay and Nieland, *Film Noir*, 64–72.

48 Fishing actually leads to a complex cluster of metaphoric associations in the film, from the name of Jeff's sleazy partner (Jack Fisher), to the fishing nets on the beach in Acapulco, to the Lake Tahoe activities of Jeff, the Kid, and Whit.

49 For an unusual gloss on this philosophical question, see Auster, *Ghosts*. Set in 1947, Auster's novella concerns a detective named Blue who finds himself in a case he cannot give up. At one point he goes into a movie theater to watch *Out of the Past*, which Auster synopsizes as a clear parallel to Blue's own situation. Auster's focus on the role of the mute Kid is worth contemplating.

50 Kathie and Jeff are slain classic gangland style, in a car riddled with bullets, but without the melodrama we find in most gangster films of the 1930s, such as *Little Caesar*.

51 Harvey, *Movie Love in the Fifties*, 26.

Chapter Five: *Bad Boy Patriots*

1 Maltz, *The Citizen Writer*, 10.

2 Greene, *A Gun for Sale*. For a comparison between the novel and the film, see Naremore, *More Than Night*, 72–74. Naremore emphasizes the differences, but given the looseness of many Hollywood adaptations at the time, this one strikes me as relatively faithful.

3 For the film's production history, see Biesen, *Blackout*, 50–57. Biesen quotes

Greene as especially disapproving of the adaptation's introducing a "female conjurer working for the FBI," although of course she works directly for a Senate committee, not the FBI per se.

4 MacDonnell, *Insidious Foes*, 153.

5 For the use of the term bad boy during the 1950s, see Medovoi, *Rebels*, especially 39–40. Medovoi points out that the term stretches back to late nineteenth-century American fiction.

6 Borde and Chaumeton, *A Panorama of American Film Noir, 1941–53*, 37.

7 Dinerstein, " 'Emergent Noir,' " 421.

8 The novel *High Sierra* was published in 1940 by the hard-boiled author W. R. Burnett, who coscripted the film *This Gun for Hire*. On Burnett, see Irwin, *Unless the Threat of Death Is behind Them*, 97–122.

9 On the central role played by domesticity in American crime narratives, see Cassuto, *Hard-Boiled Sentimentality*.

10 Although I say relatively little about the formal features of *This Gun for Hire*, I should mention that its cinematographer, John Seitz, went on two years later to shoot *Double Indemnity*, whose darkened interiors closely resemble his earlier compositions in the Tuttle film.

11 Naremore, *More Than Night*, 73.

12 Hitchcock would deploy this kind of mother-lover-spy figure to almost parodic effect in *North by Northwest* (1959).

13 Biesen, *Blackout*, 48. See also Doherty, *Projections of War*.

14 I was surprised to learn that this festival, which features the burning of a fifty-foot puppet, was started in 1924, as a modern invented tradition, although Santa Fe fiestas began in the early 1700s. For a contemporaneous French account of the film that emphasizes existential alienation, see Tailleur, "*The Pink Horse*; or, the Pipe Dreams of the Human Condition."

15 Even though Montgomery was much better known as an actor than as a director, he is underrated in the latter function, especially considering experiments like his version of Raymond Chandler's *Lady in the Lake* (1947), released a few months before *Ride the Pink Horse*, which tries to establish a subjective perspective by making Phillip's head literally one with the camera, so that we see only what he sees. Montgomery's direction is valuable, if only as an object lesson for film studies students about how cinema does not and cannot construct subjectivity in this manner. But if *Ride the Pink Horse* is more conventional in its camerawork, it also contains scenes of great power, such as the beating of Pancho by two thugs in the background as terrified children ride the rotating carousel in the foreground. Not exactly the merry-go-round scene at the climax of Hitchcock's *Strangers on a Train* (1951), but impressive nonetheless.

16 Maltby, "The Politics of the Maladjusted Text." This important line of inquiry about postwar disillusionment was initially proposed in the seminal essay of 1972 by Paul Schrader, "Notes on Film Noir."

17 In all the scenes of eating in the film (and there are plenty), Gagin hardly ever

touches his food, just as he hardly speaks, so that curing his ills (body and mind) will center on putting sustenance in his mouth, and getting words out (a version of Freud's talking cure). For a discussion of the postwar American movie gangster as businessman, see chapter 3.

18 On Truman and his committee, see Brandes, *Warhogs*, 261–62. For a contemporaneous account of wartime corruption written by a renowned popular historian, see Catton, *The War Lords of Washington*. Agent Retz was played in the film by Art Smith, who ironically was blacklisted on the basis of Elia Kazan's infamous HUAC testimony. See. Navasky, *Naming Names*, 201.

19 I borrow this term from Osteen, "The Big Secret," 81. The most famous nuclear noir is of course Robert Aldrich's *Kiss Me Deadly* (1955), which I discuss in my postscript.

20 For a recent example, see Dombrowski, *The Films of Samuel Fuller*. In her analysis of *Pickup*, Dombrowski does an excellent job of discussing camera setups, showing how Fuller intercuts fluid master shots with inserts, but she says nary a word about the film's politics, even though the plot centers on cold war espionage.

21 Stewart, *On Longing*, 102.

22 Implicitly drawing on Walter Benjamin's famous discussion of aura in "The Work of Art in the Age of Mechanical Reproduction," Stewart in examining concepts of the miniature emphasizes small books that require immense human craft and care, as opposed to photographic media such as microfilm. See Stewart, *On Longing*, 8, 11, 37–44.

23 Quoted in Truffaut with Scott, *Hitchcock*, 138–39.

24 Fuller, *A Third Face*, 304–5.

25 See Heumann and Murray, "*Cape Town Affair*." For their information about "Blaze of Glory," Heumann and Murray rely on a brief unsubstantiated speculation in Gallafent, "Kiss Me, Deadly," 245. Fuller in his autobiography acknowledges the Dwight Taylor story as the source of his script but does not mention that it was about drugs, suggesting that he changed the script simply because he found courtroom dramas boring. By 1952 the Production Code was losing force, and therefore it is unclear whether Taylor's story would have run into censorship problems. Three years earlier, for example, the same studio (Twentieth Century-Fox) was able to produce and release a film that featured drug dealers, *Slattery's Hurricane*, also starring Widmark, after making some script changes demanded by the PCA head Joseph Breen. For details, see American Film Institute, *American Film Institute Catalog of Motion Pictures Produced in the US*, 2213.

26 Fuller, *A Third Face*, 293. Fuller's retrospective confusion between trade and nuclear secrets is itself revealing in relation to the fact that after the Second World War, complex criteria for legitimizing the classification of proliferating pages and pages of documents as national security secrets came to be based on corporate patents and formulas, whose status as protected had a longer history of legal precedent. See Galison, "Removing Knowledge."

27 Rogin, "*Ronald Reagan*," the Movie, 239.

28 Enamored of Fuller's fluid camerawork, critics have been rather condescending toward his writing, often falling back on tired clichés about the director as an American primitive with brilliant visual instincts and little else. Manny Farber, for example, curtly dismissed his scripts as "grotesque jobs." See Farber, *Negative Space*, 129. But there is nothing grotesque about *Pickup*'s resonant dialogue. To cite another instance of Fuller's craft in plotting, we note how the intensely claustrophobic scene of Joey hidden in a descending apartment dumbwaiter near the end exquisitely parallels Skip's dredging up the hidden microfilm by rope and pulley near the beginning of the movie.

29 Fuller was a notorious embellisher. At one point in his autobiography *A Third Face*, Fuller says the film was screened in Washington for Hoover, who telephoned Zanuck to complain (304), but a few pages later (307–8) Fuller asserts that a lunch with the three of them took place at Romanoff's restaurant in Hollywood, a claim Fuller repeated elsewhere. See Server, *Sam Fuller*, 34. The detail about removing *damn* is from yet another interview (with Richard Schickel) reproduced in the Criterion Collection DVD edition (2004) of *Pickup*. I have not been able to corroborate this remarkable encounter, which is not mentioned in any Zanuck biography I have consulted. As Steven J. Ross has noted, Hoover from the early 1920s on routinely had his field agents file reports on specific movies. See Ross, *Working-Class Hollywood*, 9, 144. But even though Hoover was known to frequent Romanoff's when in Los Angeles, it is uncertain whether he would arrange a meeting to personally confront a director about making some changes to a script. In fact, a memo from an FBI field agent to Hoover dated May 19, 1952, indicates that during the making of *Pickup* it was Fuller who initially contacted the bureau, and not vice versa. After describing Fuller's desire to verify his depiction of FBI procedures (a request that underscores Fuller's serious investment in the cold war plot), the memo goes on to quote a friend of Fuller's that the director "was not on the left side at all, that he is an extreme individualist who is not afraid to take a stand, even though it might be very controversial." Hoover replied, "If Fuller contacts you concerning his proposed screen story advise him Bureau unable to be of assistance." Thanks to Marsha Gordon Orgeron for sharing this information, which was obtained through the Freedom of Information Act.

30 Sayre, *Running Time*, 91.

31 A French documentary on Fuller of 1982 (included in the Criterion Collection DVD) opens by showing the director clutching the first reel of *Pickup* housed inside a canister similar to the one Skip uses to hide the microfilm. Recording Fuller's comments as he reviews the reel, scene by scene, the documentary helps us see how the exterior shot of a racing subway train that begins *Pickup*, with its window frames set off in a blur of black and white, closely resemble the rushing strip of film frames that winds through the viewing apparatus operated by Fuller.

32 As a negative original, not a positive copy, the celluloid sequence of frames under Skip's scrutiny would also seem to illustrate Garrett Stewart's remarkable argu-

ment concerning what he calls cinema's "photo-synthesis," the complex relays between the single photographic cell, suppressed from our awareness, and the moving image. Surprisingly, although Stewart masterfully analyzes the role played by
still photographs and freeze frames in dozens of movies, he does not discuss
microfilm at all, a more literal trace of the frame photogram that *Pickup* high-
lights as such. See Stewart, *Between Film and Screen*.

33 It seems that *auteur* has been pushed to the margins of the current academic film
studies lexicon, to be replaced by the more impartial (and less French-sounding)
term *authorship*. For an interesting discussion that argues for a "new auteurism,"
see Polan, "Auteur Desire." For a more recent case study, see Orgeron, "La
Camera-Crayola." On Fuller's denial that the film was political, see Fuller, *A
Third Face*: "I had no intention of making a political statement in *Pickup*, none
whatsoever. My yarn is a noir thriller about marginal people, nothing more,
nothing less" (305). It therefore might seem contradictory for me to read the film
autobiographically but against the director's own stated intentions. Yet I would
argue that Fuller's statement of intention is cagey enough to warrant its own
skeptical analysis, since while explaining his design, he invokes the term *noir*
(elsewhere disavowed by him) and calls attention to his "marginal" characters in
a way that cannot help but have political and socioeconomic implications.

34 Other major lone screenwriter-directors in the 1940s and 1950s would include
Orson Welles, of course, and John Huston, most notably in *The Maltese Falcon*
(1941), based on the Dashiell Hammett novel, and *The Treasure of the Sierra
Madre* (1948), based on the B. Traven novel. Another example is Joseph L.
Mankiewicz, who both wrote and directed *All About Eve* (1948).

35 Dimendberg, *Film Noir and the Spaces of Modernity*, 21–22. For an interesting
discussion of Fuller's violent close-ups in relation to his depiction of women, see
Gordon, " 'What Makes a Girl Who Looks Like That Get Mixed up in Science?' ".
Pickup's beginning subway scene has no dialogue or music other than diegetic
sounds, much like *Ride the Pink Horse* (for the first five minutes) and *This Gun for
Hire* (for the first ninety seconds).

36 In recounting the genesis of *Pickup*, Fuller recalled that "all the newspapers at
that time in the United States were talking about Klaus Fuchs, the spy who
operated from England, selling secrets on microfilm to the Soviet Union." In the
same paragraph he also mentions Richard's Nixon's "phony exposé" of Alger Hiss
as a contemporaneous case to which his film implicitly referred. See Fuller, *A
Third Face*, 295.

37 It is interesting that in thinking about the cast for *Pickup*, Zanuck compared an
"Alan Ladd treatment vs. Humphrey Bogart treatment," the latter whom he
likens to "hard-hitting" Widmark, while the former is already deemed "conventional" a decade after *This Gun for Hire*, despite how much the French were taken
with this angelic killer. For the Zanuck quotation, see Dombrowski, *The Films of
Samuel Fuller*, 68.

38 Quoted in Powers, *G-Men*, 223.

39 Rogin, *"Ronald Reagan," the Movie*, 268; McConnell, *The Spoken Seen*, 131–33.

40 Schlesinger, *The Vital Center*, 151. Robert Corber notes how Schlesinger in this passage goes on to compare such perversion to homosexual behavior. See Corber, *In the Name of National Security*, 19–23.

41 McConnell, *The Spoken Seen*, 135.

42 In response to Tiger's prediction that Skip will soon be back in jail, Candy's breezy, departing, "You wanna bet?" (the final line of the movie), is ambiguous and could be read, perhaps, as simply a sign of her confidence in his criminal expertise. But more likely their coupling suggests his reformation.

43 Rogin, *"Ronald Reagan," the Movie*, 269.

44 McCarthy, "Naming Names," 154. As McCarthy trenchantly observed in an earlier essay ("The Contagion of Ideas"), "Once the state is looked upon as the *source* of rights, rather than their bound protector, freedom becomes conditional on the pleasure of the state" (44). The best discussion of cold war intellectuals like McCarthy remains Pells, *The Liberal Mind in a Conservative Age*.

45 It is striking, in fact, that two of the most macho filmmakers in midcentury Hollywood, John Huston (in 1948) and Sam Fuller (in 1953), each directed noirs that put older, worn women at the narrative's moral center. For these films the veteran actresses Claire Trevor and Thelma Ritter were each nominated for a best supporting actress Academy Award, which Trevor won for *Key Largo*.

46 Gary Cooper, October 23, 1947, HUAC testimony, reprinted in Bentley, *Thirty Years of Treason*, 153.

47 Schlesinger, *The Vital Center*, 201.

Postscript

1 The big-budget MGM production *Trial* (1955), for example, fans the fires of anticommunism, in the style of cold war liberalism, by showing how an earnest law professor (played by Glenn Ford, naturally) defending an innocent Mexican American teenager is manipulated and duped by the CPUSA for political gain. But it is telling that the film explicitly announces itself as set in June 1947, when domestic subversion could still be seen as something of a serious threat.

2 On Hoover and McCarthy, see Powers, *Secrecy and Power*, 320–23; and O'Reilly, *Hoover and the Un-Americans*, 111–12. For a fascinating documentary based on footage from the army hearings, see Emilio de Antonio's *Point of Order!* (1964), which emphasizes how so much of the senate investigation centered on matters of ocular proof, such as color-coded charts, a cropped photo, and a carbon copy of a letter of dubious provenance but supposedly authored in 1951 by Hoover (which he denied).

3 For one account, see Washington, *The Other Black List*. See also Dudziak, *Cold War Civil Rights*. Dudziak shows how Soviet race-baiting propaganda during the 1950s prompted mainstream American politicians to improve domestic race relations.

4 *Gun Crazy* was directed by Joseph H. Lewis and cowritten by MacKinlay Kantor and Dalton Trumbo (fronted by Millard Kaufman), whose HUAC hounding might help explain the movie's political edge, especially its perverse sympathy for the outlaw couple. Later that same year, presumably inspired by Mann's *Border Incident* (see chapter 4), Lewis directed a film about a concentration camp survivor trying illegally to gain entrance into the United States from Cuba, but *A Lady Without Passport* has neither the visual flair nor the biting satire of *Gun Crazy*. The year 1950 marks the peak of film noir production in Hollywood, although of course most of these movies were run-of-the-mill thrillers without the kind of self-reflexivity that I am attributing to *Gun Crazy*. It might seem that my argument requires a clear assumption of intentionality and agency on the part of the filmmakers, but ultimately I am more interested in affect, in how these particular noirs of the 1950s consistently mimic certain established conventions and expectations. My take on these films has been partly anticipated by Robert Kolker, who in noting the progressive institutionalization of the cycle in the 1950s, remarks how films such as *Kiss Me Deadly* and *Touch of Evil* become "deeply conscious of the way they are put together," suggesting "how disturbing the genre still can be when its forms go beyond the conventions that were established." See Kolker, *A Cinema of Loneliness*, 364. On overtly farcical noirs, see Borde and Chaumeton, *A Panorama of American Film, 1941–1953*, 122–23. For a helpful year-by-year count of film noir releases, see Spicer *Film Noir*, 28, table 2.1.

5 On the juvenile delinquency panic of the 1950s, see Gilbert, *A Cycle of Outrage.*

6 Naremore. *More Than Night*, 150. Subsequent quotations on 150, 22.

7 See Schreiber, *Cold War Exiles in Mexico*, 106. Another sign of the filmmakers' calculated slyness can be found during a conventional montage sequence of blaring newspaper headlines announcing the couple's crime spree, such as "HOLDUP PAIR CRASH / STATE LINE BARRIER!" Beneath this mock headline in smaller print we discover another more insidious one: "Taxpayers to Hear of Subversive Acts." Thanks to my student David Israel for pointing this out. For a similarly covert headline strategically inserted in the later cold war movie *Pickup on South Street*, see chapter 5.

8 For the film's reception, see Naremore, *More Than Night*, 150.

9 Alain Silver reasonably surmises that Aldrich had the photo taken to show to Borde, who had very likely sent Aldrich a copy of his coauthored book and who had been corresponding with Aldrich since 1955 as he prepared his article "Un cinéaste non-conformiste." Personal correspondence with Alain Silver, January 23, 2010.

10 On Rancière, see my introduction, note 29. For an interesting discussion on the complex relays between Hollywood and Paris during the Cold War that encouraged an emergent cosmopolitan film culture, see Schwartz, *It's So French!.*

11 Borde and Chaumeton, *A Panorama of American Film Noir, 1941–1953*, 13.

12 Ibid., 155.

13 I attribute this unusual appropriation of French feminism to the screenwriter,

A. I. Bezzerides, who in the earlier *Thieves' Highway* (1948) scripted one of the most complex and unconventional women in noir, a war refuge prostitute (named Rica) who mocks the male protagonist's desire to "save" her. The best discussion of the visual aspects of Aldrich's film remains Silver, "*Kiss Me Deadly.*" See also Silver and Ursini, *What Ever Happened to Robert Aldrich?*. For a cultural analysis of the film's regulation and reception, see Maltby, "'The Problem of Interpretation. . . .'" Maltby's contextual approach overlooks the way in which the very issues he argues are central for situating the film, especially concerns in the 1950s about the threat of mass culture to high art, are self-consciously threaded into the narrative itself, thus calling into question his assertion that reading the movie as an "act of aesthetic subversion" would not have been available to American audiences at the time of the film's release. Maltby's insistence on commercial and institutional motives as constituting the film's "cultural framework" strikes me as a bit monolithic and deterministic, ignoring, for one thing, the film's very appropriation and internalization of French attitudes toward Americans and American popular culture: Mickey Spillane channeled through Simone de Beauvoir, as it were. Not to rehash New Historicist debates about subversive potential, but if the movie could have been made in 1955, it could have been understood (by some) in 1955.

14 On the cultural impact of *Playboy*, see Gilbert, *Men in the Middle*, chaps. 4 and 9.

15 Naremore, *More Than Night*, especially chaps. 1 and 2.

16 Rancière, "Contemporary Art and the Politics of Aesthetics," 43. As an example of this sort of border crossing between high and low, Rancière mentions a Robert Rauschenberg lithograph containing an image of Venus from a Diego Velázquez painting combined with an image of car keys. This lithograph, *Breakthrough 11*, was done in 1965, a decade after *Kiss Me Deadly*'s juxtapositions created a similar sort of cognitive dissonance.

17 All quotations from Oakes and Grossman, "Managing Nuclear," 364, 368, 376, 383. For an expanded version, see Oakes, *The Imaginary War*. On the performative aspects of civil defense, see Davis, *Stages of Emergency*.

18 See, for example, Sproule, *Propaganda and Democracy*.

19 Borde and Chaumeton, *A Panorama of American Film Noir, 1941–1953*, 155.

20 See Bhabha, "The Other Question"; Denning, *The Cultural Front*, 400–402; and Pease, "Borderline Justice / States of Emergency." Along these lines, also see more recently Beckham, "Placing *Touch of Evil*, *The Border*, and *Traffic* in the American Imagination"; and Marcus, "The Interracial Romance as Primal Drama." None of these critics spend much time considering matters of affect, which has most interestingly been addressed via the movie's soundtrack. See Leeper, "Crossing Musical Borders." For the important but understudied topic of film noir and sound more generally, see Miklitsch, *Siren City*.

21 For a recent version of this argument, see Rollins, "'Some Kind of a Man.'" *Touch of Evil* was the first Hollywood studio film Welles directed since *The Lady from Shanghai* (1948), and it was to be his last.

22 Played broadly by a heavily accented Russian actor (Tamiroff), Grandi is an unnatural amalgam mixing Mexican, American, and Italian. In keeping with the film's persistent double consciousness, Quinlan's strangulation of Grandi thus not only resonates within the narrative's hazy revenge plot (evoking the "half-breed" who strangled Quinlan's wife) but also serves as Welles's comment on cinema history. Accusing the buffoonish racketeer of watching too many gangster movies, Susan during their first encounter dismisses the diminutive Grandi as a "Little Caesar," giving us a link between the familiar screen figure of the 1930s mobster and its postwar reincarnation in noir, a genealogy I discuss in chapter 3. For Welles to murder Little Caesar is to finish off the gangster genre itself. Given my focus on the self-reflexivity displayed by these three films from the 1950s, it could be argued that they represent a bridge between noir and subsequent "neo-noir," or that they are even neo-noir themselves. But I prefer to think of them as ending a cycle rather than beginning a new one, since for me nostalgia-laden movies of the 1970s, such as Roman Polanski's *Chinatown* (1974), have quite a different historical valence about them concerning questions of citizenship and therefore stand outside my emphasis on the cold war period of the 1940s and 1950s.

Bibliography

Adler, Les K., and Thomas G. Paterson. "Red Fascism: The Merger of Nazi Germany and Soviet Russia in the American Image of Totalitarianism, 1930's–1950's." *American Historical Review* 75, no. 4 (1970), 1046–64.

Agamben, Giorgio. *Homo Sacer: Sovereign Power and Bare Life*. Trans. Daniel Heller-Roazen. Stanford: Stanford University Press, 1998.

———. *State of Exception*. Trans. Kevin Attell. Chicago: University of Chicago Press, 2005.

Aleinikoff, Alexander. "Theories of Loss of Citizenship." *Michigan Law Review* 84, no. 7 (1986), 1471–1503.

Alemán, Jesse. "The Other Country: Mexico, the United States, and the Gothic History of Conquest." *American Literary History* 18, no. 3 (2006), 406–26.

Altman, Rick. *Film/Genre*. London: British Film Institute, 1999.

American Film Institute. *American Film Institute Catalog of Motion Pictures Produced in the US: Feature Films, 1941–50*. Berkeley: University of California Press, 1999.

Anderson, Henry P. *The Bracero Program in California*. New York: Arno Press, 1961.

Anderson, Maxwell. *Key Largo: A Play in a Prologue and Two Acts*. Washington, D.C.: Anderson House, 1939.

Arendt, Hannah. *The Origins of Totalitarianism*. New York: Harcourt Brace Jovanovich, 1951.

———."The Stateless People." *Contemporary Jewish Record* 8, no. 2 (1945): 137–53.

Arnold, Kathleen R. *Homelessness, Citizenship, and Iden-*

tity: The Uncanniness of Late Modernity. Albany: State University of New York Press, 2004.

Auerbach, Jonathan. *Body Shots: Early Cinema's Incarnations*. Berkeley: University of California Press, 2007.

Auster, Paul. *Ghosts*. In *The New York Trilogy*, 159–32. New York: Penguin, 1990.

Bacevich, Andrew J., ed. *The Long War: A New History of U.S. National Security Policy since World War II*. New York: Columbia University Press, 2007.

Bahr, Ehrhard. *Weimar on the Pacific: German Exile Culture in Los Angeles and the Crisis of Modernism*. Berkeley: University of California Press, 2007.

Basinger, Jeanine. *Anthony Mann*. Boston: Twayne, 1979.

Batvinis, Raymond J. *The Origins of FBI Counterintelligence*. Lawrence: University Press of Kansas, 2007.

Beckham, Jack M., II. "Placing *Touch of Evil, The Border,* and *Traffic* in the American Imagination." *Journal of Popular Film and Television* 33, no. 3 (2005), 130–41.

Bell, Daniel. *The End of Ideology: On the Exhaustion of Political Ideas in the Fifties*. Glencoe, Ill.: Free Press, 1960.

Bell, Leland V. *In Hitler's Shadow*. Port Washington, N. Y.: Kennikat, 1973.

Bennett, David H. *The Party of Fear: From Nativist Movements to the New Right in American History*. Chapel Hill: University of North Carolina Press, 1988.

Bennett, Marion T. "The Immigration and Nationality (McCarran-Walter) Act of 1952, as Amended to 1965." *Annals of the American Academy of Political and Social Science*, no. 367 (1966), 127–36.

Bentham, Jeremy. "Rewards to Informers." Chapter 13 of *The Rationale of Reward*. In *The Works of Jeremy Bentham*, ed. John Bowring, vol. 2, 189–266. New York: Russell and Russell, 1962.

Bentley, Eric, ed. *Thirty Years of Treason: Excerpts from Hearings before the House Committee on Un-American Activities, 1938–1968*. New York: Viking, 1971.

Bhabha, Homi. "The Other Question: The Stereotype and Colonial Discourse." *Screen* 24, no. 1 (1983), 7–32.

Biesen, Sheri Cinen. *Blackout: World War II and the Origins of Film Noir*. Baltimore: Johns Hopkins University Press, 2005.

Biskind, Peter. *Seeing Is Believing*. New York: Pantheon, 1983.

Blakley, Joanna, and Martin Kaplan, eds. *Warner's War: Politics, Pop Culture, and Propaganda in Wartime Hollywood*. Los Angeles: USC Annenberg Norman Lear Center, 2004.

Blum, William. *Killing Hope: U.S. Military and C.I.A. Interventions since World War II*. Monroe, Maine: Common Courage Press, 2004.

Boorstin, Daniel J. *The Americans: The Democratic Experience*. New York: Random House, 1973.

——. *The Genius of American Politics*. Chicago: University of Chicago Press, 1953.

Borde, Raymond. "Un cinéaste non-conformist: Robert Aldrich." *Les temps modernes*, no. 124 (1956), 1681–96.

Borde, Raymond, and Etienne Chaumeton. *A Panorama of American Film Noir, 1941–1953*. Trans. Paul Hammond. San Francisco: City Lights Books, 2002.

Bosniak, Linda. "Citizenship Denationalized." *Indiana Journal of Global Legal Studies*, no. 7 (2000), 447–510.

Brandes, Stuart D. *Warhogs: A History of War Profits in America*. Lexington: University Press of Kentucky, 1997.

Bregent-Heald, Dominque. "Dark Limbo: Film Noir and the North American Borders." *Journal of American Culture* 29, no. 2 (2006), 125–38.

Broe, Dennis. *Film Noir, American Workers, and Postwar Hollywood*. Gainesville: University Press of Florida, 2009.

Bronfen, Elisabeth. "Femme Fatale—Negotiations of Tragic Desire." *New Literary History* 35, no. 1 (2004), 103–16.

——. *Home in Hollywood: The Imaginary Geography of Cinema*. New York: Columbia University Press, 2004.

Brook, Vincent. *Driven to Darkness: Jewish Émigré Directors and the Rise of Film Noir*. New Brunswick, N.J.: Rutgers University Press, 2009.

Brown, Royal S. *Overtones and Undertones: Reading Film Music*. Berkeley: University of California Press, 1994.

Buchanan, Edna. "Lucky Luciano," *Time*, December 7, 1998, 130–32.

Buhle, Paul, and Dave Warner. *Radical Hollywood: The Untold Story Behind America's Favorite Movies*. New York: New Press, 2002.

Cain, James M. *The Postman Always Rings Twice*. New York: Vintage, 1992.

——. *The Postman Always Rings Twice, Double Indemnity, Mildred Pierce, and Selected Stories*. New York: Knopf, 2003.

——. *Serenade*. New York: Knopf, 1937.

Camacho, Alicia Schmidt. *Migrant Imaginaries: Latino Cultural Politics in the U.S.-Mexico Borderlands*. New York: New York University Press, 2008.

Carey, Gary. *All the Stars in Heaven: Louis B. Mayer's M-G-M*. New York: E. P. Dutton, 1981.

Carlson, John. *Under Cover: My Four Years in the Nazi Underworld of America; The Amazing Revelation of How Axis Agents and Our Enemies within Are Now Plotting to Destroy the United States*. New York: E. P. Dutton, 1943.

Cassuto, Leonard. *Hard-Boiled Sentimentality: The Secret History of American Crime Stories*. New York: Columbia University Press, 2009.

Catton, Bruce. *The War Lords of Washington*. New York: Harcourt, Brace, 1948.

Cavell, Stanley. *The World Viewed*. New York: Viking, 1971.

Ceplair, Larry, and Steven Englund. *The Inquisition in Hollywood: Politics in the Film Community, 1930–60*. Garden City, N.Y.: Doubleday, 1980.

Chan, Sucheng. *Asian Americans: An Interpretive History*. Boston: Twayne, 1991.

Charles, Douglas M. *J. Edgar Hoover and the Anti-interventionists: FBI Political Surveillance and the Rise of the Domestic Security State, 1939–1945*. Columbus: Ohio State University Press, 2007.

Chartier, Jean-Pierre. "The Americans Are Making Dark Films Too." Trans. R. Barton Palmer. In *Perspectives on Film Noir*, ed. Palmer, 25–27. New York: Prentice Hall, 1996.

Chase, Harold W. *Security and Liberty: The Problem of Native Communists, 1947–1955*. Garden City, N.Y.: Doubleday, 1955.

Chion, Michael. *The Voice in Cinema*. Trans. Claudia Gorbman. New York: Columbia University Press, 1999.

Christiansen, Jerome. *America's Corporate Art: Studio Authorship of Hollywood Movies*. Stanford: Stanford University Press, forthcoming.

Christopher, Nicholas. *Somewhere in the Night: Noir and the American City*. New York: Henry Holt, 1998.

Cohan, Steven. *Masked Men: Masculinity and the Movies in the Fifties*. Bloomington: Indiana University Press, 1997.

Conley, Tom. "Cinema and Its Discontents." In *Jacques Rancière: History, Politics, Aesthetics*, ed. Gabriel Rockhill and Philip Watts, 216–28. Durham: Duke University Press, 2009.

Copjec, Joan. "The Phenomenal Nonphenomenal: Private Space in *Film Noir*." In *Shades of Noir: A Reader*, ed. Copjec, 167–97. London: Verso, 1993.

Corber, Robert. *In the Name of National Security: Hitchcock, Homophobia, and the Political Construction of Gender in Postwar America*. Durham: Duke University Press, 1993.

Corkin, Stanley. *Cowboys as Cold Warriors: The Western and U.S. History*. Philadelphia: Temple University Press, 2004.

Costanzo, Ezio. *The Mafia and the Allies: Sicily 1943 and the Return of the Mafia*. Trans. George Lawrence. New York: Enigma Books, 2007.

Coutin, Susan Bibler. "Illegality, Borderlands, and the Space of Nonexistence." In *Globalization under Construction: Governmentality, Law, and Identity*, ed. Richard Warren Perry and Bill Maurer, 171–202. Minneapolis: University of Minnesota Press, 2003.

Cowie, Elizabeth. "Film Noir and Women." In *Shades of Noir: A Reader*, ed. Joan Copjec, 121–65. London: Verso, 1993.

Crowe, Cameron. *Conversations with Wilder*. New York: Knopf, 1999.

Crowther, Bosley. " 'Border Incident,' Adventure Film about US Immigration Service, Opens at Globe," *New York Times*, November 21, 1949.

———. *The Lion's Share: The Story of an Entertainment Empire*. New York: E. P. Dutton, 1957.

Davis, Tracy C. *Stages of Emergency: Cold War Nuclear Civil Defense*. Durham: Duke University Press, 2007.

Defert, Daniel. " 'Popular Life' and Insurance Technology." In *The Foucault Effect: Studies in Governmentality*, ed. Graham Burchell, Colin Gordon, and Peter Miller, 211–33. Chicago: University of Chicago Press, 1991.

Denning, Michael. *The Cultural Front: The Laboring of American Culture in the Twentieth Century*. New York: Verso, 1996.

Desser, David. "The Wartime Films of John Huston: Film Noir and the Emergence of the Therapeutic." In *Reflections in a Male Eye: John Huston and the American Experience*, ed. Gaylyn Studlar and Desser, 19–32. Washington: Smithsonian Institution Press, 1993.

Diamond, Sander A. "The Bund Movement in the United States: An Overview." In *Germany and America: Essays on Problems of International Relations and Immigration*, ed. Hans L. Trefousse, 183–98. New York: Brooklyn College Press, 1980.

Dick, Bernard F. *The Star-Spangled Screen: The American World War II Film*. Lexington: University Press of Kentucky, 1985.

Dies, Martin. *The Trojan Horse in America*. New York: Dodd, Mead, 1940.

"DiGiorgio Sues for $2,000,000," *Los Angeles Times*, November 8, 1949.

Dimendberg, Edward. *Film Noir and the Spaces of Modernity*. Cambridge: Harvard University Press, 2004.

Dimock, Wai Chee. "Aesthetics at the Limits of the Nation: Kant, Pound, and the *American Saturday Review*." *American Literature* 76, no. 3 (2004), 525–47.

Dinerstein, Joel. " 'Emergent Noir': Film Noir and the Great Depression in *High Sierra* (1941) and *This Gun for Hire* (1942)." *Journal of American Studies*, no. 42 (2008), 415–48.

Dixon, Winston Wheeler. *Film Noir and the Cinema of Paranoia*. New Brunswick, N.J.: Rutgers University Press, 2009.

Doane, Mary Ann. *The Desire to Desire: The Woman's Film of the 1940s*. Bloomington: Indiana University Press, 1987.

Doherty, Thomas. *Projections of War: Hollywood, American Culture, and World War II*. New York: Columbia University Press, 1993.

Dombrowski, Lisa. *The Films of Samuel Fuller*. Middletown, Conn.: Wesleyan University Press, 2008.

Dudziak, Mary L. *Cold War Civil Rights*. Princeton: Princeton University Press, 2000.

Dudziak, Mary L., and Leti Volpp., eds. "Legal Borderlands: Law and the Construction of American Borders." Special issue, *American Quarterly* 57, no. 3 (2005).

Dunn, Thomas L. *A Politics of the Ordinary*. New York: New York University Press, 1999.

Edgerton, Gary. "Revisiting the Recordings of Wars Past: Remembering the Documentary Trilogy of John Huston." In *Reflections in a Male Eye: John Huston and the American Experience*, Gaylyn Studlar and David Desser, 33–61. Washington: Smithsonian Institution Press, 1993.

Elsaesser, Thomas. *Weimar Cinema and After: Germany's Historical Imaginary*. London: Routledge, 2000.

English, T. J. *Havana Nocturne: How the Mob Owned Cuba–and Then Lost It to the Revolution*. New York: William Morrow, 2008.

Ewald, François. "Insurance and Risk." In *The Foucault Effect: Studies in Governmentality*, ed. Graham Burchell, Colin Gordon, and Peter Miller. Chicago: University of Chicago Press, 1991.

Farber, Manny. *Negative Space*. New York: Da Capo Press, 1998.

Fay, Jennifer, and Justus Nieland. *Film Noir: Hard-Boiled Modernity and the Cultures of Globalization*. London: Routledge, 2009.

Filreis, Alan. "Words with 'All the Effects of Force': Cold-War Interpretation." *American Quarterly* 39, no. 2 (1987), 306–12.

Fox, Claire F. *The Fence and the River: Culture and Politics at the US-Mexico Border*. Minneapolis: University of Minnesota Press, 1999.

Freud, Sigmund. "The Uncanny." In *The Standard Edition of the Complete Psychological Works of Sigmund Freud*, ed. James Strachey, with Anna Freud, vol. 17, 24 vols., 219–56. London: Hogarth, 1953.

Fuller, Samuel. *A Third Face: My Tale of Writing, Fighting, and Filmmaking*. New York: Alfred Knopf, 2002.

Galarza, Ernesto. *Merchants of Labor: The Mexican Bracero Story*. Santa Barbara: McNally and Loftin, 1978.

———. *Spiders in the House and Workers in the Field*. Notre Dame, Ind.: University of Notre Dame Press, 1970.

Galison, Peter. "Removing Knowledge." *Critical Inquiry* 31, no. 1 (2004), 229–43.

Gallafent, Edward. "Kiss Me, Deadly." In *The Book of Film Noir*, ed. Ian Cameron, 240–46. New York: Continuum, 1993.

Gallagher, Brian. " 'I Love You Too': Sexual Warfare and Homoeroticism in Billy Wilder's *Double Indemnity*." *Literature-Film Quarterly* 15, no. 4 (1987), 237–46.

Gary, Brett. *The Nervous Liberals: Propaganda Anxieties from World War I to the Cold War*. New York: Columbia University Press, 1999.

Gemünden, Gerd. *A Foreign Affair: Billy Wilder's American Films*. New York: Berghahn, 2008.

Gentry, Curt. *J. Edgar Hoover: The Man and His Secrets*. New York: W. W. Norton, 1991.

Gilbert, James. *A Cycle of Outrage: America's Reaction to the Juvenile Delinquent in the 1950s*. Chicago: University of Chicago Press, 1986.

———. *Men in the Middle: Searching for Masculinity in the 1950s*. Chicago: University of Chicago Press, 2005.

Giovacchini, Saverio. *Hollywood Modernism: Film and Politics in the Age of the New Deal*. Philadelphia: Temple University Press, 2001.

Goodman, Walter. *The Committee: The Extraordinary Career of the House Committee on Un-American Activities*. New York: Farrar, Straus and Giroux, 1968.

Gorbman, Claudia. *Unheard Melodies: Narrative Film Music*. Bloomington: Indiana University Press, 1987.

Gordon, Marsha. " 'What Makes a Girl Who Looks Like That Get Mixed up in Science?': Gender in Sam Fuller's Films of the 1950s." *Quarterly Review of Film and Video* 17, no. 1 (2000), 1–17.

Gosch, Martin A., and Richard Hammer. *The Last Testament of Lucky Luciano*. Boston: Little, 1974.

Graebner, William S. *The Age of Doubt: American Thought and Culture in the 1940s*. Boston: Twayne, 1991.

——. *The Engineering of Consent: Democracy and Authority in Twentieth-Century America*. Madison: University of Wisconsin Press, 1987.

Greene, Graham. *A Gun for Sale*. 1936. New York: Viking, 1982.

Grieveson, Lee, Esther Sonnet, and Peter Stanfield, eds. *Mob Culture: Hidden Histories of the American Gangster Film*. New Brunswick, N.J.: Rutgers University Press, 2005.

Grobel, Lawrence. *The Hustons*. New York: Charles Scribner's Sons, 1989.

Grossman, Julie. "Film Noir's 'Femme Fatales' Hard-Boiled Women: Moving beyond Gender Fantasies." *Quarterly Review of Film and Video*, no. 24 (2007), 19–30.

Gunning, Tom. *The Films of Fritz Lang: Allegories of Vision and Modernity*. London: British Film Institute, 2000.

Gutiérrez, David G. *Walls and Mirrors: Mexican Americans, Mexican Immigrants, and the Politics of Ethnicity*. Berkeley: University of California Press, 1995.

Hacking, Ian. "Biopower and the Avalanche of Printed Numbers." *Humanities in Society* 5, nos. 3–4 (1982), 279–95.

Hantke, Steffen. "Boundary Crossing and the Construction of Cinematic Genre: Film Noir as 'Deferred Action.'" *Kinema* (fall 2004), www.kinema.uwaterloo.ca.

Harvey, James. *Movie Love in the Fifties*. New York: Alfred Knopf, 2001.

Henriksen, Margot A. *Dr. Strangelove's America: Society and Culture in the Atomic Age*. Berkeley: University of California Press, 1997.

Herrera-Sobek, María. *The Bracero Experience: Elitelore versus Folklore*. Los Angeles: UCLA Latin American Center Publications, 1979.

Heumann, Joseph K., and Robin L. Murray. "*Cape Town Affair*: Right-Wing Noir, South African Style." *Jump Cut*, no. 47 (2005), www.ejumpcut.org.

Higham, John. *Strangers in the Land: Patterns of American Nativism, 1860–1925*. New York: Atheneum, 1963.

Hiney, Tom. *Raymond Chandler: A Biography*. New York: Grove, 1997.

Hoover, J. Edgar. "Letter to Sidney Souers, July 7, 1950." *New York Times*, December 22, 2007.

——. *Persons in Hiding*. Boston: Little, Brown, 1938.

Horton, Robert., ed. *Billy Wilder: Interviews*. Jackson: University Press of Mississippi, 1999.

Huston, John. *An Open Book*. New York: Alfred Knopf, 1980.

Irons, Peter. *Justice at War: The Story of the Japanese American Internment Cases*. New York: Oxford University Press, 1983.

Irwin, John T. *Unless the Threat of Death Is behind Them: Hard-Boiled Fiction and Film Noir*. Baltimore: Johns Hopkins University Press, 2006.

Jameson, Fredric. "The Synoptic Chandler." In *Shades of Noir: A Reader*, ed. Joan Copjec, 33–56. London: Verso, 1993.

Kanstroom, Daniel. *Deportation Nation: Outsiders in American History*. Cambridge: Harvard University Press, 2007.

Keller, William W. *The Liberals and J. Edgar Hoover: Rise and Fall of a Domestic Intelligence State*. Princeton: Princeton University Press, 1989.

Kemp, Philip. "From the Nightmare Factory: HUAC and the Politics of Noir." *Sight and Sound* 55, no. 4 (1984), 266–70.

Kessler, Ronald. *The Bureau: The Secret History of the FBI*. New York: St. Martin's Press, 2002.

Koch, Howard. *As Time Goes By: Memoirs of a Writer*. New York: Harcourt Brace Jovanovich, 1979.

Kolker, Robert. *A Cinema of Loneliness: Penn, Stone, Kubrick, Scorsese, Spielberg, Altman*. 3rd ed. New York: Oxford University Press, 2000.

Koppes, Clayton R., and Gregory D. Black. *Hollywood Goes to War: How Politics, Profits, and Propaganda Shaped World War II Movies*. New York: Free Press, 1987.

Koszarski, Richard. *Hollywood Directors, 1941–76*. New York: Oxford University Press, 1977.

Kozloff, Sara. *Invisible Storytellers: Voice-Over Narration in American Fiction Film*. Berkeley: University of California Press, 1988.

Kracauer, Siegfried. *The Salaried Masses: Duty and Distraction in Weimar Germany*. Trans. Quintin Hoare. London: Verso, 1998.

Krutnik, Frank. *In a Lonely Street: Film Noir, Genre, Masculinity*. London: Routledge, 1991.

Krutnik, Frank, et al., eds. *"Un-American" Hollywood: Politics and Film in the Blacklist Era*. New Brunswick, N.J.: Rutgers University Press, 2007.

Kuhn, Fritz. "Address." In *Free America! The German American Bund at Madison Square Garden*, 15–20. New York: n.p., 1939.

Lawrenson, Helen. *Latins Are Still Lousy Lovers*. New York: Hawthorn Books, 1968.

Leeper, Jill. "Crossing Musical Borders: The Soundtrack for Touch of Evil." In *Soundtrack Available: Essays on Film and Popular Music*, ed. Arthur Knight and Pamela Robertson Wojcik, 226–43. Durham: Duke University Press, 2001.

Lewis, Jon, and Eric Smoodin, eds. *Looking Past the Screen: Case Studies in American Film History and Method*. Durham: Duke University Press, 2007.

Lipman, Jane K. *Guantánamo: A Working-Class History between Empire and Revolution*. Berkeley: University of California Press, 2009.

Lott, Eric. "The Whiteness of Film Noir." *American Literary History* 9, no. 3 (1997), 542–66.

Lowe, Lisa. *Immigrant Acts: On Asian American Cultural Politics*. Durham: Duke University Press, 1996.

Lowenthal, Max. *The Federal Bureau of Investigation*. New York: William Sloane, 1950.

Lunbeck, Elizabeth. *The Psychiatric Persuasion: Knowledge, Gender, and Power in Modern America*. Princeton: Princeton University Press, 1994.

MacDonnell, Francis. *Insidious Foes: The Axis Fifth Column and the American Home Front*. New York: Oxford University Press, 1995.

MacShane, Frank. *The Life of Raymond Chandler*. New York: E. P. Dutton, 1976.

Maddux, Thomas R. "Red Fascism, Brown Bolshevism: The American Image of Totalitarianism in the 1930s." *Historian*, no. 40 (1977), 85–103.

Maltby, Richard. "The Politics of the Maladjusted Text." 1984. In *The Book of Film Noir*, ed. Ian Cameron, 39–48. New York: Continuum, 1993.

——. " 'The Problem of Interpretation . . .': Authorial and Institutional Intentions in and around *Kiss Me Deadly*." *Screening the Past*, no. 10 (2000), www.latrobe.edu.au/screeningthepast.

Maltz, Albert. *The Citizen Writer: Essay in Defense of American Culture*. New York: International Publishers, 1950.

Manon, Hugh S. "Some Like It Cold: Fetishism in Billy Wilder's *Double Indemnity*." *Cinema Journal* 44, no. 4 (2005), 18–43.

Marcus, Alan. "The Interracial Romance as Primal Drama: *Touch of Evil* and *Diamond Head*." *Film Studies*, no. 11 (2007), 14–26.

Marx, Leo. *The Machine in the Garden: Technology and the Pastoral Ideal in America*. New York: Oxford University Press, 1964.

May, Lary. *The Big Tomorrow: Hollywood and the Politics of the American Way*. Chicago: University of Chicago Press, 2000.

McCann, Sean. *Gumshoe America: Hard-Boiled Crime Fiction and the Rise and Fall of New Deal Liberalism*. Durham: Duke University Press, 2000.

——. "Dark Passages: Jazz and Civil Liberty in the Postwar Crime Film." In *"Un-American" Hollywood*, Krutnik et al., eds. (New Brunswick, N.J.: Rutgers University Press, 2007), 113–29.

McCarthy, Mary. "The Contagion of Ideas." In *On the Contrary*, 43–54. New York: Farrar, Straus and Cudahy, 1961.

——. "Naming Names: The Arthur Miller Case." In *On the Contrary*, 147–54. New York: Farrar, Straus and Cudahy, 1961.

McCarthy, Todd, and Charles Flynn, eds. *King of the Bs: Working within the Hollywood System; An Anthology of Film History and Criticism*. New York: E. P. Dutton, 1975.

McConnell, Frank D. *The Spoken Seen: Film and the Romantic Imagination*. Baltimore: Johns Hopkins University Press, 1975.

McCoy, Alfred W. *The Politics of Heroin: CIA Complicity in the Global Drug Trade*. Brooklyn: Lawrence Hill Books, 1991.

McKale, Donald M. *The Swastika Outside Germany*. Kent, Ohio: Kent State University Press, 1977.

McWilliams, Carey. *North from Mexico: The Spanish-Speaking People of the United States*. Philadelphia: Lippincott, 1949.

Medovoi, Leerom. *Rebels: Youth and the Cold War Origins of Identity*. Durham: Duke University Press, 2005.

Miklitsch, Robert. *Siren City: Sound and Source in Classic American Noir*. New Brunswick, N.J.: Rutgers University Press, 2011.

Miller, Char Roone. *Taylored Citizenship: State Institutions and Subjectivity*. Westport, Conn.: Praeger, 2002.

Miyamoto, Yoichiro. "Papa and Fidel: Cold War, Cuba, and Two Interpretational

Communities." In *Hemingway, Cuba, and the Cuban Works*, ed. Larry Grimes and Bickford Sylvester. Kent, Ohio: Kent State University Press, forthcoming.

Momen, Mehnaaz. "Are You a Citizen? Insights from Borderlands." *Citizenship Studies* 9, no. 3 (2005), 323–34.

Munby, Jonathan. *Public Enemies, Public Heroes: Screening the Gangster from "Little Caesar" to "Touch of Evil"*. Chicago: University of Chicago Press, 1999.

Murphet, Julian. "Film Noir and the Racial Unconscious." *Screen* 34, no. 1 (1998), 22–35.

Murphy, George, with Viktor Lasky. *Say . . . Didn't You Used to Be George Murphy?* New York: Bartholomew House, 1979.

Murphy, Marion Emerson. *The History of Guantanamo Bay*. 3rd ed. Guantánamo Bay, Cuba: United States Naval Base, District Publications and Print Office, 1968.

Naremore, James. *More Than Night: Film Noir in Its Contexts*. Berkeley: University of California Press, 1998.

Navasky, Victor. *Naming Names*. New York: Viking, 1980.

Neale, Steve. *Genre and Hollywood*. London: Routledge, 2000.

Nemerov, Alexander. *Icons of Grief: Val Lewton's Home Front Pictures*. Berkeley: California University Press, 2005.

Neve, Brian. *Film and Politics in America*. London: Routledge, 1992.

Ngai, Mae M. *Impossible Subjects: Illegal Aliens and the Making of Modern America*. Princeton: Princeton University Press, 2004.

Ngai, Sianne. *Ugly Feelings*. Cambridge: Harvard University Press, 2005.

"North of the Border," *Time*, November 1, 1948.

Nugent, Frank S. "Review of *I Was a Captive of Nazi Germany*, prod. Malvina Pictures." *New York Times*, August 3, 1936.

Oakes, Guy. *The Imaginary War: Civil Defense and American Cold War Culture*. New York: Oxford University Press, 1994.

Oakes, Guy, and Andrew Grossman. "Managing Nuclear Terror: The Genesis of American Civil Defense Tragedy." *International Journal of Politics, Culture, and Politics* 5, no. 3. (1992), 361–403.

O'Brien, Charles. "Film Noir in France: Before the Liberation," *Iris*, no. 21 (1996), 7–21.

Ogden, August Raymond. *The Dies Committee: A Study of the Special House Committee for the Investigation of Un-American Activities, 1938–1944*. Washington: Catholic University of America Press, 1945.

Ogle, Maureen. *Key West: History of an Island of Dreams*. Gainesville: University Press of Florida, 2003.

Oliver, Kelly, and Benigno Trigo. *Noir Anxiety*. Minneapolis: University of Minnesota Press, 2003.

O'Reilly, Kenneth. *Hoover and the Un-Americans: The FBI, HUAC, and the Red Menace*. Philadelphia: Temple University Press, 1983.

Orgeron, Devin. "La Camera-Crayola: Authorship Comes of Age in the Cinema of Wes Anderson." *Cinema Journal* 46, no. 2 (2007), 40–65.

Osteen, Mark. "The Big Secret: Film Noir and Nuclear Fear." *Journal of Popular Film and Television* 22, no. 2 (1994), 79–81.

Palmer, R. Barton. *Hollywood's Dark Cinema: The American Film Noir*. New York: Twayne, 1994.

Pease, Donald E. "Borderline Justice / States of Emergency: Orson Welles' *Touch of Evil*." *New Centennial Review* 1, no. 1 (2001), 75–105.

Pelizzon, V. Penelope, and Nancy M. West. "Multiple Indemnity: Film Noir, James M. Cain, and Adaptations of a Tabloid Case." *Narrative* 13, no. 3 (2005), 211–37.

Pells, Richard H. *The Liberal Mind in a Conservative Age*. New York: Harper and Row, 1985.

Pérez, Louis A., Jr. *Cuba and the United States: Ties of Singular Intimacy*. 2nd ed. Athens: University of Georgia Press, 1997.

——. *Cuba in the American Imagination: Metaphor and the Imperial Ethos*. Chapel Hill: University of North Carolina Press, 2008.

——. *On Becoming Cuban: Identity, Nationality, and Culture*. Chapel Hill: University of North Carolina Press, 1999.

Plumly, Stanley. *Old Heart: Poems*. New York: Norton, 2007.

Polan, Dana. "Auteur Desire." *Screening the Past*, no. 12 (2001), www.latrobe.edu.au/screeningthepast.

——. "Commentary." On *Border Incident* DVD, dir. Anthony Mann. Warner Home Video, 2006.

——. "The Limitless Potentials and the Potential Limits of Classical Hollywood Cinema." In *Film Analysis*, ed. Jeffrey Geiger and R. L. Rutsky, 363–79. New York: W. W. Norton, 2005.

——. *Power and Paranoia: History, Narrative, and the American Cinema, 1940–1950*. New York: Columbia University Press, 1986.

——. "Review of *The Noir Thriller*, by Lee Horsley." *Intensities*, no. 2 (2004), www.cult-media.com / issue2.

——. "Stylistic Regularities (and Peculiarities) of the Hollywood World War II Propaganda Film." In *Warner's War: Politics, Popular Culture, and Propaganda in Wartime Hollywood*, ed. Joanna Blakley and Martin Kaplan, 38–47. Los Angeles: USC Annenberg Norman Lear Center, 2004.

Powers, Richard Gid. *Broken: The Troubled Past and Uncertain Future of the FBI*. New York: Free Press, 2004.

——. *G-Men: Hoover's FBI in American Popular Culture*. Cardondale: Southern Illinois University Press, 1983.

——. *Secrecy and Power: The Life of J. Edgar Hoover*. New York: Free Press, 1987.

Pratt, Ray. *Projecting Paranoia: Conspiratorial Visions in American Film*. Lawrence: University Press of Kansas, 2001.

Putnam, Robert D. *Bowling Alone: The Collapse and Revival of American Community*. New York: Simon and Schuster, 2000.

Quirk, Robert E. *Fidel Castro*. New York: W. W. Norton, 1993.

Rancière, Jacques. "Contemporary Art and the Politics of Aesthetics." In *Commu-*

nities of Sense: Rethinking Aesthetics and Politics, ed. Beth Hinderliter et al, 31–50. Durham: Duke University Press, 2009.

——. *Film Fables*. Trans. Emiliano Battista. Oxford: Berg, 2006.

——. *The Future of the Image*. Trans. Gregory Eliott. London: Verso, 2007.

Reisler, Mark. "Always the Laborer, Never the Citizen: Anglo Perception of the Mexican Immigrant during the 1920s." In *Between Two Worlds: Mexican Immigrants in the United States*, ed. David G. Gutiérrez, 23–44. Wilmington, Del.: Scholarly Resources, 1996.

Robinson, Greg. *By Order of the President: FDR and the Internment of Japanese Americans*. Cambridge: Harvard University Press, 2001.

Rogge, O. John. *The Official German Report*. New York: Yoseloff, 1961.

Rogin, Michael. *"Ronald Reagan," the Movie, and Other Episodes of Political Demonology*. Berkeley: University of California Press, 1987.

Rollins, Brooke. " 'Some Kind of Man': Orson Welles as *Touch of Evil*'s Masculine Auteur." *Velvet Light Trap*, no. 57 (2006), 32–41.

Ronning, C. Neale. *José Martí and the Emigré Colony in Key West: Leadership and State Formation*. New York: Praeger, 1990.

Ross, Steven J. "*Confessions of a Nazi Spy*: Warner Bros., Anti-fascism, and the Politicization of Hollywood." In *Warner's War: Politics, Pop Culture, and Propaganda in Wartime Hollywood*, ed. Joanna Blakley and Martin Kaplan. Los Angeles: USC Annenberg Norman Lear Center, 2004.

——. *Working-Class Hollywood: Silent Film and the Shaping of Class in America*. Princeton: Princeton University Press, 1998.

Rossiter, Clinton. *Constitutional Dictatorship*. Princeton: Princeton University Press, 1948.

Rovner, Sáenz Eduardo. *The Cuba Connection: Drug Trafficking, Smuggling, and Gambling in Cuba from the 1920s to the Revolution*. Trans. Russ Davidson. Chapel Hill: University of North Carolina Press, 2008.

Salemson, Harold J., ed. *Thought Control in the U.S.A.* Beverly Hills: Hollywood ASP-PCA, 1947.

Sarris, Andrew. *The American Cinema: Directors and Directions, 1929–1968*. New York: E. P. Dutton, 1968.

Saxe, Robert Francis. *Settling Down: World War II Veterans' Challenge to the Postwar Consensus*. New York: Palgrave MacMillan, 2007.

Sayre, Nora. *Running Time: Films of the Cold War*. New York: Dial Press, 1982.

Schary, Dore. *Heyday: An Autobiography*. Boston: Little, Brown, 1979.

Schatz, Thomas. *The Genius of the System: Hollywood Filming in the Studio Era*. New York: Henry Holt, 1988.

Schickel, Richard. *Double Indemnity*. London: British Film Institute, 1992.

Schlesinger, Arthur, Jr. *The Vital Center: The Politics of Freedom*. Boston: Houghton Mifflin, 1949.

Schrader, Paul. "Notes on Film Noir." *Film Comment* 8, no. 1 (1972), 8–13.

Schrecker, Ellen, ed. *The Age of McCarthyism: A Brief History with Documents.* Boston: Bedford/St. Martin's Press, 2002.

Schreiber, Rebecca M. *Cold War Exiles in Mexico: U.S. Dissidents and the Culture of Critical Resistance.* Minneapolis: University of Minnesota Press, 2008.

Schuck, Peter H., and Rogers M. Smith. *Citizenship without Consent: Illegal Aliens in the American Policy.* New Haven: Yale University Press, 1985.

Schwartz, Vanessa R. *It's So French!: Hollywood, Paris, and the Making of Cosmopolitan Film Culture.* Chicago: University of Chicago Press, 2007.

Selby, Spencer. *Dark City: The Film Noir.* Jefferson, N.C.: McFarland, 1984.

Server, Lee. *Sam Fuller: Film Is a Battleground.* Jefferson, N.C.: McFarland, 1994.

Shumway, David R. "Disciplinary Identities; or, Why Is Walter Neff Telling This Story." *Symploke* 7, nos. 1–2 (1999), 97–107.

Sikov, Ed. *On Sunset Boulevard: The Life and Times of Billy Wilder.* New York: Hyperion, 1999.

Silver, Alain. "*Kiss Me Deadly*: Evidence of Style." In *Film Noir Reader*, ed. Alain Silver and James Ursini, 209–36. New York: Limelight Editions, 1996.

Silver, Alain, and James Ursini. Introduction to *Film Noir Reader*, ed. Silver and Ursini, 3–15. New York: Limelight Editions, 1996.

——. *What Ever Happened to Robert Aldrich?* New York: Limelight Editions, 1996.

Silver, Alain, and Elizabeth Ward, eds. *Film Noir: An Encyclopedic Reference to the American Style.* Woodstock, N.Y.: Overlook Press, 1979.

Silverman, Kaja. *The Acoustic Mirror: The Female Voice in Psychoanalysis and Cinema.* Bloomington: Indiana University Press, 1988.

Simmel, Georg. "The Stranger." In *The Sociology of Georg Simmel*, ed. and trans. Kurt Wolff, 402–8. New York: Free Press, 1950.

Skierka, Volker. *Fidel Castro: A Biography.* Trans. Patrick Camiller. Cambridge: Polity, 2004.

Sklar, Robert. "Havana Episode: The Revolutionary Situation of *We Were Strangers*." In *Reflections in a Male Eye: John Huston and the American Experience*, ed. Gaylyn Studlar and David Desser, 63–77. Washington: Smithsonian Institution Press, 1993.

Smigel, Edwin O., and H. Laurence Ross, eds. *Crimes against Bureaucracy.* New York: Van Nostrand Reinhold, 1970.

Sobchack, Vivian. "Lounge Time: Postwar Crises and the Chronotrope of Film Noir." In *Refiguring American Film Genres: History and Theory*, ed. Nick Browne, 129–70. Berkeley: University of California Press, 1998.

Sollors, Werner, ed. *Interracialism: Black-White Intermarriage in American History, Literature, and Law.* Oxford: Oxford University Press, 2000.

Somerville, Siobahn B. "Queer Loving." GLQ: *A Journal of Lesbian and Gay Studies* 11, no. 3 (2005), 335–70.

Spicer, Andrew. *Film Noir.* Harlow, United Kingdom: Pearson, 2002.

Sproule, J. Michael. *Propaganda and Democracy: The American Experience of Media and Mass Persuasion*. Cambridge: Cambridge University Press, 1997.

Steinberg, Peter L. *The Great "Red Menace": United States Persecution of American Communists, 1947–1952*. Westport, Conn.: Greenwood Press, 1984.

Stephan, Alexander. *"Communazis": FBI Surveillance of German Émigré Writers*. Trans. Jan van Heurck. New Haven: Yale University Press, 2000.

Stewart, Garrett. *Between Film and Screen: Modernism's Photo Synthesis*. Chicago: University of Chicago Press, 1999.

Stewart, Susan. *On Longing: Narratives of the Miniature, the Gigantic, the Souvenir, the Collection*. Baltimore: Johns Hopkins University Press, 1984.

St.-George, Maximilian, and Lawrence Dennis. *Trial on Trial: The Great Sedition Trial of 1944*. N.p.: National Civil Rights Committee, 1946.

Studlar, Gaylyn. "A Gunsel Is Being Beaten: Gangster Masculinity and the Homo-erotics of the Crime Film, 1941–1942." In *Mob Culture: Hidden Histories of the American Gangster Film*, Lee Grieveson, Esther Sonnet, and Peter Stanfield, 120–45. New Brunswick, N.J.: Rutgers University Press, 2005.

Sutherland, Edwin H. *White Collar Crime*. New York: Dryden Press, 1949.

——. "White Collar Criminality." In *White-Collar Crime: Offenses in Business, Politics, and the Professions*, Gilbert Geis and Robert F. Meier, 38–49. New York: Free Press, 1977.

Szalay, Michael. *New Deal Modernism: American Literature and the Invention of the Welfare State*. Durham: Duke University Press, 2000.

Tailleur, Roger. "*The Pink Horse*; or, the Pipe Dreams of the Human Condition." In *Perspectives on Film Noir*, ed. R. Barton Palmer, 39–43. New York: Prentice Hall, 1996.

Telotte, J. P. *Voices in the Dark: The Narrative Patterns of Film Noir*. Urbana: University of Illinois Press, 1989.

Theoharis, Athan G. *The FBI and American Democracy: A Brief Critical History*. Lawrence: University Press of Kansas, 2004.

——. "The FBI's Stretching of Presidential Directives, 1936–1953." *Political Science Quarterly* 94, no. 4 (1976–77), 649–72.

——. *Spying on Americans: Political Surveillance from Hoover to the Huston Plan*. Philadelphia: Temple University Press, 1978.

——, ed. *The Truman Presidency: The Origins of the Imperial Presidency and the National Security State*. Stanfordville, N.Y.: Earl M. Coleman Enterprises, 1979.

Theoharis, Athan G., and John Stuart Cox. *The Boss: J. Edgar Hoover and the Great American Inquisition*. Philadelphia: Temple University Press, 1988.

Tratner, Michael. *Crowd Scenes: Movies and Mass Politics*. New York: Fordham University Press, 2008.

Truffaut, François, with Helen G. Scott. *Hitchcock*. Rev. ed. New York: Simon and Schuster, 1985.

Tyler, Parker. "Hollywood as a Universal Church." *American Quarterly* 2, no. 2 (1950), 165–76.

——. *Magic and Myth of the Movies*. New York: Henry Holt, 1974.

"U.S. Ship in Caribbean Is Sunk by Torpedo," *New York Times*, April 20, 1943.

Vernet, Marc. "*Film Noir* on the Edge of Doom." In *Shades of Noir: A Reader*, ed. Joan Copjec, 1–31. London: Verso, 1993.

Viertel, Peter. *Dangerous Friends: At Large with Huston and Hemingway in the Fifties*. New York: Doubleday, 1992.

Vincendeau, Ginette. "Noir Is Also a French Word: The French Antecedents of Film Noir." In *The Book of Film Noir*, ed. Ian Cameron, 49–58. New York: Continuum, 1993.

Wald, Priscilla. *Constituting Americans: Cultural Anxiety and Narrative Form*. Durham: Duke University Press, 1995.

Waldman, Diane. "'At Last I Can Tell It to Someone': Female Point of View and Subjectivity in the Gothic Romance of the 1940s." *Cinema Journal* 23, no. 2 (1983), 29–40.

Warshow, Robert. "The Gangster as Tragic Hero," (1948). In *The Immediate Experience: Movies, Comics, Theatre and Other Aspects of Popular Culture* (Cambridge, Mass.: Harvard University Press, 2001), 97–104.

Washington, Mary Helen. *The Other Black List: African American Literacy and Cultural Artists on the Left in the 1950s*. New York: Columbia University Press, forthcoming.

Weyl, Nathaniel. *The Battle against Disloyalty*. New York: Tomas Y. Crowell, 1967.

Whitfield, Stephen J. *The Culture of the Cold War*. 2nd ed. Baltimore: Johns Hopkins University Press, 1996.

"Who is the Good Guy?," *Time*, October 16, 1964, 36.

Wicking, Christopher, and Barrie Patttison. "Interviews with Anthony Mann." *Screen* 10, nos. 4–5 (1969), 32–54

Wilder, Billy, and Raymond Chandler. *Double Indemnity: The Screenplay*. Berkeley: University of California Press, 2000.

Williams, Raymond. *Marxism and Literature*. Oxford: Oxford University Press, 1977.

Williams, Tony. "1947: Movies and the 'Enemy' Within." In *American Cinema of the 1940s*, ed. Wheeler Winston Dixon, 182–99. New Brunswick, N.J.: Rutgers University Press, 2006.

Wilson, Christopher P. *Cop Knowledge: Police Power and Cultural Narrative in Twentieth-Century America*. Chicago: University of Chicago Press, 2000.

Wylie, Phillip. *A Generation of Vipers*. New York: Rinehart, 1942.

Young, Paul. "(Not) the Last Noir Essay: Film Noir and the Crisis of Postwar Interpretation." *Minnesota Review*, nos. 55–57 (2002), 203–21.

Youngkin, Stephen D. *The Lost One: A Life of Peter Lorre*. Lexington: University Press of Kentucky, 2005.

Zimmer, Karl E. *Affixal Negation in English and Other Languages: An Investigation of Restricted Productivity.* Suppl. *Word: Journal of the International Linguistic Association* 20, no. 2 (1964).

Žižek, Slavoj. *The Universal Exception: Selected Writings, Volume Two.* Ed. Rex Butler and Scott Stephens. New York: Continuum, 2006.

Index

Jonathan Auerbach is a professor of English at the University of Maryland. He is the author of *Body Shots: Early Cinema's Incarnations* (2007), *Male Call: Becoming Jack London* (1996), and *Romance of Failure: First-Person Fictions of Poe, Hawthorne, and James* (1989).

Library of Congress Cataloging-in-Publication Data

Auerbach, Jonathan, 1954–
Dark borders : film noir and American citizenship / Jonathan Auerbach.
p. cm.
Includes bibliographical references and index.
ISBN 978-0-8223-4993-8 (cloth : alk. paper)
ISBN 978-0-8223-5006-4 (pbk. : alk. paper)
1. Film noir—United States—History and criticism.
2. Motion pictures—United States—History. I. Title.
PN1995.9.F54A947 2011
791.43'6556—dc22
2010038071